The Seventh Enemy

The Seventh Enemy

The Human Factor in the Global Crisis

Ronald Higgins

50477

McGraw-Hill Book Company
New York   St. Louis   San Francisco
Dusseldorf   Mexico

1 2 3 4 5 6 7 8 9 0 B P B P
7 8 3 2 1 0 9 8

Library of Congress Cataloging in Publication Data
Higgins, Ronald.
The seventh enemy.
Includes bibliographical references and index.
1. International relations.   2.   Social problems.
3.   Conservation of natural resources.   I.   Title.
JX1395.H49   327'.17   78–17305
ISBN 0–07–028780–5

Extract from "Choruses from 'The Rock' " in *Collected Poems 1909–62* by
T. S. Eliot, copyright 1936, by Harcourt Brace Jovanovich, Inc.; copyright
© 1963, 1964 by T. S. Eliot. Reprinted by permission of Harcourt Brace
Jovanovich, Inc., and Faber and Faber Ltd. Extract from "The Hand that
Signed the Paper" from *The Poems of Dylan Thomas.* Copyright 1939 by
New Directions Publishing Corporation. Reprinted by permission of New
Directions Publishing Corporation and J. M. Dent & Sons Ltd. Extract from
"The Second Coming" reprinted with permission of Macmillan Publishing
Co., Inc., and A. P. Watt & Son Ltd., from *Collected Poems of William
Butler Yeats.* Copyright 1924 by Macmillan Publishing Co., Inc., renewed
1952 by Bertha Georgie Yeats.

To my parents

Acknowledgments

I am indebted for help and encouragement to numerous friends of whom I must name Mimi Barker, Dr. Glin and Linda Bennet, Yorick and Helene Blumenfeld, Dr. Joan Feldman, Diana Ferguson and the late Dr. Irene Champernowne. Eva Tayler typed the final manuscript.

I owe special gratitude to Jacqueline Barton's diligent research and astute criticism. Walter C. Patterson of Friends of the Earth and Graham Searle of Earth Resources Research Ltd. gave invaluable technical advice. My debts to others, including former colleagues in Whitehall and at *The Observer*, are no smaller for being less specified. I also thank the authors and publishers of works from which I have quoted.

My association with Bruce Lee of McGraw-Hill and Rivers Scott of Hodder and Stoughton has been close, happy and valuable. Responsibility for errors, misjudgments and other insufficiencies is however solely mine.

A last note. Sympathisers (like myself) with the Women's Movement will I trust forgive my use of 'man' and 'his' to cover both sexes. To identify both every time is otiose; to write constantly of 'persons' seems clumsy. Personkind has troubles enough.

LITTLE REEVE, VOWCHURCH, HEREFORD.

Contents

PART FIVE: *The Assault on the Seventh Enemy* 221

PART SIX: *An Inclusive Sensibility: The Seven Lamps* 239

Introduction

Mankind is blundering headlong towards multiple calamity. In the twentieth century it has already suffered upheaval, repression and barbarism on a massive scale. The human cost of the decades of neglected desolation amongst the poor of the world has been even higher than that of the deliberate atrocities committed from Auschwitz to Hiroshima, from the Gulag Archipelago to Vietnam. Yet we blindly resist the mounting evidence that worse is almost certainly in store. We have erected line upon line of psychological defences to avoid recognising the realities and the demands of our time. Even the 'doomsayers' who have so vigorously warned us of the perils to 'Spaceship Earth' have tended to encourage expectations that saving action is likely to be taken in time. I am compelled to doubt it.

The gathering crisis is unique, the first in history involving the whole earth and the entire species. The next two or three decades will witness the convergence of six immense and seemingly remorseless threats. Only through the most drastic yet sensitive action would we substantially moderate their impact. The human factor will be decisive in both its aspects, the personal and the collective. But the behaviour of twentieth century man does not encourage confidence. Quite the opposite: in our individual blindness and the frightening inertia of our political institutions we must locate the greatest of all the dangers, what I have called the Seventh Enemy.

Mankind seems afflicted by a sort of madness which may be more menacing because individually most of us appear so respectably sane. We pass our daily lives in a measured enough fashion, soberly adjusting to immediate circumstances, playing some part as citizens and caring for those around us. We are not unkind or lunatic.

Yet the final results of our individual reasonableness seem

like the product of a collective insanity. We have somehow created a world of profound and increasing inequalities, in which the top third of our fellow men and women live in restless affluence and the bottom third in degrading poverty. It is a world in which absurd expectations, compulsive appetites and human multiplication are exhausting scarce resources and endangering the land, the waters and the atmosphere. It is a world where deprivation and injustice have become so profound and so public that they make even more precarious the balance of nuclear terror which has become the extraordinary and permanent context of our lives.

These are familiar propositions. Taking them one by one, many will admit they are true. Yet we rarely weigh them up together. And we know them with mind, not heart. Sometimes by night we may detect the rising dread, the awful Yeatsian awareness that 'things fall apart; the centre cannot hold; Mere anarchy is loosed upon the world. . .' But then we are swiftly reassured or distracted by the conventional bustle of meeting the next morning's needs. We are apt to say things are never as bad as they seem.

They are a great deal worse. I believe we must prepare ourselves for a world of rapidly mounting confusion and horror. The next twenty-five years, possibly the next ten, are likely to bring starvation to hundreds of millions and hardship, disorder or war to most of the rest of us. Democracy, where it exists, can have little chance of survival. Nor in the long run can our extravagant urban-industrial way of life. We of the rich world are probably the last comfortable generation. We could well witness the last act in the strange and in some ways glorious drama of modern materialist man. The evidence as a whole strongly suggests that an era of anarchy and widespread suffering is swiftly coming upon us.

Such judgments may sound alarmist, even hysterical. That is not what we call a doctor who diagnoses a terminal cancer. Either his facts and interpretation are right or they are not. He may under-estimate the resilience of the patient. He may over-estimate it. Either way it is not his business to encourage false hopes.

Many, however, while accepting this argument, will find my forebodings intrinsically implausible. After all, they will say, mankind can control its own destiny; injustice can be remedied, dissensions mediated, dangers averted. With our astonishing intelligence and adaptability we have solved a multitude of problems — in medicine, for example — over the last two or three centuries. Are not the current threats equally susceptible to vigorous treatment? Has there not been over a decade of encouragingly realistic debate about the global condition? Have not dozens of experts in human ecology pointed out the paths we ought to take? Surely there is time to avoid catastrophe?

There *is* still time to save ourselves but that fact may prove no more than the last twist in the knot of tragedy. The challenge is so immense and is gaining such momentum that a sufficient response at this late stage seems increasingly unlikely. Unless something quite extraordinary happens to transform our consciousness of the human plight, I believe we shall do much too little, much too late. Nor can we *expect* such a transformation, not with the speed or on the scale that the situation now demands.

The reasons for this stark conclusion are the main subject of this book but one of them must be mentioned at once. It is our complacent addiction to the secular optimism which our thrusting Western civilisation invented and has profoundly depended upon. The idea of inevitable progress was buried in the quagmires of the First World War but the flow of technical and material successes has preserved a foolish confidence in our capacity to solve almost any problem through the exercise of will and reason alone and has sustained a common obstinate determination not even to contemplate the possibility of humanity's defeat.

I believe this sort of optimism is now obsolescent, indeed dangerous. It mists our perception of disturbing facts and menacing trends, lessens our sense of urgency and reduces our willingness to take sacrificial action.

We are constantly told we have a duty to hope but this confuses spiritual and temporal hope. Spiritual hope is a matter of faith. It often begins with despair about human nature but ultimately it refuses outright cynicism. Temporal hope, hope for one's own time, for society *en masse*, must be one of balanced calculation about the factual realities. We can respond to claims about man's unquenchable spirit without taking a sanguine view of mankind's collective future. In 1933 Franklin D. Roosevelt said, 'The only thing we have to fear is fear itself'. This common view is, I think, no longer appropriate. Now we must fear hope. We have reached the point when the only source of rescue may lie precisely through fear: a wholesome fear, not a neurotic despondency; a courageous willingness to face the full and terrible dimensions of humanity's plight.

We may need to revive what Henry James called the imagination of disaster, to see the skull beneath the skin, to recognise with feeling as well as thought the real possibility of mankind's failure. This unblinkered view should not be seen as morbid or unconstructive, but as a terrible necessity for driving us to consciousness of our perilous position and its awesome demands. It is an idea strange and difficult to the contemporary mind: that fear may work what love has not and light appear from the depths of darkness.

Any advocate of what Albert Camus called 'courageous pessimism' must meet one especially powerful objection. When I was talking to a distinguished liberal academic a year or so ago about the threat of famine he said something like this, 'The problem is worse than you say. We shall have to write off South Asia for a start. But we should not say so. It would paralyse the will to act.' In his book *The Doomsday Syndrome* John Maddox's central charge was likewise that the 'doomsday movement' was sapping the will to get things done.[1]

There is no easy answer to this contention. Optimism has certainly so far been the spur to problem-solving in our civilisation. Now, however, it is obscuring a self-destructive course. Writing about the alleged perils of self-analysis, the psychiatrist Karen Horney said,

> If a patient recognises . . . he has been secretly driving at self-destruction, his clear recognition of that drive is much less dangerous than letting it silently operate. The recognition is frightening, but it is bound to mobilise counteracting self-preserving energies, provided there is any will to live.[2]

What is true of individuals is not necessarily applicable to people in the mass but surprises are possible. In Bristol once, I addressed a large, mostly graduate, women's conference. ('I suppose you could call us caring suburbia.') The previous speaker was an ebullient technologist who jollied the audience with typical reassurances that all would be well. I became angry, told him so, tore up my cautiously balanced notes and declared to the conference that I would risk spoiling their ease of mind, would probably crack few jokes and would explain just how slim I thought our chances were and why. The silence lasted throughout the lecture and a full minute after. Then they rose from their seats, clapping and stamping their feet.

Any personal pride about this response was pushed aside by surprise and sheer relief. They were prepared to stare the realities in the face. The response was of people glad to be taken seriously at last. Despite their comfortable mode of life, many said they knew inside that the world was sick and its foundations shaking. They needed to have their fears brought into the open where they might begin to grapple with them.

Perhaps then we may dare to tell the truth — as we see it — rather than insult healthy adults by concealing it for fear of their reaction. We must all know that our civilisation is no more immune to destruction than earlier ones. Why indeed should our species be exempt from extinction? Through its unique ingenuity? That is just as likely to work against us. Ingenuity is exactly what has enabled our generation to create the Promethean means through which absolutely all life could be extinguished from the planet — another of those immense facts of our day we have allowed to grow dull. The super-powers' capacity for overkill (a unique term for a unique time) is already ample.

I do not however believe nuclear extinction is immediately likely. The current leaders of the super-powers seem rational enough not to intend what could profit no one. It would take another romantic megalomaniac like Hitler to stage a deliberate world-suicide. True, the chances of a nuclear Third World War erupting before the end of the century must be high. But its proportions, if unprecedented, are unlikely to be so great as to raze or fatally irradiate all the earth. Many remote communities, perhaps extensive regions, could remain unscathed.

There will be survivors — possibly a large majority — from

any of the calamities we yet need to envisage. That is one ground for reassurance. Another is that there would then be new possibilities for human society. Moreover, amidst the signs of breakdown there are already parallel signs of breakthrough. (It is said the Chinese write 'crisis' with two ideograms, one meaning 'danger', the other 'opportunity'.)

Over the past twenty years or so a new global perspective has been taking shape, bringing a new vocabulary of concern about 'Planet Earth', and the impact of man's 'technosphere' on nature's 'biosphere'. There are many in whom anxiety for nation is being transcended by anxiety for mankind. There are new insights into the kind of policies and appropriate technologies which could relieve the distress of the poor and reduce the dangers to all. There are all sorts of experiments with new kinds of resource-conserving alternative living. There are new styles of thought and patterns of practice bearing on almost every aspect of life; creative developments which could offer better chances of man achieving a more balanced relationship with the natural environment, a more sustainable economic system and a safer international order.

However, I must say at the outset that I find it hard to see these various reassurances as more than limited consolations: the potentialities of a post-cataclysmic society could as well be dark as bright. Nor are the many new insights and experiments very reassuring. I do not contest their value or the need to pursue them. What I profoundly doubt is that the likely scale of their application will do more than postpone and diminish the likely calamities.

Intellectually I am as sure of this black assessment as one can be about any necessarily speculative judgment. The case, I shall show, is powerful. Emotionally, however, I feel a distress about it that may be immature. Born and bred in the security of the West, I have always expected too much and still cannot reconcile myself to the prospect of our descending into brutal circumstances of life even though these may be no harsher than those endured by most of our forebears and half of our contemporaries. It is not easy to accommodate the expectation of a worst-ever future at the time of the best-ever present.

The irony is strange. We have been enjoying the greatest benefits that political civilisation has ever offered to ordinary people, especially perhaps in the Atlantic community. Not only prosperity and, apart from Vietnam, a long period without large-scale war; but a stable and, despite its faults, a benign social order. Our politics have been accessible, our freedoms considerable and, for all but a few, our opportunities and ease of life have been unprecedented. Yet ours is a feast that the earth's limited resources cannot long sustain and a privileged order that is now as vulnerable as it has always been unjust.

In contemplating the awesome realities of the present global condition we are bound to feel dismay. One must of course resist the dismay when it threatens reasoned judgment but I think it should be controlled, not repressed. As an authentic personal response, either in writer or reader, it may be built upon. Perhaps, after all, we must allow the global crisis to produce a personal crisis. Unless we can allow it to reverberate in our innermost selves we may not measure, or respond to, its depths.

Nor otherwise shall we avoid the snares of self-righteous anger. Anger has its uses and fit targets but is not a safe guide to diagnosis. It hungers to identify and punish the guilty even before it has clearly established the nature of crimes. Indeed it too easily assumes that every horror must be the result of others' deliberate wickedness rather than often the product of impersonal forces or of unwitting acts of omission or commission in which all, including the accusers, may have played their part.

It is bold, perhaps reckless, for anyone to attempt an overview of the global condition. All the traditions from which I come are sceptical about such undertakings. The English culture is essentially cautious, empirical, reverent towards detail. My universities, London and Oxford, reinforced the claims of humbly narrow focus with their suspicions of general theory and approximate methods. The same wariness of large judgment was inculcated by twelve years in the British Diplomatic Service and eight at *The Observer* newspaper.

Why then do I undertake the task? Because, unless one is to live in a state of bewildered anxiety or deliberate indifference, the only recourse is to try to make some coherent sense out of the total situation and begin drawing conclusions for one's own life. The daily headlines of the late twentieth century are like a nightmare of portents. I feel driven to try to bring some order to this nightmare: to distinguish and weigh the threats, to relate them to each other and to begin to define what changes in outlook we need.

I shall suggest we consider the essential components of our common danger under seven broad headings. First there are six impersonal threats: the population explosion; the maldistribution of food; the shortage of vital resources; the degradation of the environment; the misuse of nuclear power; and the growing tendency of science and technology to escape humane control. Theoretically all six may be susceptible to direct attack but, as I have said, our actual response depends ultimately on the human factor. The seventh of the threats lies here, in that combination of political inertia and individual blindness which constitute the Seventh Enemy.

Part I of the book discusses the recent political background, some of the previous debate about our prospects, and points up some of the most disturbing features of the world arena in which the drama of the coming decades will unfold. Part II examines each of the six impersonal threats in turn and Part III, the characteristics of the Seventh Enemy. In Part IV I look at the sort of world we are likely to see over the next two or three decades and in Parts V and VI at the choices, political, moral and spiritual, that we face — or decline to face.

I begin however by describing some of my experiences as a diplomat. With a vast subject there are dangers in too much abstraction. As we explore the various hazards to world order, I would like readers to have some idea of the inside workings of government — of what it is like to share in its responsibilities and to operate within its limitations. It is not my purpose to expose state secrets or make startling revelations but to convey some feel for the realities of the international apparatus to which we largely, and naïvely, entrust our future.

Prologue

Diplomatic Realities

> The hand that signed the treaty bred a fever,
> And famine grew, and locusts came;
> Great is the hand that holds dominion over
> Man by a scribbled name.
>
> Dylan Thomas,
> *Collected Poems 1934–1952*[1]

At a party in London not long ago I bearded a British Defence Minister about the possibility of terrorists building their own 'backyard' nuclear bombs.

The minister said he thought his experts were sceptical about it but he had never looked into the subject. He would try to do so. He paused. Then, sounding tired, he said it was never easy to spend time weighing hypothetical dangers. He had a lot on his plate. He had to be practical.

I suddenly felt torn between sympathy and apprehension. Sympathy for an over-worked minister caught up in the hectic tumble of events. Apprehension about the number and scale of the 'hypothetical' dangers to which governments in general are giving so little attention. His remarks revived my memories of what it is like to work in the Foreign Office and I realised how far my thinking about the world's problems had strayed from the severely pragmatic approach of those engaged in the daily exercise of power.

While I had been thinking about tomorrow's nuclear terrorism, ministers were working out means to cope with today's hi-jackings. While I had been worrying about the long-term population-food equation, they had been arguing with their European partners over next month's butter price.

It is said of politics that 'the squeaky wheel gets the grease'; problems are tackled as they arise. This approach is plainly inadequate in the late twentieth century. The whole machine is in danger of being thrown off the rails. Governments now have an inescapable responsibility to safeguard the human future, not just to sustain some sort of present order.

That is easily said and too easily tempts us to thrust the whole blame for our troubles on the short-sightedness, neglect or incompetence of governments. Of course many governments are open to these charges but even the best are human institutions from which we persistently expect too much. The perennial cries for a 'fresh start', 'new leadership', electoral reform or revolutionary change usually betray ignorance of the treacherous difficulties of managing human affairs. How often has the new dawn — the French or Russian Revolution, the election of a Kennedy or a Giscard d'Estaing — produced the expected benefits? The grand conceptions and the would-be heroes are soon diminished by the intractabilities of political reality, the corruptions of power or, at best, the constant need for inglorious compromise.

The days of hope are succeeded by years of disillusion. President Eisenhower was derisively accused of 'delusions of adequacy' but adequacy should be rated an achievement. All politics is untidy and government especially so: even more conflicting aims and pressures have to be taken into account. Few problems present themselves to ministers in the neat, self-contained form in which they are packaged for instant judgment in the newspapers. There are few great moments of decision, rather a series of hurried improvisations. There are few solemn conclaves where an administration boldly decides on a radical change of course and fewer still where the issues are seen as moral. For the most part those who rule us are swept up in the stream of events, trying to keep head above water, trying most of all to look confident and active however uneasy and helpless they feel.

Twelve years service in the Foreign Office and in British embassies abroad gave me many opportunities to see governments under pressure. It taught many daunting lessons about the limits to their capacities, lessons which therefore bear closely on our collective prospects. There may seem a great gulf between an individual's experience in diplomacy and questions about the human fate but without a mental picture of how government is actually done, the reader will focus too much on the nature of the challenges and too little on the problems of effectively responding to them.

Let me describe what it was like to serve in three rôles: as a duty officer in the Foreign Office, as a private secretary to a senior minister and as a political officer in time of war — during the Suez affair of 1956.

The Resident Clerk's View

In 1963 I became one of the four officials who took turns as the Foreign Office duty officer, or Resident Clerk. At precisely six p.m. on Friday my sitting room on the top of the Foreign Office became the weekend operations room. From Downing Street, four stories below, I could hear colleagues exchanging farewells as they walked away for their buses and trains. I often had a sudden feeling of chilling isolation, of being left alone with a dangerous world. Silence settled on the great Victorian building as if it had slid under the ocean.

The silence never lasted long. Soon the telephones would begin to ring; the ordinary black and the special green with its 'scrambler' for secret, if always guarded, conversations. Within ten minutes or so the frock-coated messenger would clatter along the marble-tiled corridor towards my door with the first locked boxes of telegrams from the cypher section down below. I would fumble for the right keys from a fat bunch wondering what nastiness foreigners were cooking up. Until Monday morning every telegram from all the British embassies, consulates and other diplomatic missions around the world would be brought to me to assess their urgency and importance, to decide in effect whether anything was to be done about them and with what priority. The task could bring no glory: sensible decisions were taken for granted. It could bring disgrace: a single oversight or misjudgment might have untold — or widely told — repercussions.

World events are continuous; they have no respect for Civil Service Establishment Codes. For forty hours of each week many hundreds of political and economic specialists are immediately on hand to react to whatever happens. For the remaining 128 hours — every night and every weekend — a single Resident Clerk looks after the shop.

The Foreign Office is an extraordinary structure built last

century as an Italianate palace devoted to the intended permanence of the British Raj. Soberly impressive rather than elegant, my rooms overlooked the splendid spires and towers of Whitehall beyond the roof of the Chancellor's and the Prime Minister's house just opposite. The communal dining room faced west across St. James's Park to Buckingham Palace beyond which each evening the sun insolently insisted on setting.

Clerks are required to be bachelors (though not chaste) and of some years experience (as diplomats). I had had two postings abroad and therefore enough service behind me to acquire the vital familiarity with the communication and intelligence-gathering systems. I had also learned how to simulate calm when trouble breaks. As the Resident Clerk I had to cope as best I could but was not authorised to take any decisions of substance or policy. Unfortunately it is not always apparent which those are.

If a telegram plainly demanded instant action I telephoned at once to the official or minister most concerned to put them in the weekend picture for that area and get their instructions. Marginal cases were often tricky. Officials are sometimes touchy about being disturbed and it does one's career no good to generate a reputation for nervous misjudgment. One took risks. Ministers were invariably polite; some even seemed to enjoy being woken in the small hours, getting a sense of being in on the action.

Occasionally they take the initiative, waking the Clerk. In the middle of one night I was telephoned by a Cabinet minister of hawkish reputation about intelligence reports of a massing of Turkish warships and tank-landing craft in their ports opposite the northern coast of Cyprus. The civil war on the island had again flared up and Turkish aircraft had recently flown attacking missions in support of the hard-pressed Turkish minority. The minister was sure the Turks were about to launch a seaborne invasion. He asked me to tell the Foreign Secretary that he thought we should put the Royal Navy in at once to stop it.

If only as one of nature's doves I doubted both the diagnosis and the proposed remedy. I suspected the Turks were only staging an elaborate warning to the Greeks but I was no more an expert on the Cyprus imbroglio than he and in no position to argue. Feeling dozy and irritated I just said I would call back as soon as I could.

Instead of waking the Foreign Secretary at once I paused to think, putting myself into his shoes, or bed socks. In the dead of night he was going to be asked to put British warships in the way of an alleged invasion fleet. Could their mere presence be expected to persuade the Turkish armada meekly to return to port? Should we be prepared to fire? Might that not lead to war? With a NATO ally? The speculations became bizarre. What should I say if the Foreign Secretary asked my views?

Then I realised there was a simpler question he should ask first. Had we enough ships? Could we in fact establish an adequate naval presence there in time? Ten minutes had ticked by. I had better get on with it.

I telephoned the Duty Officer at the Ministry of Defence. They always sounded so cheerful, like blasé characters out of those class-ridden Second World War films. 'Hello, old boy. What can I do for you? Can't you sleep or something?'

'Look,' I said, 'one of our masters is feeling dynamic. How many naval vessels have you got within twelve hours sailing time of North Cyprus?'

'Wait one,' he said as he put down the telephone to get his maps. 'For the top right hand corner of the Med, eh? Well, old chap, not much. A frigate off Malta but she's got engine trouble. A destroyer and a tank-landing craft — rather bent — at Gib but that's even further. There's an aircraft carrier off Aden but she'd take three days. No luck I'm afraid. Bad time. Sorry.'

I thanked him, left the Foreign Secretary asleep and telephoned the minister back. I broke it gently. You have to. There was a practical problem. The Navy ruled fewer waves than we thought. Terrible pity, but there it was. He somehow combined a snort with a sigh and we agreed to go back to our beds. As it happened, the Turks did likewise; their fleets stayed in port. It could have been touch and go. Some years later they did invade the island.

I had done little more than circumvent a high-level overnight rumpus in Whitehall but the episode may suggest how the handling of any international emergency can often depend as much on the judgment of inconspicuous public servants as on the men at the top. Nor are the eminent always available. The Resident Clerk or his equivalent in the Foreign, Defence and Internal Security Ministries around the world are in temporary control of powerful institutions. (No outward telegram can be issued without the Clerk's written authority.) We sometimes discussed how we might best exert our leverage to contrive a *coup d'état*! Certainly no one should ever be surprised that it is so often the young officers, in the Third World especially, who find themselves in a position to overthrow apparently secure regimes.

What most impressed me as a Resident Clerk was the immense volume and range of the international activity to which any Foreign Ministry continually has to respond — coups, insurrections, military movements, arms sales, hijackings, natural disasters, threats to commercial interests, awkward twists in economic or financial negotiations, new and often hostile alignments and unexpected changes of policy by any of 150 sovereign states on any of dozens of contentious issues from disarmament to the law of the sea. Moreover any single response might demand prior consultation with many other government departments and many friendly — and less friendly — powers.

In 1782 the British Foreign Office consisted of a Permanent Under Secretary, a Chief Clerk and only nine 'clerks'. Foreign Secretaries made their own foreign policy. In the mid-nineteenth century the volume of traffic was sufficiently small for Lord Palmerston to read all the reports from posts abroad and to instruct his relatively few ambassadors personally.

Sir Edward Grey, Foreign Secretary in the spacious Edwardian years before the First World War, was already complaining of being so pressed that he could not remember having taken any step that was not of immediate urgency. That staggering statement must disturb us the more because the pressure has gone on growing relentlessly. When Anthony Eden became Foreign Secretary once again in 1951 he remarked that the work load had about doubled in six years. The rumbustious George Brown, Foreign Secretary in the mid-sixties, insisted on new systems to reduce the mass of paper reaching him. Even so he said he was still having to read telegrams and policy submissions until two or three in the morning.

The intricacy of international transactions has also grown. Take for example the mounting of a straightforward 'bush fire' peace-keeping operation.

One weekend in January 1964 I received an 'emergency' telegram from our acting High Commissioner in Dar-es-Salaam, capital of Tanganyika (now Tanzania) to say the 1st Battalion of the Tanganyikan Rifles had mutinied. Tanganyika had obtained its independence from Britain only about a year before and its army was by agreement still commanded by British officers. The report said the mutineers had detained some of these officers, had broken out of barracks and were roaming angrily around the town. Our representative had been unable to contact President Nyerere but one of his ministers had asked for the urgent help of British army units stationed in neighbouring Kenya to restore order.

I immediately telephoned senior officials and ministers in London and asked my opposite number at the Ministry of Defence to warn the military staffs to be ready for action. Our ministers at once decided they should meet the request and got the Prime Minister's agreement. Then I received a new telegram from Dar-es-Salaam saying another of Tanganyika's ministers had declared that the situation had improved and that outside help was not needed after all. Which minister should we believe? Was one of them playing politics? Yet another telegram resolved any doubt; the position was deteriorating fast and mutineers had seized the airport.

Tanganyika's troubles were worrying enough but the contagion could swiftly spread among our other former colonies in East Africa. Zanzibar, independent only since the previous month, had already witnessed a rebellion. There was a danger of the new African armies in Uganda and Kenya following the example of the Tanganyikans. We did not know whether the unrest was a matter of pay and conditions or of ambitious African soldiers resenting their white officers, or if there was a conspiracy, perhaps involving the Communists. Whatever the cause, the whole structure of East African order was in peril.

That this last fear was not exaggerated became apparent two days later when trouble broke out in Uganda and British troops had to be flown in from Kenya. Then there was a mutiny amongst Kenyan troops stationed near Nairobi. A British unit restored order there but the need for reserves from outside became even more acute.

Desire to help is one thing, ability another. Could we make enough forces available and get them to the right places in time? Undertaking any new commitment means a painful reappraisal of existing ones. A game of chess has to be played in which conflicting priorities, distance and time are dimensions as potent as the strength of the pieces moved around the board.

Naval units including an aircraft carrier, HMS *Centaur*, had already been despatched to Tanganyikan waters from Aden. Troops presented a greater logistical challenge. A battalion of the Scots Guards on military exercise in Aden was promptly sent back to Kenya but the other forces in Aden were engaged in countering an Arab nationalist revolution assisted by Cairo. Another possible source was Libya where British troops were stationed under a treaty with King Idris. The official concerned in London happened to be my own week-day boss. He was unsympathetic when I telephoned him. He said our relations with the king were highly sensitive, there might be legal complications and so on. He made me feel I was somehow personally to blame for the commotion. I became angry but was anyway forced to cut him short. Yet more telegrams were arriving and I had no time to argue, whatever he may say on Monday. Moreover I was sure his own seniors would put East Africa first. There were more serious obstacles to extracting troops from our sovereign bases in Cyprus where they were helping to stabilise a civil war which had again erupted violently. Any troops we borrowed from there would have to be replaced fast.

Once the necessary units had been earmarked, we and the Ministry of Defence had to organise an involved sequence of military transport flights between bases in Britain, Libya, Cyprus and East Africa. These required diplomatic clearance from all the countries they would overfly. Some of these countries would be cooperative, others suspicious or antagonistic. This meant carefully but quickly instructing our embassies in these places to explain all the sudden military activity: it was not 'neo-colonialism'. Similar explanations had to be given to allied powers and to several hostile ones who might otherwise misinterpret our intentions. The details no longer matter and all those mutinies were soon safely over. It was only one now-forgotten episode in an unusually hectic week but the total strain on the human systems, on our network of communications and on our available resources and means of pressure was immense.

The Private Secretary's View
An ideal place to watch the decision-making process is as a Private Secretary to a senior minister, especially one conducting major negotiations. In January 1961 I was appointed to the staff of Edward Heath who was later to become leader of the Conservative Party and, thereafter, Prime Minister.

Heath had recently been moved to the Foreign Office by Harold Macmillan who seemed to admire him as if he were an unexpectedly promising newcomer to a prep-school cricket team. The Foreign Secretary at the time was a peer, Lord Home, who under Britain's quaint and seemingly unalterable constitutional arrangements was not entitled to speak in the House of Commons. Edward Heath, already a fellow member of the Cabinet, was to fill this gap but his main task was to be, in effect, Minister for Europe.

A few months after I joined him, the government made one of those rare decisions that change the direction of policy: Britain would apply for membership of the European Economic Community. From then on, I seemed to be constantly flying with Heath between London and the European and North American capitals in connection with the ensuing negotiations.

Heath was hard to keep up with, a man of inexhaustible energy and fierce ambition, driven by a remarkably simple patriotism. I did not need to share his Conservative politics; mine was an official not a political appointment and we often argued. He enjoyed it: he called me his 'angry young man'. Some ministers feel their way quietly to the point of decision or tamely accept their department's advice. Heath preferred hard questioning, brain-storming, the exhaustive exploration of every option, especially with his younger advisers.

The Brussels negotiations were the most adventurous that Britain had embarked on since the war and an army of civil servants from all over Whitehall was delighted at last to take part in building something new, not just in dissolving an empire and managing the country's descent to second-class status. The early days were invigorating. Heath, long a committed European, radiated enthusiasm. The difficulties of reconciling Britain's Commonwealth and other interests with those of the original continental members were formidable but ultimate success was not questioned. 'Europe must unite or perish,' Heath told the first session in Paris.

The vision was noble but we soon learned the rhetoric bore little relation to the mundane and sometimes sordid business of bargaining the terms of Britain's admission. The gulf between oratory and reality had its comic side. Paul-Henri Spaak, the Belgian Foreign Minister, once told me over dinner that he spoke sufficient English to call for a lasting peace but barely enough to order a cucumber sandwich.

As leader of the British team, Heath's first call on the Foreign Office was for its accumulated wisdom on the conduct of large-scale negotiations. Virtually none was to be had: the newcomer to international affairs has to learn there are no special rules, no frameworks to guide him, no store of historic battle plans. He must depend on his own judgment of men, motives, situations and timing; use his own instinct as to when to stick and when to budge.

We soon learned secrecy was impossible to ensure. The temptations on the various participants to leak whatever parts of the proceedings most suited them were too great even though, in the end, this made all of them more vulnerable to outside pressures. We were also forced to recognise that no new pattern can be made without painfully breaking the old. To obtain entry, Britain would have to wriggle out of solemn commitments to her Commonwealth partners — notably about their trading preferences. To compensate for the Commonwealth's losses, all sorts of special arrangements had to be negotiated with the EEC for seemingly absurd items. High-powered politicians had to sweat for days about Australian canned peaches and East Indian kips (a sort of leather, it transpired). It was all a far cry from the 'great adventure' Heath had spoken of at a Conservative Party rally.

And so it went on, month after month, often into the early hours in the crowded conference room on the seventh floor of a monstrous building in Brussels; convoluted arguments about the tariffs on tea from India, canned salmon from Canada or sultanas from Cyprus. Every step demanded sensitive consultation with other governments, endless briefings of Commonwealth and other representatives and careful handling of the world's press. Hours of explanation seemed necessary for every minute of actual bargaining.

Working in perpetual proximity to Heath, opening all the mail and monitoring, by established convention, all his telephone calls, I was astonished by the constant juggling act he had to perform. The domestic pressures were not the least burdensome. The Conservative Party was less suspicious of continental entanglement than the Labour opposition but large parts of it still resented the end of Empire and strongly felt the Commonwealth connection should have priority. The Cabinet itself was not wholly united and some of his fellow-enthusiasts had departmental responsibilities they felt bound to defend to the hilt, or pretend to. Deep in the negotiations we had a sudden, absurd crisis about the terms affecting British tomato growers.

Heath also had to woo and propitiate almost every interest group in the country. I became used to hauling out the whisky for his regular morning briefings of trade union leaders and attending endless fattening lunches with big-wigs pressing the always 'special' needs of banking or fisheries, shipping or sugar. Each occasion demanded that Heath master an intricate brief. In retrospect it now seems that this preoccupation with the domestic factors, the economics and the multiplying details distracted him and all of us from some of the larger political realities of the time.

The Dutch were as helpful as their national needs allowed. The Belgians and Italians often conciliated with skill. The Germans were keen on final success. Throughout it was the French who were least amenable to compromise and most annoyingly pious about the sanctity of the Rome Treaty which had created the Community. That the treaty's original terms had greatly favoured French interests was hardly unconnected with this and in the autumn of 1962 the talks got steadily more bogged down.

Heath had always recognised the French as the greatest obstacle and from the outset did all he could to appease them (except learn French). We seemed to visit Paris every week — if only for a few hectic hours. However, it gradually became apparent that the French reservations were as much political as economic. France under the pompous nationalism of President de Gaulle feared Britain might replace her as the leading power in the Community. As one of his ministers remarked, 'No cock likes sharing his hens'. The French also wanted a different sort of Community, one independent of the US and not reliant on her nuclear umbrella. Britain favoured a united Europe working in active inter-dependence with America. De Gaulle therefore saw Britain as a sort of Trojan horse of American power.

This conflict of basic outlook between London and Paris was like a secret drama concealed by all the tedious haggling in Brussels. And the British never faced out the issues with the French until it was too late. The thinking was that if an economic settlement was reached at Brussels, Paris would be forced to reconcile itself to British entry.

In January 1963 I flew with Heath for a critical private lunch at the British Embassy in Paris with Couve de Murville, France's haughty Foreign Minister. As soon as it was over Heath came into the outer office to tell us about it. He had asked Couve whether, if the economic negotiations were successful, there could be any question of a political veto. Couve had said no. Heath had said this was a profoundly important statement. There must be no misunderstanding; their two Ambassadors, from London and Paris, were present and he must ask the question again. Couve had made an identical reply; if the technical problems were overcome 'no power on earth could prevent you coming in!' Heath's report brought relief. Perhaps the great enterprise would succeed after all. One colleague expressed doubts. I thought him cynical: Couve had spoken.

The cynic proved right. Only three days later President de Gaulle amazed the world by formally declaring at a press conference at the Elysée Palace that Britain was not ripe for Community membership. Britain was 'insular and maritime' and 'her habits and traditions were very special and very original'. If Britain came in, he intoned, the Community would lose its cohesion and become prey to 'a colossal Atlantic grouping, under American dependence and control'.

The shock to France's five Community partners was immense. To the British negotiating team it was shattering. If Couve had not been clear about de Gaulle's real intentions I thought he should have confessed his uncertainty or at least muddied his response to Heath's direct question. If, on the other hand, Couve had known the General's intentions, he must have been lying. That seemed unthinkable. Or did he regard the President as more than 'a power on earth'?

Soon after the news of de Gaulle's sensational veto came through to us in London, I accompanied Heath to a television interview out at the BBC's Lime Grove studios. We of his personal staff could scarcely believe what had happened. We had worked frantic hours over fourteen long months of non-stop travel and negotiation and had helped to drive and coordinate the work of hundreds of officials in the diplomatic equivalent of a D-Day landing. Thousands on the continent had shown the same dedication. Was it credible that one stubborn and remote old man should declare in effect that we had been wasting our time from the start?

I felt close to unprofessional tears at de Gaulle's cynicism and perhaps no less for the tragedy it seemed to represent for Heath personally. He had been a devoted European since entering the House of Commons. British entry to the Community had been his supreme goal. He saw it, perhaps optimistically, as the key to Britain's future and to Western Europe's. Success seemed no less vital to his own future. The task had been the most testing challenge yet made to his powers. A lonely, undemonstrative bachelor, he had given everything he had. There is not much idealism in politics; this venture had been an exception. On the journey I tried gently to draw him out but his eyes and voice were dead; a chill had descended through him. Intellectually he may have recognised the possibility of de Gaulle's veto; emotionally he was quite unprepared. He said there was still a chance of rescuing something from the wreck. He must have known there was none. It would be years before the damage to Europe and unity would be mended. Even now, with Britain safely inside, the original vitality of the Community has not been recovered.

I cannot look back on that frustrating saga except as a profound caution to those who speak lightly of what may be achieved between nations granted good will, common sense and all the other clichés of international worthiness. The original inspiration may often be fine, whether in 1945 of the United Nations as a world forum for peace or today of the proposed New International Economic Order as a means to cure world poverty. Yet the realities of power soon obscure, diminish and corrupt the great visions. Most progress depends on slow and tortured accommodation in small matters, on unglamorous compromise between hard-bitten men more alive to prices than values.

At least that is to speak of progress. There is regress too. Even the most settled and experienced governments are capable of extraordinarily wild and dangerous acts.

The Political Officer's View

It was in October 1956 that I first directly experienced the eruption of the irrational into world affairs — or played any part in it. My rôle was not conspicuous, yet few diplomats have ever had to present a friendly government with a sudden ultimatum threatening armed intervention, let alone discover they have been sucked into a plot of Byzantine intricacy.

The Suez crisis resulted in fierce actions by the armed forces of Israel, Egypt, Britain and France and led to those of several other nations, including the super-powers, being put on alert. The conspiracy that lay behind it was a potentially tragic one and carries disturbing implications for what we must expect of governments under the growing stresses of our time.

I had been sent to the British Embassy in Tel Aviv as a political officer, Third Secretary in Chancery, in April 1956. I was hugely excited that my first posting should be to a young state enduring siege. Israel's borders with the surrounding Arab states were constantly penetrated by terrorists known as *fedayeen*. Dodging Israeli night patrols, they emerged with their grenades, dynamite and machine guns to attack isolated settlements, ambush unescorted vehicles and mine the roads and tracks. The toll and tension rose as the summer grew more torrid. At intervals the Israelis mounted ferocious reprisal raids on Arab villages just over the borders. At the UN and elsewhere, denunciations and exhortations were uttered in growing number and futility at both sides.

Whenever I could, I drove round the country (with a borrowed sub-machine gun) to learn its crazily exposed geography. Once, with a girl friend, I missed a fatal ambush by an hour. The somewhat melodramatic sense of sharing the Israelis' beleaguerment added to my sympathy for their efforts to forge a sovereign-refuge for the survivors of Hitler's holocaust. The sympathy was not always reciprocated. Sometimes it was as well to muddy the little Union Jack on one's diplomatic licence plates. Britain's relations with one of Israel's antagonists, Jordan, were still close and the Israelis (rightly) suspected the British of some willingness to compromise with the Arabs at Israel's cost for the sake of their wider interests in the area.

The whole Middle East had been especially unstable for some time. Britain, then still the predominant power, was at odds with the radical Arab nationalism of Egypt and Syria. The nationalists themselves were in conflict with the traditionally conservative regimes of Jordan, Iraq, Saudi Arabia and the Gulf States. There were differences between London and Washington. For commercial reasons the Americans were keen to reach an accommodation with all the Arabs. There was also the historic rivalry between Britain and France. More recently, however, their minds had come closer. The French had become embittered by the Arab nationalists' support of the Algerians' independence struggle. France had therefore started providing Israel with modern aircraft. The Russians, who were supplying arms to Egypt, were standing by, as always, to profit from disturbance in general and Western disunity in particular. This then was the powder-keg to which any outbreak of open war between Israel and the Arabs might put the spark.

Egypt's ruler, President Nasser, was the outstanding leader of Arab nationalism. Since achieving power in 1954 he had done all he could to sever Britain's colonial strings. By means of a terrorist campaign he had forced Britain to agree to withdraw its forces and supply dumps from the Canal Zone. The withdrawal was still going on when Anthony Eden (later Lord Avon) succeeded Winston Churchill as Britain's Prime Minister in April 1955.

Eden's efforts to conciliate Nasser had failed by March 1956. Though basically anti-Communist, Nasser had been refused arms by the West and had turned to Russia for them. By July he found that the US and Britain (and hence the World Bank too) had decided not to finance the Aswan Dam which Nasser thought the key to rescuing his masses from poverty. The West was adamant. John Foster Dulles, the American Secretary of State, had responded to Egyptian threats to turn to Moscow by saying the US did not submit to blackmail.

Heady talk of this rebuff to Nasser being a 'victory for the West' was suddenly stilled on July 26. In a three-hour speech denouncing America, Britain and imperialism, Nasser announced his nationalisation of the Suez Canal Company, ostensibly to finance the dam. The blow was bitter and startling, especially for Eden. He heard the news in the middle of a dinner party in London and was reported to say, 'The Egyptian has his thumbs on our wind-pipe.'[2] Most of the British press and public took the same inflated view, at once comparing Nasser to Mussolini, even Hitler.

Britain had had powerful feelings about the canal ever since Disraeli's legendary purchase of a controlling interest in 1875. The canal had been Britain's artery of empire. (By 1956 India and Pakistan were free but the Union Jack still flew over many parts of Asia and Africa.) It was also the artery for Britain's oil and Eden believed she had only six week's reserves.

At the Tel Aviv Embassy we watched the storm gathering but our prime concern had to be narrower — the escalating border violence and the attempt to dissuade the Israelis from 'over-reacting', especially to the assaults across the Jordanian border. We argued that our friend King Hussein had only limited capacities to curb the mostly Egyptian-sponsored terrorists.

On October 26 the Israelis began to commandeer buses and lorries for a full-scale mobilisation of its citizen army. There was immediate debate in Tel Aviv's diplomatic community as to who they would attack. The common assumption was Jordan. At an American party I declared my own guess to be Egypt — the main source of threat. There was disbelief. The next day, with a Swedish girl friend as cover, I drove south to scout the Negev Desert approaches to the Egyptian border. The streams of armour and singing infantry suggested the guess was plausible. For an hour or so Israeli security detained me, demanding my camera. I had not got one, had not of course needed one.

On October 27 my ambassador was instructed especially to warn the Israeli Prime Minister, Ben Gurion, against attacking Jordan and to add that an attack on Egypt would lead to British action under the 1950 Tripartite Declaration. At this point, to the ambassador's puzzlement, Ben Gurion remarked, 'I think you will find your government knows more about this than you do'.[3]

Back at the embassy we sandbagged the ground-floor windows, blacked out the rest and worked out an evacuation plan for British subjects, not forgetting the tea urns. (Though hundreds of Americans were soon to be flown to Greece, few of our people actually decided to leave.) Telegrams were flooding in and the wireless and cypher staff were working flat out on instant coffee, toffees and not a little whisky in the dark hours.

Two hectic days later, on October 29, the Israelis attacked Egypt, dropping a crack parachute force from sixteen Dakota aircraft at the crucial Mitla Pass in the Sinai Desert thirty miles east of Suez. Israeli Mystère aircraft secured air superiority and patrolled the Canal Zone. Asked about their final objective at an official briefing that evening, the Israeli spokesman moved his pointer across the wall map and said, 'Cairo is there.'

What we now expected was for the British, French and American governments to act together under their Tripartite Declaration, against Israel as the obvious aggressor. However, on the afternoon of October 30, we received emergency telegrams from London, *en clair* — not in cypher — to say that the British and French governments had issued an ultimatum to *both* Israel and Egypt. The text crisply demanded the withdrawal of their forces from any positions within ten miles of the Suez Canal and their agreement to British and French forces establishing themselves along both sides of it. If either Israel or Egypt did not submit, Britain and France would be obliged to intervene in whatever strength was necessary. They were given only twelve hours to decide. Oddly, the telegram referred neither to the Americans being consulted nor to the Tripartite Declaration.

The ultimatum had been delivered to the Israeli and Egyptian embassies in London. There was nothing for us to do in Tel Aviv except await word of their replies. After a long day the ambassador and his deputy drove away through the blackout to their homes on the hill at Ramat Gan. I, the junior, was left holding the fort for the night shift.

Late that evening the telephone rang down in the embassy's bleak foyer. It was the Deputy Head of the Israeli Foreign Office. Had we got anything for him? Any message? Puzzled, I said no. What then, he asked, was all this press agency talk about an ultimatum? Heavens, I said, had he not received it from his embassy in London? No, nothing.

I gasped, outlined the content from memory and warned him that several of the twelve hours granted had already elapsed. Asking him to hold on, I rushed up the four floors to the strong room for the definitive text. I carefully read this to him, with such solemnity as a sense of history demanded and my puffing allowed. Then I remarked that something must have gone drastically wrong with Israeli communications. To play safe with our own, I must ask him to try to obtain his government's response within an hour. So far as I knew, the Royal Air Force's Canberra bombers were already warming up on our airfields in Cyprus, just over the horizon.

I sent an emergency telegram at once to the Foreign Office to report this extraordinary situation, telephoned the ambassador at home to tell him the form and then waited for the Israeli to come back. About an hour later he did so, saying he had his government's answer. Impetuously I asked if it was yes or no, thinking I could get that off at once to London and send the full text later. He declined. It was not, he said, the way diplomacy was done.

He started to dictate the text and comedy broke in. After a few sentences, me scribbling away, he broke off. That wording was not right, was it? Should it be 'not however unless' or 'always providing'? What did I think? The rival variations seemed of little significance and the minutes were ticking by.

By this time I had been joined in the grimly sandbagged lobby by a senior but non-political colleague who, worried about his children, was begging me to get a quick plain answer out of the Israelis. I asked the ministry to hold on, turned to my colleague and said that was not the way diplomacy was done. Somewhat later, with the whole text before me, I was at last able to flash it to London.

It was some weeks before I discovered what had gone amiss on the Israeli side. Their London embassy had wrongly assumed the ultimatum to be secret. (Eden had told Parliament of it at once.) So, to send it in their cypher, the Israelis had first to translate it carefully into Hebrew. Then there had been difficulties with their radio transmission, perhaps due to atmospheric conditions. Then, once received and decyphered in Jerusalem, what was still thought to be a secret document had to be brought down by the winding road through the Judean Hills to Tel Aviv where the ministers were spending the night. It was never an easy journey and there was a fog. Through such series of unpredictable mistakes and accidents can the course of history be altered.

My big moment had come and gone. I fondly thought it might one day warrant a paragraph in some history of the period. Neither I nor anyone else in the embassy knew we had been playing parts in an extraordinary charade, a massive deception. Nor had the Foreign Office, except for two or three senior officials. Nor had most British ministers; nor had the Americans, other allies or the Commonwealth. Nor had Hugh Gaitskell, Leader of the Opposition. Nor, of course, had Parliament, the press or the public.

According to his memoirs, Eden had already told Eisenhower on the day after the canal's nationalisation that in the last resort Britain must use force to bring Nasser to his senses and that military plans had therefore been commissioned.[4] It also transpired that through that summer Britain had held extremely secret top-level meetings with the French government of Guy Mollet and contacts had been made, mostly through the French, with Israeli leaders. According to Professor Hugh Thomas, who privately interviewed many of the participants, the three powers finally agreed at Sèvres on October 22, a week before the Israeli thrust into Sinai, that their actions would be coordinated. Israel's strike against Egypt code-named 'Operation Kadesh' would be employed as the excuse for the Anglo-French operation 'Musketeer', also against Egypt.

The first suspicions of the concealed truth arose from the

nature of the ultimatum. President Nasser was being ordered under threat of force to withdraw from critical areas of his own sovereign territory and release it to the occupation of foreign, Anglo-French, forces. However, the Israelis were being asked no real concession. Though deep into Egypt, their armies were much more than ten miles from the canal. Nasser could never accept such outrageous demands. Moreover British and French hostility towards him had been obvious for months. Both were bent on attacking Egypt, not merely to occupy the canal zone but to overturn Nasser's Arab nationalist regime.

At first Nasser thought Eden was bluffing and threw his forces across the canal against the Israelis. On the night of October 31, however, he withdrew most of them to defend Cairo. The Anglo-French aerial assault on Egyptian airbases had begun that evening. (It had been delayed by another unexpected factor, the presence of US evacuation aircraft at Cairo West airfield.) It went on for two days. Anglo-French naval units meanwhile attacked Egyptian vessels in the Mediterranean and the Gulf of Suez. A massive campaign of vituperation against Nasser was launched over Egypt by radio and aerial leaflet. Israeli forces meanwhile seized the Gaza Strip on their right flank and swept west through Sinai towards the canal but without getting close enough to compromise the Anglo-French cover story. (The French themselves were less fastidious: many of their aircraft are believed to have operated from Israeli airfields.)

Meanwhile an immense Anglo-French invasion fleet had been sailing from Malta, Gibraltar and even Southampton. It was agonisingly slow and immense pressure for a cease-fire was building up at the UN. President Eisenhower — a few days away from his second term election — was incensed at the action, the deception and perhaps especially by the timing of his previously trusted allies.

By November 5 the Israelis had seized all their vital objectives including the Egyptian positions at the head of the Gulf of Aqaba which had formerly stopped them using their only southern port, at Eilat. Ben Gurion was therefore by then disposed to accept the UN's demand for a cease-fire despite the British and French being far from achieving their own objectives. He was persuaded to make difficulties and at dawn British and French paratroops were dropped around Port Said. They were supported the next day by sea bombardments and waterfront landings of infantry and an Anglo-French armoured column was at once launched towards Suez at the other end of the Canal. But it had all taken too long. Political pressure had caught up with military tardiness — another unreckoned factor. At midnight the nerve of the British Cabinet snapped; they decided to accept the UN cease-fire.

The reasons were several. Israeli-Egyptian fighting, the expedition's pretext, had ceased. The international community was outraged. Eisenhower had used barrack-room language. The Russians had been at first preoccupied by the Hungarian uprising — they had marched into Budapest the previous day. Now they were believed to be considering armed intervention in aid of Egypt and to have alerted their missile forces. The United States had therefore also readied herself for war. There was a more immediate danger facing Britain's now divided Cabinet. Sterling was threatened and American support depended on an immediate cease-fire. Eden, weakened by ill health, was exhausted. Much of British opinion, and the press, had supported his audacious venture — certainly after 'our boys' had been despatched to the fray — but the storm of international complication had sapped his will to see the thing through even though the French were still keen to do so.

Fighting ceased and was not resumed. Under American pressure, including a threat to cut off oil supplies, Britain and France were compelled to pull out and to hand over to a UN force. Israel also withdrew to her previous frontiers though the UN secured her new access to the Gulf of Aqaba and assumed control of the troublesome Gaza Strip. Israel thus gained substantially. France lost much in prestige. Britain was especially humiliated despite her hastily contrived excuse that she had acted only to prepare the path for a laggardly UN intervention. Her enemies were delighted, her allies appalled, her friends anguished. There was petrol rationing and a balance of payments crisis. The nation had been belatedly compelled to recognise the limits of its post-war power. By December, Anthony Eden, in broken health, had to retire after only nineteen months in office.

Fairness to him would require a fuller account. Eden's concern about Nasser was acute: the subterranean hostility throughout the Middle East, the arbitrary seizure of the Suez Canal Company and the constant demands for the annihilation of Israel. Nor was the United States willing to act with any international boldness before her election was over — a stultification of foreign policy evident in every election year.

Nevertheless I hold to my description of the Anglo-French operation as an eruption of the irrational. It had many results quite opposite to those intended. Instead of installing a safe international regime for the canal, it led to the physical blocking of the waterway and a reinforcement of Nasser's hold on it. Instead of shattering Nasser's position in Egypt, it made him a hero. Instead of weakening Arab nationalism, it inflamed it. If it was intended to reassert British and French determination to assert their will in the world — to stop, as Eden said, 'the long, dismal, drawling tides of drift and surrender'[5] — then the failure of the expedition brought both of them as much contempt as opprobrium. If it was meant to re-establish international order, the method chosen was in blatant disregard of it. If it was meant to preserve peace, the Suez expedition could have precipitated a Third World War.

The operation was rooted in a false analysis. There was a false appreciation of the canal's importance, of the political harm Nasser was doing, of Britain's financial solidity and of the likelihood of overt hostility from Washington. But beneath the cerebral miscalculations there were crucial emotional factors which blinded Eden and Mollet to the realities.

They had come to regard Nasser as a political cancer. Eden insisted on seeing the threat to the canal as equivalent in menace to Hitler's occupation of the Rhineland in 1936. He thought that only ruthless surgery could extirpate the evil and danger. Eden saw himself acting for legality, order, stability. He would not appease the transgressor. There would be no more surrenders, no more Munichs. A brave and experienced minister, he had become set in the pre-war framework of thought: it was as if he had to use Nasser to replay the drama of Hitler's rise to show that, with decision and courage, the Nazi nightmare might have been prevented.

Eden had become doctrinaire. In seeking to restore international morality he became unscrupulous and exposed the world to greater perils. And if he had *not* exaggerated the original dangers it was absurd, having launched the expedition, not to have completed it. The vanguard of a great army had been called back after barely a day of land fighting. The irrationality was confirmed rather than redeemed by this ultimate lack of resolution: tragedy became farce.

At first sight the Suez affair may seem to reassure us about the prospects of preserving world order. The Anglo-French resort to violence was halted by world pressures and the long-run consequences were not as severe as either the pro- or anti-Suez factions had predicted. But it was a close-run thing. The super-powers could easily have been dragged in. In the late twentieth century a failure of crisis-management can lead to unprecedented destruction and Suez illustrates how difficult that management is becoming.

Modern crises are astonishingly complex, due partly to the proliferation of states with the end of empire. A dynastic struggle in pre-industrial Europe could involve a dozen countries. In our time a crisis may quickly involve the vital interests of thirty or forty and potentially of all. The complexity is enhanced by the multiplying connections and interdependencies of modern societies. Interdependence can make for stability but it also brings mutual vulnerabilities and apprehensions which are intensified by inherited antagonisms, competitive appetites and ideological differences.

Complexity adds to unpredictability, produces more scope for chance and miscalculation to take a hand and bewilders those who would wish to act for restraint. Then there is the heightened volatility of a powerfully-armed world in which elemental public passions can be instantly aroused through the universality of radio and television. A global village is inflammable.

Much of the pre-Suez turmoil was caused by the behaviour of new nations. Whatever sympathy we may have for their struggle for national identity and strength, we cannot but fear their lack of experience and of respect for the traditional obligations of international politics. Egypt was seeking upheaval in Iraq and Jordan, Libya and Lebanon.

The Saudis (with American help) were trying to undermine the Gulf States. Iraq was plotting against Syria. Israel, for that matter, was hankering for the wider frontiers of Eretz Israel.

Much of the developing world is a seed bed of subversion and insurrection, of coup and counter-coup, of domestic repression and virulent propaganda, of confiscation of property and repudiation of agreements. It is a world of nationalistic fervour, of passionate self-righteousness and frequent ruthlessness, as well as one of pathetic need. We have to respond to its calls for justice without ignoring its threats to international order.

The most elementary fairness however demands recognition that, in the Suez affair itself, reckless impatience was just as evident in London and Paris as in any of the Middle East capitals. Two of the most mature and democratic states resorted to the wilful aggression of the bully boy and showed themselves just as vulnerable to the gaudy emotions of party conferences, the grandiloquent calls to courage and unity and the hunger for glory. A leading article in *The Times* earlier that year had sounded this note. In discussing the 'Egyptian dictator' it warned of 'a deplorable flight from responsibility' and ended,

> Doubtless it is good to have a flourishing tourist trade, to win Test matches. . . But nations do not live by circuses alone. The people in their silent way, know this better than the critics. They still want Britain great.[6]

For years Americans read and responded to editorials like that about their 'responsibility' in Vietnam. The language is high flown; the emotions beneath it are primitive. As individuals, whether politicians or citizens, we share a frightening blindness not only to the realities of the world scene but to our own motivations. But to this aspect of the Seventh Enemy, as to that of political inertia, we must later return. What I hope has emerged from these snapshots taken from the Resident Clerk's mess, the Minister's Private Office and from the smoke of Suez is a sense of the tortuosities of international dealings and of the many obstacles to the vast saving actions that the human condition now demands. If in turn this understanding induces somewhat greater patience with the problems of those who rule us, it must also reinforce our doubts about their capacities to cope with unprecedented difficulties in civilised and effective ways.

Part One
The First Global Crisis

1 The Approach to Chaos

> There is a question in the air, more sensed than seen, like
> the invisible approach of a distant storm . . . the question
> asks whether we can imagine the future other than as a
> continuation of the darkness, cruelty, and disorder of the
> past; worse, whether we do not foresee in the human
> prospect a deterioration of things, even an impending
> catastrophe of fearful dimensions.
>
> Robert Heilbroner,
> *An Inquiry into the Human Prospect*[1]

Apocalyptic cries of woe and urgent proclamations that 'The
End is Nigh' have been so perennial in the human story that
we could be forgiven scepticism about their modern doomster
versions. They could reflect no more than a melodramatic
tendency to read vast significance into transient troubles.
Indeed many would argue that all prophecy is bunk, that
whether gory or golden the future cannot be known.

In the strict sense this is manifestly true. We cannot hope to
predict specific events. We can however assess the general
direction of some of the forces at work in our time. The
enterprise is fallible but not irrational. History is not the
remorseless machine painted by, say, the Marxists. But nor is
it a lucky dip from which any future is equally likely to
emerge. For at least two or three decades ahead, much of
mankind's course will be largely determined by choices
already made.

We must of course avoid projecting past trends into the
future automatically. (Whatever else it has done, the increase
in urban traffic has not buried New York or London in horse
manure as looked likely at the beginning of the century.)
Nevertheless, forecasting of a less naïve kind is not only
possible but essential. Reason does not demand we sit

stupidly awaiting fate. All active life depends on intelligent anticipation. Few decisions would make sense without it. All planning involves some forecasting. A new power station can take ten years to come on stream; a new weapons system or educational pattern likewise.

In the sense of forecasters, we are all 'prophets' nowadays. We cannot escape it. It is at least unconscious prophecy to assume in our attitudes and behaviour that tomorrow will be roughly like today. We think, speak and act on broad, if mostly unspoken, assumptions about how the future will turn out. These assumptions affect what we spend or save, give or keep, spoil or re-use. They affect how we do our work and bring up our children. They influence, directly or indirectly, what we say, what we buy, how we vote. They make a difference to what we do and what we don't.

Our action or inaction inevitably affects our own future and that of others. We can't help making a difference, whether by design or neglect. It is our petrol-guzzling cars that lead to disastrous oil blow-outs at sea. Our appetite for energy spreads nuclear hazards. It is our indifference that sustains poverty, disease and hopelessness across half the world. Jean-Paul Sartre's text is central to the modern situation, 'Not to act is also to act'. The individual's involvement in global society, in shaping the collective future, is intricate and inescapable.

The Pace of Change
What especially demands that we look ahead is the now frantic pace of change. If the history of the universe were to be shown on a timechart one mile long, the whole story of modern man would appear as only the last fraction of an inch. The earth is older than 4,500 million years. Mammals date back about eighty million years and the first primitive men and women emerged between one and four million years ago. But Homo sapiens sapiens evolved only about 35,000 years ago and it was after 9000 BC that our species first turned from hunting and gathering to a settled life of herding and farming. Since then it has been man's cultural rather than biological evolution that has shaped (and misshaped) the world. Change has so accelerated that the signal characteristic of our century has been expotential growth, operating like compound rather

than simple interest. A world population growth rate of two per cent a year may sound modest until one realises this could double our numbers in thirty-six years.

Our century has seen doublings in population, production, consumption, the speed of communication, the numbers of scientists, the size of business corporations and the growth of bureaucracies and centralised control. Our century began mostly horse drawn and has already placed powered vehicles on the moon. It began with primitive radio and has enabled us to witness an (absurdly contrived) Apollo/Soyuz handshake in space. It began with the Wright brothers' flight and had fabricated the jet engine within four decades and the Jumbos within seven.

We forget how recent are so many of the most familiar furnishings of our existence: moving pictures, 1905; mass produced cars, 1908; plastics, 1911. The first commercial wireless broadcast was in 1920 and the first television transmission in 1927. Only in 1938 arrived nylon, the Xerox copiers, the ball point pen. The transistor dates back only to 1948; the first laser to 1960.

It is of course the same story amongst weapons of war. In 1914 the military first achieved an efficient machine gun; in 1915 the first sinking of a ship by submarine and the first tanks. In 1938 came the first deliberate aerial bombardments of civilian populations, in Spain and Ethiopia. In 1944 the first supersonic missile, the German V2, was launched on London.

The acceleration in the size of a single explosion is perhaps the most dramatic of all illustrations of the age of doubling. Talking in 1932 of major war, the British Deputy Chief of Air Staff said that no bomb heavier than 500 pounds would be needed. By 1945 we were using 'block busters' containing 22,000 pounds, about ten tons of TNT. On February 13 of that year 800 tons of high explosives and incendiary bombs gutted Dresden and killed 30,000 people in about twenty-four hours. On August 6 the atomic bomb that razed Hiroshima was equivalent to 13,000 tons of TNT. It killed 80,000 or more in forty-three seconds.

By the early 1950s another prodigious technological leap produced bombs of megaton calibre — equivalent to an unimaginable million tons of TNT. The first real hydrogen bomb, exploded at Bikini in March 1954, was expected to have the power of eight million tons of TNT. It actually proved equivalent to fifteen million tons. We all make mistakes.

The largest American thermo-nuclear weapons now believed to be in service, the Titan IIs, have a yield of ten megatons. The Russian SS9s have a yield of between twenty and thirty-five megatons. A bomb of that size on a major city would kill millions and create a fire ball which would ignite hundreds of square miles. It is technically easy to make much larger explosions. The largest yet was of fifty-seven megatons produced by the Russians in October 1961. Had it been wrapped in an outer casing of uranium this device could have released over a hundred megatons.

Single bombs of that size make little strategic sense. More to the point is the total megatonnage accumulated since 1945. By 1961 the world's then four nuclear powers had already stockpiled about 30,000 megatons of nuclear explosive, the equivalent of 30,000,000,000 tons of TNT and hence nearly ten tons of TNT for every person then on earth.[2] A pound of the stuff is enough for a single killing so on that criterion our overkill capacity had already been exceeded by a factor of thousands.

That apparently was not enough. Since 1961 our overkill capacity has doubled, possibly trebled. US strategic forces alone are believed to wield a mind-blowing explosive power about half a million times greater than that used on Japan in 1945. The Russians probably have a larger megatonnage (though fewer warheads and less accuracy of delivery). Meanwhile the recently 'backward' Chinese managed to go from a first primitive nuclear explosion to a thermo-nuclear device in less than three years.

The World Today

How has the rising pace of change affected the political arena? If a Resident Clerk in the late seventies should look up from his cluttered, over-burdened desk, what sort of a world would he see? Would humanity look safer than in 1954, a generation before, when I first entered the Foreign Office?

The intervening years have certainly registered some achievements. The remainders of great colonial empires have been freed, in the British case with the spilling of remarkably little blood. A number of constructive regional groupings have emerged. Some heat has been taken out of the ideological conflict between Capitalism and Communism and the super-powers have become reconciled to neutralism amongst the developing countries. Most vital of all, Washington and Moscow found it possible to reach the limit of confrontation, notably in the Cuban missile crisis of October 1962, without precipitating a Third World War.

However the Clerk already feels less reassured when, mindful of the bulging world armouries, he notes that there are still dozens of unstable situations which could ignite a spluttering fuse to a potentially engulfing war. Few of the post-war disputes have been finally resolved: tensions of varying intensity remain for example over or in Korea, Berlin, Namibia, South Africa, Taiwan, Kashmir, Cyprus, Indo-China, Israel, Cuba, the Sahara, Somalia and Rhodesia. Many other territorial disputes and religious, racial and doctrinal hatreds continue to fester.

The incidence of war has been increasing. According to one study, between 1945 and 1975 there were 119 civil and international wars involving the territory of sixty-nine states and the armed forces of eighty-one.[3] By comparison there were only twenty-four wars between 1900 and 1941. The wars of the last three decades have killed tens of millions; more than the Second World War. In that period mankind spent around 6,000 billion dollars (six million million) on arms — the equivalent of 1,500 dollars for every man, woman and child. About a third of this has been on major weapons: tanks, aircraft, ships and missiles. International trade in these has boomed since the Arab-Israeli War of 1973. Ninety-five countries imported major weapons in 1975.

The Clerk notes that the Middle East and Southern Africa are especially inflammable. The basis of East-West tensions remains essentially unchanged. New nuclear tests are reported. There are periodic talks on strategic arms limitation but the gargantuan arms race continues, complicated by the neutron bomb, the Cruise missile and other new weapons. Negotiations for the mutual reduction of forces in Europe make little headway. In Asia, Africa and Latin America there is constant unrest. There were some 300 coups and attempted coups between 1945 and 1972. Military dictatorships are common. Repressive regimes cling to their power and privilege. Revelations multiply of the ruthless (and perturbingly gauche) activities of intelligence agencies and of their special departments for subversion, misinformation and concealed assassination. There is a growing use of sophisticated torture. Uncounted thousands of political prisoners moulder in camps and cells from Indonesia to Chile, from the Soviet Union to South Africa. Cambodia is one vast concentration camp. The UN splutters along in passionate disarray and near impotence.

Meanwhile the Soviet Union has come close to strategic parity with the US and shown herself confident enough to enter new hunting grounds in Africa. The US, humiliated in Vietnam, has had to recognise the limits of her power. Of course the ambitious idea of rolling back the tide of Communism from Eastern Europe and China had died with Dulles at the end of the fifties but America's passivity over Angola, whether well or ill-judged, suggested at least a temporary weakening of the will even to contain it.

Another notable change has been the emergence of the Chinese from isolation, their acquisition of nuclear forces and their bitter engagement in an ideological as well as territorial conflict with their former Soviet patrons. The relative strength of both Japan and the European Community has also grown. The solidarity of neither Eastern nor Western bloc is what it once was.

All these factors have contributed to a movement away from the severe bi-polarity of world politics of a generation before. Whether the diffusion of power will make for greater stability in super-power relations the Clerk will think questionable. Moreover not only China but India and Israel have devised nuclear weapons. Many other nations are quickly acquiring the capacity to follow them, putting more fingers on more triggers. The increasing incidence of terrorist outrage, political assassination and hi-jacking adds yet more unpredictabilities.

These are only some of the new factors which shake the contemporary Clerk's confidence. He notices that the poor world's problems of over-population, poverty and under-development are still regarded more as a matter for occa-

sional rhetoric and calculated gesture than urgent international action. Deprivation, hunger and disease are rarely
the subject of messages unless there is a natural disaster, an
especially dramatic famine or an official delegation at some
conference or other wants approval of the (pious but non-
committal) line it proposes to take.

The Clerk has also learned of a host of other alleged threats
to the economic and social foundations of world order. He has
seen for himself the deterioration of our natural surroundings
and has read about the vulnerability of the atmosphere and
global weather patterns. There are constant revelations about
poisons hidden in the effluents of industry and talk of
potentially calamitous accidents with nuclear power or experiments in molecular biology. He knows that some of the new
weapons systems may upset the fateful calculations of strat-
egists. There is growing anxiety about the dwindling of the
earth's oil reserves. Fuel prices have soared. Bad grain
harvests in the Soviet Union reduce the stocks available to
meet famine elsewhere. Inflation surges on and the world's
financial and trading system appears unexpectedly precarious.

In short, the Resident Clerk is confronted with questions
scarcely dreamed of only a generation earlier. Are we
destroying the biological basis of life? Are vital resources
running out? Are we coming to the end of affluence? Should
we go for zero-growth? Can we still hope to see the poor
world brought up to our own standards of living? Can we even
expect to feed it? If not, what numbers may die? And where
and with what politically convulsive results? Might food
follow oil as a scarce resource used as a weapon of power
politics? Who will decide who is to starve?

Faced with an eruption of such great and unaccustomed
issues, it can seem impossible to make any sense at all of
mankind's situation. The Clerk may rightly suspect that some
of what he has read is the self-interested exaggeration of the
media or the theatrical utterance of eco-freaks with a down on
a system in which they cannot succeed. Some may be the
calculated hyperbole of politicians and committed ideologues
seeking a passing advantage. (Does Peking believe its often
declared prediction of a war between the two super-powers?)
He may ask if there is really a world crisis at all. Are we

confronted with mostly unrelated and perennial problems in new forms? After all, societies have almost always lived with distress and conflict, pestilence and deprivation, suffering and the chance of sudden death.

The Doom Debate

Most people do not attempt to judge such questions and it is hard to blame them. Contemplation of the world's ills was never easy on the feelings. A sense of powerlessness also deters. What could one do about it all? The contemporary Clerk, like the rest of us, finds it hard enough to make a coherent picture of daily events. How can any of us come to grips with the larger trends and tensions which lie beneath? When these are discussed, the language is often abstract and technical. The details, the jargon, the percentages, can be baffling. And the experts often disagree. It seems impossible to keep proportion. It is easy to stop listening, tempting to stop trying to assess the situation at all.

Somehow we must try. For, as I have intimated, events will take over unless we begin to understand and to act. A growing number of writers, scholars, institutes and think-tanks have been engaged on the task. Naturally enough they have taken a wide variety of paths and reached varying conclusions.

Some, like Herman Kahn of the Hudson Institute, do not think the prospects ominous and remain convinced, for instance, that economic growth can be and should be sustained. The first Club of Rome report, *The Limits to Growth*, was far less sanguine.[4] It gave new emphasis to the seeming insatiability of the affluent economies' appetite for the planet's finite reserves of natural resources and caused a stir by arguing that on recent trends they would be doomed to collapse. The Club's second report *Mankind at the Turning Point* explored the world outlook in a more sophisticated way, taking it region by region.[5] This, too, concluded however that failure to take radical action would cost immense suffering.

Both these reports employed elaborate computer simulations or models taking account of as many as possible of the major measurable variables and relationships which are shaping our fate. Most of the other global studies have been less dependent on intricate mathematics and more accessible

to the general reader. Several have been no less comprehensive, notably *Only One Earth*, a brilliant survey on 'the
care and maintainance of a small planet'.[6] Others have
concentrated on specific threats, or on particular lines of
remedy like E. F. Schumacher's influential study of economics 'as if people mattered'.[7] One or two have focused on
spiritual aspects of the drama as did Theodore Roszak in an
eloquent discussion of the sterility of the modern cast of
mind.[8]

The size like the range of the literature is vast. Although the
doom debate began with Rachel Carson's *Silent Spring* in
1962, it raged most fiercely between 1965 and 1972.[9] There
were of course always those who thought the doomsayers
hysterical. I have already mentioned John Maddox's charge
in *The Doomsday Syndrome* that they sap the will to
survive.[10] But whatever the differences about the severity of
the various threats, both sides have agreed in placing a great
deal of hope if only implicitly, in the response of people and
governments.

It is here I part company with most in the field. We simply
cannot assume that intelligent prescription will eventually be
translated into constructive policies, much less that it will be
done in time.

My sketch of recent world politics already warns us against
any such expectation. Fervent nationalism, widespread
unrest and mutual fear make an unpromising basis for most of
the remedies we are offered. The ecologists should note that
the doom debate, though vigorous, has resulted in remarkably little government action beyond the convening of a few,
mostly abortive, world conferences. True, that is something,
yet to make much of it is to speak as if time were on our side.

U Thant, then Secretary-General of the UN, had this to say
in 1969,

> I do not wish to seem over dramatic, but I can only
> conclude from the information that is available to me as
> Secretary-General, that the Members of the United
> Nations have perhaps ten years left in which to subordinate
> their ancient quarrels and launch a global partnership to
> curb the arms race, to improve the human environment, to
> defuse the population explosion, and to supply the required

momentum to development efforts. If such a global partnership is not forged within the next decade, then I very much fear that the problems I have mentioned will have reached such staggering proportions that they will be beyond our capacity to control.[11]

Most of that decade has been wasted and almost all the problems U Thant listed are now more severe than when he spoke.

So-called doomsayers are usually accused of excessive pessimism. What puzzles me is their underlying optimism. Perhaps some are more fearful about the dismal waste of the years than they publicly say, but most not only seem sure that saving action will be taken but that meanwhile we shall accommodate disturbance without too much commotion. Michael Allaby, for example, finds hope in the adaptability shown by the British to the high cost of fuel and the general inflation which followed the oil crisis of 1973. 'The moral of this story is that people, and nations, are more resilient than theorists imagine them to be.'[12]

This is true to a degree but the impact of a relatively brief oil crisis on a well-governed and rich society was puny compared with our coming travails. And though people are fairly adaptable, the adaptations often take mean or destructive forms. Rich societies under pressure are perhaps capable of enduring a progressive decline in their standard of living without civil collapse but they are not in the process likely to prove generous or far-sighted about the troubles of others.

The American economist Robert Heilbroner makes this crucial point in his incisive study *An Inquiry into the Human Prospect*. Talking about the magnitude of the coming changes and the resulting competitive struggle for advantage and existence, he says '. . . the bonds of national identity are certain to exert their powerful force, mobilising men for the collective effort needed, but *inhibiting* the international sharing of burdens and wealth.'[13] (My italics.)

Heilbroner is one of the few analysts of mankind's plight who treats not just the threats but the question of human response with the sombre gravity required. He fears only one kind of social system could meet the growing pressures, one combining a 'religious' orientation and a 'military' discipline, the monastery and the barracks. (It is one to which, so far, he sees the Chinese system coming closest.)

Even so, I am not sure Heilbroner quite plumbs the depths of our probable prospect. He sees the dangers coming to a head some way into the next century and his prime anxiety is the fearful price in liberty we shall have to pay for our collective survival. I cannot help fearing that the crisis will be brought much closer than that and be positively intensified by human action. This is another point where I differ from most writers on the subject.

I think we must consider the terrible possibility of quite savage reversal. In situations of rising stress, human action can as easily hasten as slow the processes of disintegration. Strange forces sometimes erupt in human affairs. The horrors of Hitler's Final Solution or of Russia's barbaric prison camps in the Gulag Archipelago reflect something latent in humanity at large, not just in the regimes which created them. We do not like to think about this. Germany before the Nazis had been one of the world's most cultivated societies. The Russian Revolution was rooted in high ideals of human liberation from oppression. Alexander Solzhenitsyn describes the transportation by barge of political prisoners to the Vorkuta complex:

> People were thrown into the trough-like holds and lay there in piles or crawled around like crabs in a basket. . . The journey in such a barge was no longer prisoner transport, but simply death on the installment plan . . . they gave them hardly anything to eat. Then they tossed them out in the tundra. . . They just left them there to die, alone with nature.[14]

Savagery may break out anywhere. In Northern Ireland men are shooting others through the knee caps as 'warnings'. From the recent Lebanese civil war there were hideous reports of cold-blooded massacre and mutilation. Likewise in the Indonesian occupation of East Timor. Such phenomena are not to be written off as exceptional aberrations; they are symptoms of a darkness which may overcome any society, any individual. As the psychologist Anthony Storr has said,

The sombre fact is that we are the cruellest and most ruthless species that has ever walked the earth; and that, although we may recoil in horror when we read in newspaper or history book of the atrocities committed by man upon man, we know in our hearts that each of us harbours within himself those same savage impulses which lead to murder, to torture and to war.[15]

Despite all this our minds seem to remain obstinately contaminated with the peculiar heresy that all problems are soluble. The zoologist Angus Martin has interestingly suggested that our dogged optimism, our will to dominate difficulties, has been bred into us in the course of human evolution. He fears we may be unable to escape from its genetically-rooted arrogance and destructiveness however grave our situation becomes.[16]

Be that as it may, in theory all of the six impersonal threats are capable of solution. The next doubling of population is virtually inevitable, for reasons I shall explain, but we do know how we might prevent the one after. We have enough food and, shared equitably, all could be adequately fed, for the present anyway. Other scarce resources could be used more slowly, conserved more carefully, divided more fairly. Technologies could mend much of the environmental damage they have caused. Nuclear weaponry and other dangerous innovations could be curbed.

So much for theory. Yet any one of the six threats we failed to meet could by itself bring calamities. Moreover the threats are deeply interlocked. Most solutions bring new problems. The conquest of plague and malaria has intensified the population explosion. Anti-pollution measures can be extravagant with energy. Nuclear alternatives to fossil fuels bring their own hazards. Furthermore, some remedies take decades to have marked effect — like birth control programmes.

'Wild' Problems

It may be thought that the extraordinary and accumulating powers of science and technology must be capable of untying these knots. But the problems are not purely technical and need much more than the ingenuity of clever people in white coats. We must distinguish between 'tame' and 'wild' problems. Take the sending of men to the moon. Once it was decided to make the necessary investment of money and skill (an important proviso) this task was indeed purely technical, essentially straightforward, a matter of design. Apart from risking the lives of the astronauts, it was not going to hurt anyone. It raised no questions about its impact on a complex society and posed no awkward choices between priorities or evils. It was a 'tame' problem, not entangled with either social reality or human values.

But most of our problems are 'wild' ones, entangled with both. Consider that of feeding the world's hungry. Research created new 'miracle' strains of cereals for doubling yields. In the early days some heralded this as the glorious answer. What happened in practice? For the most part, the extra grains went to feed the livestock of the rich rather than the bellies of the poor. The rich, including the industrial proletariats of Capitalist and Communist states alike, could easily afford the conversion of large amounts of grain into small amounts of meat. The poor, virtually excluded from the cash nexus, could not afford to feed the grain to their children let alone to animals. The problem of hunger is less that of increasing the volume of production than of the ability of the poor to buy. Here as elsewhere, technical innovation without social change — such as land reform — can make matters worse.

We must therefore reject the idea of there being a simple 'technological fix'. Human choice, individual and collective, decides where and how our technical powers are applied, to what social ends and in accordance with what values. The question is not whether we have the ingenuity and tools but whether we have the necessary penetration of analysis, the far-sightedness, the capacity to organise, the generosity of spirit and the will.

2 North and South: A Collision Course

> When the rich assemble to concern themselves with the business of the poor it is called charity. When the poor assemble to concern themselves with the business of the rich it is called anarchy.
>
> Paul Richard,
> *The Scourge of Christ*

The century of doubling has brought no change more outrageous or potentially inflammable than the still widening gulf between the world's rich and poor. In producing unparalleled wealth we have created unprecedented inequality. Humanity has been split into two camps in which the wasteful affluence of the one is as conspicuous as the corrosive poverty of the other.

Giradoux, the French playwright, said, 'The privilege of the great is to watch catastrophe from a terrace.' The rich world has been watching catastrophe for a long time. It is scarcely too strong a term for the protracted desolation and bereavements of millions of families across the continents. The great should not imagine their superior position will give them unlimited immunity. Their attention has been too much devoted to how precisely to share out the bounty amongst their own ranks. For below their terrace the hungry throng has been gathering in rising anger: its appeal for charity has become a demand for justice.

Viewed historically, the proportions of our affluence are extraordinary. So is the way we take it for granted. Our horizons of expectation have become ludicrous: we regard as tribulation even the minor losses brought by recession. Nor are we always live to the grossness of the glossy advertisements inviting us to yet new extravagances and yet new illusions of satisfaction. The artificial contrivance of 'needs' is the dynamo of our economic system. But we all play a part in this. Only the other day I read of a doctor warning that children might be 'sensorily deprived' unless they got their television in colour!

The prime beneficiaries of affluence have been the relatively few nations comprising about a quarter of humanity, which stretch across the Northern hemisphere from North America, through Western and Eastern Europe to the Soviet Union and Japan. These societies of the 'Rich North' have much in common. They have their ideological and other differences but are all heavily industrialised, highly urbanised, intensive in agriculture, profoundly committed to science and technology and powerfully armed. They deploy vast treasuries of capital and skill to produce immense quantities of consumer goods and services. They absorb in the process, vast proportions of the earth's limited resources. The affluence has not been shared evenly either between these nations or within them. But they constitute the world's privileged. Even their poor are rich.

In contrast there is the world's 'Poor South', consisting of most of the nations of Asia, Africa and Latin America. They too are various in history and culture but are broadly non-industrialised, still mostly rural (though that is changing fast) and primitive in agriculture. They employ much less science and technology and are militarily weak. They have little capital or trained manpower. They produce, per head, few goods and services and consume, per head, a tiny proportion of the earth's resources. Many of them have wealthy minorities but also vast numbers who are trapped by poverty, illiteracy, under-employment, disease and high birth rates in a remorseless cycle of deprivation.

In terms of literal geography, some nations fit no more tidily into a North-South than an East-West division. Australia, New Zealand and South Africa (that is, its reigning white minority) are essentially parts of the Rich North, which spawned them. On the other hand, China must be counted in the Poor South and may well become its most potent champion.

There are of course many countries in a transitional or ambiguous position between South and North. Conspicuous amongst these are the oil-rich states of OPEC (the Organ-isation of Petroleum Exporting Countries) such as Iran, Saudi Arabia, Nigeria and Venezuela. Following the oil-price boom of 1973, they acquired immense Northern incomes and financial power. Nevertheless, the majority of their people still endure Southern poverty and, for the present at least, their governments have identified themselves with the ambi-tions of the South in what is already widely called 'the North-South dialogue'.

Despite inevitable simplifications (and the different con-notations of the 'South' for Americans), the distinction between North and South is as useful as that between East and West. It draws attention to what Soviet Communism and Western Capitalism have in common in the eyes of the deprived. It also helps us to avoid talking of the 'Third World'. This term (like the 'Fourth World' — meaning the very poorest nations) is not wholly objectionable yet it often suggests the under-developed world is somehow of tertiary importance, a somewhat accessory and less important frac-tion of mankind.

In fact, the nations of the Poor South already comprise over two-thirds of humanity and their fate will affect us all. There are not three — or four — 'worlds' but one.

Tragically, the North-South division of this one world is also racial. The Rich North is overwhelmingly white — even the South Africans so regard the Japanese — while the Poor South is black, brown or yellow. This dreadful coincidence of privilege with white skin is made more ominous by remem-bered history. The North includes all the recent imperialist powers and the South their recent vassals. In the view of many in the South, Northern colonialism persists, even if it has changed its means from frank conquest to political interven-tion, economic pressure and military 'assistance'. Nor, despite double standards, do the Russians always escape this charge.

The Development Gap
The Northern nations achieved their prosperity through initial environmental advantages, not special virtue. We do not 'deserve' our wealth nor the Southerners their poverty. They are neither witless nor feckless. The North was favoured by a temperate climate, a more reliable agriculture and so a

more settled basis for generating trade. Capital was accumulated, skills developed, technology applied. Over the last two
centuries the combination of these within an effective if crude
risk-taking market system produced industrialism and rapid
growth. The North shot ahead and has continued to do so.
British people were probably not much richer than Indians in
the eighteenth century. Now their income per head is about
twenty-five times higher.[1]

Northern industrialism deliberately inhibited similar
advance in the South. Whatever benefits colonies received
from imperial administration they did not include indigenous
industrial development. Their economies were frankly subordinated to the interests of the mother countries, first as
primary producers, with their plantations and mines, and
second as captive markets. When, in the last century, Indian
textile producers proved capable of competing successfully in
Britain, a tariff wall was erected against their embryo
industries.

In our century the gap has continued to widen. The
capital-intensive Northern economies have thrust ahead
while relatively the Southern ones have crawled. Most of their
growth has been absorbed by their rapidly growing populations. The average Asian is probably not much better off
than a century ago.

There is, of course, an enclave of modernity in most
Southern economies — some factories and luxury hotels, a
television service of a kind, perhaps an airline and a few other
prestige projects. What is not evident to the casual visitor is
that this modern sector produces little if any benefit for the
majority. The masses remain dependent on the traditional
sector — the almost separate subsistence economy of primitive agriculture and small-scale 'informal' trading.

The free play of market forces — so far as they are 'free' —
is effective in generating wealth, not at sharing it equitably.
The market system operates in terms of money and things,
not of human beings and their needs. Its defenders claim that
if enough wealth is created it will somehow 'trickle down' to
all. In relation to the North-South division, at least, this is
demonstrably untrue. Under the present economic world
order 'to him who hath shall be given': the market system
tends to concentrate wealth more than it disperses it.

Precise measurement of the resulting gulf in development and living standards between North and South is difficult. Data on the poor economies is often unreliable and comparisons can be treacherous, especially of personal incomes. It costs much less to survive in a semi-tropical village than a cold Northern city. Nevertheless the North-South disparities are so wide that statistical niceties cannot obscure an extraordinary and intolerable state of affairs.

Income is generated by production. The South has been able to produce little and therefore earns little. The usual way of measuring average income is to divide the gross national product (GNP) of a country by its population. According to the World Bank's provisional estimates for 1975 the GNP per head in the United States was 7,060 dollars; in France it was 5,760; in Britain 3,840; in the Soviet Union it was about 2,620. The equivalent figures for Southern nations were very much lower. In Brazil it was 1,010 dollars; in Zambia 540; in China 350; in Nigeria 310; in Indonesia 180, in India 150. Fifteen countries had even smaller average incomes.[2]

These figures conceal even more staggering facts. In 1971 the production of each of the top ten multi-national companies was greater than that of over eighty sovereign states. In 1972 the low income countries, with over two-thirds of the world's people, accounted for under seven per cent of all manufacturing output and only seventeen per cent of world trade. The Northern minority consumes about nine-tenths of the world's production of oil, most of its minerals, about four fifths of the available fertilisers and three quarters of the fish catch.

The US alone, with six per cent of the world's population, consumes about a third of its production of energy and raw materials. Directly or indirectly the average American has hundreds of mechanical slaves working for him. When millions of the impoverished want for the simplest working implements, it is instructive to count just the domestic machines we take for granted — the heaters, Hoovers, shavers, food mixers, hair driers, radios, mowers and so on. Over a lifetime the average Northerner consumes perhaps fifty times more of the world's scarce resources than an Asian peasant.

We are apt to think the South is gradually catching up. It is not. The gap is widening. In the industrialised countries, with an average income over 4,500 dollars, total production has been growing faster than in the poorer countries, with under 200 dollars per head. Moreover, in the latter, output *per person* almost stagnated between 1968 and 1974.

The incomes quoted for the poor countries are low enough in all conscience. They conceal a worse picture because they are averages. The majority get less, vast numbers far less. At just over 1,000 dollars, Brazil's average income looks relatively high. It hides profound poverty in its north-east region.

Nearly one in four of what some call the human family subsist on an annual income of around a hundred dollars per head. Robert McNamara has said, 'They are the absolute poor, living in situations so deprived as to be below any rational definition of human decency.'[3] They include half the populations of four great countries: India, Pakistan, Bangladesh and Indonesia. Tens of millions in Africa and Latin America struggle on the same margins of existence.

Abstract statistics obscure human degradation. They stand for legions of children dying in infancy from malnutrition and disease; for survivors harmed in body and mind; for parents demoralised in squalid shacks without basic services; for debilitation amongst the prematurely aged and for death and bereavement before its necessary time.

From Morocco through most of North Africa and the Middle East to India and Thailand I have observed the evidence of deprivation. In East Java I have seen pot-bellied infants with flies on their sores calling to anaemic mothers with empty breasts. In Surabaya youngsters in rags scavenged for scraps and stripped an unlocked car in seconds. In Delhi the emaciated stared out unattended by the side of the road. In Morocco eight-year-old girls, under-nourished and unschooled, make carpets for a dollar a day. In Colombo children are sometimes sold as slaves to save them from starvation. In Dacca the death wagons tour unmade streets to collect the corpses for burial.

We are speaking of people with little education or modern skill or work or hope. In earlier decades most of them would have been able to scratch a subsistence from the earth but pressure of numbers has diminished land holdings and over-strained the soil.

About 700 million of the absolute poor live in rural areas. Over half of them have less than one hectare (about two and a half acres) of land per family. The average size of these families is seven. As the families grow up, the land has to be divided yet again. Those who get none have to trek to the squalid settlements growing up around almost every city of the South; another 200 million of the absolute poor already live in them.

The Crisis of Human Settlement

Most Southern cities are now swelling to bursting point. In 1950 only sixteen held more than a million. Today over sixty do. By the end of the century about 200 will.[4] They usually have a few salubrious suburbs for those who run the modern sector. In the least favoured parts, in swampy areas, on derelict land, on rocky heights, there are sprawling shanty towns cobbled up out of flattened oil drums, wooden crates, cardboard and scrap timber. This is the new urban jungle, the festering settlements called *kampongs* in Indonesia, *callampas* in Chile, *favelas* in Brazil, *barracas* in Tripoli, *barong-barongs* in the Philippines. It is the same picture in Cairo, Lagos, Caracas, Karachi, Rio and Rangoon.

The *bustees* of Calcutta run for sixty miles along the Hooghly River and the conurbation now holds over eight million. In the centre there are 85,000 to the square mile. Hundreds of thousands sleep in the streets. Much of the area has no sewers. Garbage and night soil removal services constantly break down. So does the water supply, where it exists. A municipal system built for a fraction of present numbers is falling apart at the seams.

The worst is yet to come. Explosive population growth and the continuing daily influx of the rural poor are compounding a world-wide crisis of human settlement. Southern cities already vastly overstrained by a total population of 700 million are expected to have to cope with 1,800 million by the turn of the century.

The life of the urban poor is wretched but for most seems preferable to the utter helplessness of rural poverty. At least the city affords useful rubbish, opportunities for theft, a market for prostitution and the occasional soup kitchen. It rarely provides regular employment. At best the new urban dwellers will become casual labourers, porters, pedlars or the drivers of tricycle-rickshaws, like the *betjaks* I sometimes hailed in Jakarta when my (chauffeur-driven) car was out of action. Yes, I had servants — seven of them. It seemed a sort of contribution.

The Cycle of Deprivation
In urban and rural areas alike, the billion absolute poor have to live on so little because they are not enabled to do productive work. In most Southern nations twenty-five to thirty per cent have no work or too little. The World Bank fears this figure will rise in the coming years.

Modern economic forces have done little to help. Most Northern investment is made in the already rich countries where it is thought safer. When it has gone to the South, it has mostly been made in typically Northern capital-intensive industry employing little labour. Southern governments have encouraged this, believing a steel mill or oil refinery essential to national dignity. Such enterprises can add a lot to the GNP without benefiting any except skilled and managerial people. Indeed modern investment often adds to unemployment: a single plastic footwear plant may displace thousands of traditional cobblers and the suppliers of their working materials.

For similar reasons most international aid seems to have done little for employment. A new six-million-dollar fishport built at Manila by Japanese contractors cost 2,000 people their jobs. Investment in agriculture has tended to benefit big farmers rather than small peasants. Major public works — new roads, bridges and irrigation projects — provide only temporary labouring and after completion often have scant relevance to the lives of the poorest. Paved roads speed the movement of security forces, officials with briefcases and the crops from plantations. They make less difference to those who have always had to walk.

Ill health is another heavy burden on the world's poor. Some of the killer diseases such as plague, cholera, malaria and yellow fever have been brought under control but in one way the crippling diseases have worse effects: the dead are not a burden on the living. Leprosy, trachoma, elephantiasis and bilharzia undermine the capacity to work of hundreds of millions. A million are afflicted with river blindness in the Volta River basin of Africa alone. Dozens of less dramatic diseases, left untreated, cause lassitude and debilitation. Even measles can kill or cripple the malnourished. In the South up to half of all deaths occur before the age of five.

Medical services for the Southern poor are grossly deficient. Expenditure on them is generally less than one per cent of typical Northern levels. Dental and opthalmic care is minimal; psychiatric help nil. The simplest injury from field or workshop can bring vile complications.

In Britain there is one doctor for every 900 people. In India there is one for 5,000, in Haiti one for 13,000. Some African countries have one doctor for every 2,000 people in their large towns but one per 50,000 or more in their rural areas. India alone has 560,000 villages, many of them far from help. Even ten miles may be too many to survive for a sick man lashed to an ox-drawn plough. Doctors acquire middle-class values and expectations; few wish to serve in the backlands. They prefer to cater for the prosperous in the cities, muttering about 'modern facilities'. In a Jakarta hospital it cost a Singhalese friend of mine two years' pay to have his kidney stones removed. (A pint of my blood saved him another three months' worth.)

Health critically depends on clean water. In the cities this means a piped supply, ideally of over 200 litres (say forty-four gallons) per person per day. That is expensive, so many Southern municipalities provide it only to middle-class areas and abandon the majority to the mercy of exploitative water carriers. These may charge twenty times the municipal price and are still unreliable: cholera is often endemic in shanty towns. Poor sanitation makes things worse: 1,200 millions lack adequate access to drinking water and 1,400 millions have no sewage system.

Other services too are perversely denied to the most needy. Transport systems tend to be geared to the interests of the well off. The private car takes precedence. There are cities which provide motorways but no buses, or buses only to the wealthier areas. The poor typically spend hours every day walking to and from work. As to public housing, impressive blocks are sometimes erected but at standards so proudly 'modern' that the poor cannot hope to rent it. Their needs are more humble: a cessation of police and bulldozer raids on their self-made settlements; a chance of legal title to their scraps of ground; some water stand-pipes, perhaps electricity; decent tracks and some basic building materials for them to use themselves.

Illiteracy is another vicious component of the cycle of deprivation. It further reduces the chances of a job or self-improvement, inhibits political activity and often induces a sense of helplessness and shame. Over a third in the South are illiterate; in some Arab states and Africa up to three quarters. The proportion amongst women is especially high. There are more illiterates today than ever in history.

Nor is the outlook promising. UN figures show that in 1970 forty per cent of Asian children of primary school age were not enrolled. The schools did not exist. The figure for Africa was bigger. About half of those who do enroll, drop out before finishing. The position over secondary schooling was worse. Over half that age group in Latin America and Asia were not enrolled; in the Arab states and Africa about three quarters. Meanwhile the educational gap between North and South widens.

The Southern Elites

The manifold plight of the poor is apt to make us become patronising towards them. Yet their apparent helplessness is not intrinsic to them; it is imposed by circumstances. They are not a special sort of people. They share the same wide range of natural intelligence, personality and good and ill will as we do. They are penniless, not pathetic. Much less are they contemptible. There is an extraordinary resourcefulness and spirit alike in the rural hovels and the foetid *kampongs*, *bidons* and *favelas* of the cities. Given a chance, granted a minimum of relevant help and a small share of their due, they can make a viable sort of life with very little. The tragedy is their powerlessness. The squalor of their existence cries out at the economic and political system which creates and sustains it.

Responsibility for this system does not lie in the North alone. There are exceptions but most Southern nations have their own internal North of privilege just as most Northern societies have their own internal South of deprivation. A small ruling class of politicians, professionals, and proprietors runs government, controls industry and commerce and owns much of the fertile land. It is they who allocate the national revenues, place fat government contracts, handle the import and export trade, control the customs, negotiate special terms for the multi-nationals and get the commission on arms sales. They distribute the jobs: they decide who does what, who gets what. They dominate the modern sector and share its bounties with their friends and allies. Southern politics are volatile; family and tribal loyalties are strong. It seems to make sense to look after your own. There is, after all, a long way to fall and 'everyone does it'.

The ruling élites also exploit, while despising and otherwise neglecting, the traditional sector in which the majority is trapped. It is the place-men and bureaucrats who make the municipal rules, grant the waivers, collect the taxes and issue the licences for the street traders, the craftsmen and porters. They fix the charges for many commodities and what public services there are. Corruption is endemic. It becomes a way of life. At every level of society there is someone looking for his percentage, his *douceur*, his return favour.

At the top the rewards of power are immense. Take Kenya. President Jomo Kenyatta's family and its Kikuyu allies have accumulated huge fortunes and great estates. Sardonically they are called the Royal Family. The *Sunday Times* has shown how they profit from plantations, casinos, hotel construction, insurance, shipping, agricultural supplies, pharmaceuticals and deals in gems, ivory and charcoal. International anxiety at the destruction of the elephants and the rain forests appear to make little impact. A few brave Kenyans have protested including the politician J. M. Kariuki who was found murdered in March 1975.

There are even greater disparities of income within Southern than Northern societies. In the South the top ten per cent of the population take about forty per cent of the total pre-tax income. In the North the figure is about thirty per cent.

What of the under class, say the bottom forty per cent? In some of the countries of Eastern Europe it receives as much as twenty-five per cent of the national income. In Britain and the US it gets about twenty per cent. In Brazil, Peru, Gabon, Iraq and South Africa it has to make do with about six per cent.[5]

These extreme inequalities show no clear sign of narrowing. A radical redistribution of both income and wealth is needed in many Southern countries, especially in Latin America where there is more to share. The concentrations of land and other ownership would need to be broken up, and those of arbitrary power.

It is doubtful however whether the Southern élites would voluntarily relinquish either riches, power or privilege. Many are becoming more bourgeois, not less. Over the years their original radical zeal has been diminished by what the Danes call the 'mayonnaise cure'.

Nor, by itself, would the most drastic but purely internal reform do much to reduce the glaring disparities between North and South. Even if the South achieved two per cent more growth a year than the North — which it shows no sign of doing — *it would still take over a century to catch up*.

A Collision Course

Events in the last few years have made things worse. While the surge in the price of oil damaged all Northern economies, it placed crippling burdens on the South. Its already massive debts were further increased by the zooming costs of manufactured imports and by smaller returns from its exports to a world economy in recession. The North can live off its fat. The South, in general, has none.

Its aggregate trade deficit quadrupled between 1973 and 1975. For a while the poor nations borrowed much of the oil cash that was floating about. They were soon having to pay back in interest charges alone a sum larger than the total official Western aid in the other direction. The debts of some of the poorest countries are much larger than their annual national incomes. Bankers say these countries must pull in their belts. Try translating that to a skinny woman searching anxiously for a few sticks.

With Southern needs at their most acute the rich nations became so obsessed with their own problems of inflation, unemployment and balance of payments that they effectively reduced their aid and assistance. In 1975 there was some improvement in Western aid but it was still insultingly minimal in the light of Southern conditions. Amounting to only 0·36 per cent of the donor countries' GNP, it was only half of even the modest (and never attained) target recommended years before by the UN.

A report by the OECD in December 1975 said, 'the prospects ahead for most developing countries are black'. The World Bank said the poorest nations could expect 'virtually no increase at all in their desperately low per capita incomes for the rest of the decade'. For the billion absolute poor it forecast an increase of annual income per head from 105 dollars in 1970 to 108 dollars in 1980. For the people of the developed world in the same period it forecast a rise from 3,100 dollars to 4,000 dollars.

The decade would be worth three dollars to the destitute and 900 dollars to the rich.

Whatever the failings of Southern governments (which widely vary), there is no doubt where most of the responsibility lies. Because the nations of the Rich North control about three quarters of the world's wealth, they also dictate the rules of world trade and finance. They decide what investments are made and where, what prices are charged for industrial goods and what prices the South will receive for their raw materials. The industrialised nations do not intend the economic stagnation of the South. They operate a system which has precisely that result.

This is the (only slightly exaggerated) nub of the analysis which lies behind the South's rising demand for a New International Economic Order. In the 'Group of 77', now comprising over 110 developing countries, it has formed a sort of trade union of aggrieved nations which see Northern aid as little more than the means to patch up an essentially unjust system. They do not seek a new deal, but a new order. They utterly reject the conventional view expressed by Henry Kissinger in Kansas City in May, 1975, that 'the present economic system has served the world well', much less that 'poorer nations benefit most from an expanding world economy'. This is a convenient philosophy with only one disadvantage. It is not true.

The Group of 77 is determined to rescue the South from the economic hegemony of the North — especially the West — whether by voluntary agreement or a combination of political and monopoly pressure. However the protracted North-South dialogue about all this turns out, we would probably be mistaken to imagine the Southern poor will go on passively watching the present outrageous disproportions of wealth endure, let alone grow. Complacent Southern régimes will receive no less of a shock. Never before has material injustice been so widespread and profound. Never before has it been so obvious to its victims. On the village television set even the poorest see the extravagance of Northern life and the Mercedes, villas and the Savile Row suits of their own rulers. They are quickly learning that their anguish is not the will of God but the product of human choices.

In a decade or two's time we may well look back on the emergence of the Group of 77 as the first and neglected warning of a growing North-South conflict, one fuelled by past as well as present humiliations. Giscard d'Estaing has rightly warned us to watch out for 'the world's revenge on Europe for the nineteenth century'. The US has already accused the developing countries of 'bitter and accusatory rhetoric' and 'confrontational' tactics.

North and South seem set on a collision course. The division between East and West is perilous enough but that between North and South may prove longer lived and more fundamental. It involves all humanity, is complicated by race and is derived from a longer and more bitter history. It has probably caused even more suffering. Its healing would require not only intelligent accommodation but marked material sacrifice.

Sacrifice from both West and East: in the eyes of the South both are fat. There are already Southern calls for a tax on all industrialised countries, Capitalist and Socialist alike, and already, too, signs of Soviet outrage at this idea. The Russian Politburo indignantly if comically reject the notion that Eastern wealth is equivalent to Capitalist wealth and have intimated that it will be a hard and sad world if 'solidarity' has to be abandoned.

It is unlikely that either West or East will act in time to redress the central scandal of our age. If so, the outcome can only be growing upheaval and violence. In its early stages this may well be localised, taking varying shapes in different parts of the world. Strange temporary alliances may be formed, and unexpected enmities. But the lines of an eventual world-wide battle are already being drawn.

In essence we seem to be heading for a North-South, white-black version of Marx's class struggle of which we have so far witnessed and perhaps misunderstood only the early skirmishes. The world arena has become one of blatant injustice and profound instability at precisely the time when the six impersonal threats to mankind's survival are converging with dreadful momentum.

A lost stranger asked an Irish peasant for the road to Dublin. 'Now sure if I was going to Dublin,' replied the Irishman, 'I wouldn't be starting from here.' If humanity hopes to arrive at safety, despite the six threats, it too could have wished to start from elsewhere.

Part Two
The Six Threats

3   The First Threat: Population Explosion

May you have seventeen sons and sixteen daughters.
Indonesian Wedding Toast

In 1964 a leading family planner held up 'the Loop' declaring it would 'change the history of the world'. But parents praying for many children do not welcome the loop, the pill or the condom. Beneath all the thundering global statistics and the claims for new devices, the population crisis is the result of what countless individuals will go on deciding for themselves — their family size. Personal choice will remain the crux, however many contraceptives we may offer around.

The crisis is, however, also about the sheer numbers, about the collective consequences of all those individual decisions. It raises questions of how the new billions are to be fed, clothed, sheltered, educated, employed, governed; of how they will live and ultimately of how they will die. It concerns the size of our resources and how they are to be shared. The crisis of population is also a crisis of politics, especially the politics of poverty.

Between 1966 and 1967 I spent a harrowing year in Java, Indonesia's most densely populated island. Of all the Indonesians, apart from the Balinese, the Javanese are perhaps the most finely featured and the most exquisite in taste, manner and movement. They have a delicate sense of the mysterious which can make the Westerner feel a coarser being. Yet through rapid multiplication these quiet, smiling people had made their capital, Jakarta, a frightening bedlam. Streets, alleys and gutters streamed with jostling masses. Dust, diesel smoke and the smells of rotting rubbish clogged the humid air. When the rains came, the rich mud gathered across pitted roads. Hundreds of thousands slept on rough bunks in tin and cardboard hovels in the *kampongs*, the slum settlements crowded into empty lots and along the railway lines.

Into these *kampongs* each day arrived yet more babies and yet more job-hungry peasants crowded off the rice fields of central Java. By night, thousands of beggars and thieves, pedlars and prostitutes, prowled the streets until hustled back into the shadows by the military. It was said there were tens of thousands of young girls 'on the game' and that they were 'finished' at eighteen.

A particular moment of shock came one day when I called on the late and unlamented President Sukarno in his magnificent Independence Palace with a somewhat less magnificent British Member of Parliament. The founding father of his country took us round his lavish collection of paintings and art-objects in the State Rooms. Inside, all was spaciousness and splendour and Sukarno's bubbling hospitality. Then, looking out beyond the well-guarded gates, I suddenly saw with different eyes the usual hundreds of people squatting in rows, defecating, scrubbing their clothes and washing their cooking pots along the banks of a stagnant canal.

As Batavia, the city had been built by Dutch colonisers for at most a third of a million people. By 1967 there were already ten times that number. There was tapped water for about one in seven and little proper sewerage. 'My heart bleeds for Jakarta', said an editor friend of those days. 'It was a lovely city. You could walk and eat under the big shady trees. Now it's all gone. I love this city, but I think it is lost.'

Are mankind's hopes also becoming lost to sheer numbers? Most people do not realise it but for immediate purposes birth control is already a story of too little, too late. Contraception could produce substantial results some way into the next century but it is almost certainly too late for governments, with or without new contraceptive technologies, to stop the next doubling of mankind's numbers. Not, that is, by restraining births. By design or neglect they could do a lot to hasten deaths. That, in effect, is what they are now doing.

The Arithmetic of Population

What is the background to this extraordinary situation? From the densities of the remaining hunting and gathering tribes it has been estimated that the total human population by the advent of agriculture was between five and ten million. By the time of Christ it was probably about 300 million.[1] It went on rising relatively slowly, with reverses from epidemics like the plague, and it took until 1750 to reach a total of 800 million.

It then rose fast. By 1850 there was 1·3 billion (1,300 million) of us. By 1900 there were nearly 1·7 billion. By 1950 there were 2·5 billion. By 1975 there were 4 billion.

The amazing thrust of the acceleration shows in the contraction of the doubling time. After 1 AD the doubling of mankind's numbers took about 1,200 years. After 1650 it took about 200 years. Now it is taking about thirty-six years.

Every morning there are over 210,000 extra mouths to feed. Every three days we add the equivalent of America's dead in all the wars she has ever fought. Every year we are adding over seventy-six million, equivalent to another US every three years.

The most reliable projections of future growth, from the UN and elsewhere, suggest a world population of five billion by 1988 and approaching 6·25 billion by 2000. That is to expect two and a quarter billion more people before today's babies have reached their middle twenties.

A continuation of this growth rate into the next century would be horrifying. The total could climb to nearly thirteen billion by 2035, twenty-six billion by 2070 and nearly fifty billion by 2100. Further projections become astronomic but I think it silly to pursue them; obviously present growth rates could not continue without calamity.

The latest indications suggest that fertility, though still very high, may have been declining sufficiently to enable mankind to achieve what is called replacement-level fertility (basically, one surviving and fertile daughter per mother) by about 2020. But for reasons we shall come to, the total population would not stabilise until about three generations later, in around 2090, at eleven billion compared with todays four. As Robert McNamara as head of the World Bank has said, that's 'a world none of us would want to live in'. Granted immense efforts, we could stabilise the population at eight billion by 2070: to think of doing better is to pipe-dream. I doubt whether we shall do anything like so well.

World population grows to the extent that births exceed deaths. A deferred death has the same effect on immediate numbers as an extra birth. We always have to look at both. In 1972 the estimated world birth rate was about thirty-three per thousand and the death rate thirteen per thousand. The difference of around twenty per thousand gives an annual growth rate of just under two per cent and a current doubling time of around thirty-six years.

To stop ourselves reaching eight billion already by 2015, we would have to slash the birth rate *and* multiply the death rate. Birth control alone could now do no more than slow the doubling. If, miraculously, the average birth rate were slashed overnight to replacement levels — the famous 2·1 children per couple — the population would go on climbing for sixty years or more. Why? Because, for a start, the next generation of mothers has already been born. Short of mass sterilisation, plagues, slaughter or famine we are already committed to receiving their children.

Critical, also, is age structure, especially the proportion of young to old. A stable population has fairly even numbers in each age range. Once, in the glorious Iranian city of Isfahan, I saw so many children flooding through the narrow *suks* that I imagined walking on their heads as over a human sea. It was the same teeming picture from Marrakesh to Borneo. In many poor countries forty to forty-five per cent are aged under fifteen. Most of these youngsters will have their own children, many some grandchildren, by the turn of the century.

Population, North and South
The geographical distribution of the human overload is politically crucial. Nearly three quarters of our present numbers live in the Poor South. Well over half of mankind is Asian. Underdeveloped Asia alone (excluding Japan and other rich enclaves) contains about two billion in a land area smaller than Africa's. It is a region blighted with some of the worst destitution and the slightest hope of early relief from it.

Within their extensive territories the thirty or so countries of the Rich North contain only about one billion people. A quarter of these are in the Soviet Union and a fifth in the US. (These two populations combined are much smaller than

India's.) Over the last two or three centuries the white races so arrogantly spread themselves across the earth by colonisation and emigration that they are scarcely aware of the unfair vastness of the estates they occupied — and retain — in North America, Australasia and Southern Africa. By 1970 over half the Caucasians lived outside Europe.

The South, already overwhelmed with people, is burdening itself with an utterly disproportionate share of the new millions. About nine out of every ten of the two and a quarter billion extra people expected by the turn of the century will be born to the South.

Why is this? The North seems to be coming to the end of what is called the 'demographic transition'. It has moved from the high birth and death rates of the eighteenth century, first to low death rates and now, on the average, to low birth rates, too. This has encouraged some to expect the North's total population quickly to fall. It will not, in fact, become stable for another two generations or so.

The South, moreover, has seemed trapped in the explosive middle stage of transition. Its birth rates have remained very high while in recent decades its death rates have been dropping fast. In the 1920s Southern expectation of life at birth was about twenty-seven years; by 1945 it had risen to thirty-two; since then it has climbed to just over fifty. Medicine and especially public health are still relatively cheap compared with food. Their spread will continue to reduce premature Southern death, especially in Africa and Asia and not least amongst infants. Until famine or war stretches wider, more Southern babies will tend to survive into maturity — albeit with millions stunted in body, mind and vitality.

Birth rates are very high in the South but we should not accept facile talk about them 'soaring'. If slowly, they are falling in many, perhaps most, poor countries. Southerners have not started 'breeding like rabbits'. They have stopped 'dying like flies'.

In short, the main cause of the population explosion is declining death rates with too little compensating reduction in birth rates. Nothing more sophisticated or expensive than the spraying of a malarial swamp may slash death rates. The control of births is much more complex and is often resisted with deep suspicion.

Birth Control: Myths and Realities
It is all too easy for Northerners to imagine that, granted education in 'family planning', ready availability of contraceptives and a few pecuniary incentives, Southern parents will 'see sense' and curb their family size. Yet parents have the size of family they think they need. It is no use declaiming national let alone global statistics to harassed peasants who want children to help with their land and to care for them in old age. And if they bear more than need seems to require, it is because they must expect many of their previous offspring to die young, as in Victorian England. High infant mortality actually encourages further pregnancies. In some regions five out of seven children die in infancy.

Whatever the collective consequences, the individual parent decides according to the family's interests and within that perspective sensibly. If your bank were failing would you loyally hold tight for the sake of its over-all solvency or go it alone, swiftly extracting your life's savings? So even where contraceptives are freely available many will not use them.

One of India's first big field projects, the Khanna study, concentrated for six years on seven 'test' villages containing 8,000 people. Someone went there to find out why the project failed. He concluded that the villagers had large families because they needed them. Why then had most of them accepted the contraceptives? Because otherwise they were classified as 'resistance cases' and went on getting long and tedious monthly talks on the need for restraint!

What happened to the contraceptives? One day the researcher was squatting on the floor sipping tea with a family when through the gloom he saw a religious sculpture in the corner made of boxes and bottles. One of the men explained, 'Most of us threw the tablets away, but my brother here, he makes use of everything.' Another said, 'But they were so nice, you know. And they came from distant lands to be with us. Couldn't we even do this much for them? Just take a few tablets. Ah! even the gods would have been angry with us. They wanted no money for the tablets. I lost nothing and probably received their prayers. And they, they must have got some promotion.'[2]

A world-wide survey carried out in 1972–3 showed only thirty-one per cent of couples to be practising contraception and half of these by unreliable methods.[3] Throughout Africa, the Middle East, Latin America and much of Asia the figure was under twenty per cent. Abortions are extraordinarily common: there are four abortions, legal or illegal, to every ten live births and a hideous toll of women with massive haemorrhaging, laceration, perforation of the uterus, sepsis and renal failure.

Some believe family planning should never have been tied to the medical profession and its self-interested paternalism. The presence of a clinic on the map of, say, Uttar Pradesh does not mean contraceptives are 'available' to the woman who lives many hot miles and hours away and anyway resents medical examination by strangers.

More imagination is being shown in pilot projects like that in the Banglamoong district of Thailand, where distribution has been entrusted to village headmen, school teachers and shopkeepers who are permitted a small commission.[4] The scheme aims at removing the stigma attached to contraceptives by showing ways of re-using them. Condoms are coloured and used, after washing, as balloons or to store clean water. The ring at the top is torn off for tying hair or parcels. Pill packets are marked along the edge as school rulers. The essence of this approach is community self-help, using the people to reach the people.

The Rôle of Development
Over recent years it has been recognised that, short of compulsion, birth control programmes are unlikely to get far unless accompanied by radical social and economic changes which encourage individuals willingly to choose later marriage and smaller families. The potent factors seem to be higher living standards; better education; greater urbanisation in decent conditions, not slums; increased mobility; more and better paid employment; heightened consumer expectations and the fuller participation of women in the labour force.

These are the kinds of changes which seem to have occurred in those few Southern countries like Taiwan, Sri Lanka, West Malaysia and Colombia which have had clear success in restraining fertility. Even so, their birth rates remain worryingly high and most countries are economically way behind them. There is a vicious circle in which poverty and high fertility reinforce each other. Poverty fosters children-for-insurance; the extra mouths often intensify the immediate poverty.

A voluntary stabilisation of mankind's numbers would also depend on much higher status for women. Here too the outlook is not bright. A disproportionate number of women are illiterate and male chauvinist attitudes are deeply rooted. Mao once said women suffer the same oppressions as men, plus one — men themselves. The women's subjection is thought to signify man's virility, his *machismo*.

The inferior position of women is often reinforced by culture and religion and is implicit in the law on voting and property rights, divorce and so on. Even in India, which had a woman Prime Minister for many years, an official report in March 1975 had to admit that its society regards 'female lives as an expendable asset'. Nutrition levels for girls were especially low and their mortality consequently high. Male chauvinism is reflected in official publications: a New Delhi family planning poster said, 'One leopard is stronger than twelve jackals. One son is better than twelve daughters'.

The Politics of Population
Some governments have tackled their population problems with vigour, going far beyond propaganda. For agreement to a vasectomy, Kerala State offers each man a week's food, an umbrella and a bright sari for his partner. Elsewhere in India, six week's wages have been given or a transistor radio. Singapore, very much richer, has employed sanctions rather than bribes, discriminating against large families in, for example, the provision of public housing.

In recent years there have been experiments with much more coercive measures. With its population rising by over a million a month, India has raised the minimum marriage age and was coming close to compulsory sterilisation before Mrs. Gandhi was defeated in the election of March 1977, partly due to its clear unpopularity. There had been terrible scenes. A vasectomy booth in a Bombay suburb was burned down when it transpired that a youth of sixteen had been persuaded to get himself sterilised for a reward of 100 rupees (about ten dollars). Forty died as police fought rioting crowds at

Muzaffarnagar in October 1976. In many remote areas the young just fled when the family planning vehicle arrived. True, seven million were sterilised in nine months but the human and (for the Congress Party) the political price was immense.

Examples of strenuous action should not encourage us to believe that most governments consider their populations too large. Of 150, only a third officially do so. This anti-natalist minority does, it is true, represent about two-thirds of the world's population but, because most governments are indifferent or hostile to family planning, international agreement on a firm global policy is prevented.

In some countries resources are too short or the administrators are caught in a web of conservatism, prejudice and short-sightedness. Others who are privately more enlightened are politically vulnerable to cultural taboos and religious pressures, especially in Latin American and other Catholic countries. Some states have laws on public morals and obscenity which restrict information and access. Ireland is among them. Laws bearing on inheritance, taxation and adoption often encourage greater fertility, sometimes unintentionally.

Many governments are frankly pro-natalist — they positively want enlarged populations. For some, such as Israel, this is for obvious reasons of national security. Argentina likewise intends, if she can, to double her present twenty-five million by the end of the century out of fear of Brazil's potential to dominate Latin America. Brazil could well more than double her present 110 million in that period. Her high national aspirations and reluctance to see her problems as demographic as well as economic are paralleled widely in the Middle East and in Africa. Of the nineteen sub-Saharan African countries only three or four have official family planning programmes.

The Soviet Union and some of the East European countries have openly encouraged big families as an aid to industrial development and national power. Many have given financial incentives. Romania has campaigned for larger families for over a decade.

It is the Chinese experiments that have spread most hope that the poorest countries could effectively stem the human tide. Peking's remarkably eclectic programmes have featured 'paper pills', injectable contraceptives, spermicides, male and female sterilisation, liberal abortion, late marriage and an astonishing consensus against pre- and extra-marital intercourse. The childless are respected and large families regarded as irresponsible. The message is carried by national campaigns and reinforced by community pressures and the efforts of medical auxiliaries.

The programme has been neither as consistent nor as sustained as many imagine. The Cultural Revolution interrupted it badly. Nor, for example, has it been applied to minority races like the Mongols along the frontier with the Soviet Union. The over-all scale of achievement is hard to determine; there has been no national census since 1953 and few figures are published. Foreign specialists calculate China's current numbers at around 850 million and her annual growth rate at two per cent. Peking aims at halving that by the year 2000. It would still be high. Moreover the Chinese, as Marxists, profess to believe people the most valuable form of capital and the notion of over-population a bourgeois heresy. Their present policy is dictated by immediate national interest; they might promptly reverse it when this suited their ultimate world revolutionary purposes.

It is doubtful whether Chinese successes could be repeated elsewhere in the poor world without similar domestic upheaval, regimented discipline and ideological fervour. Few Southern regimes would be willing or able to adopt a social system so alien to their own national traditions (and so contrary to their own sectional interests).

Indeed, revolutionary emotions are just as likely to attach themselves to the opposite, pro-natal, policy. Many Southerners see birth control as some sort of trick by the white and rich to keep down the numbers of the coloured poor and preserve their own privileges. Their attitude was once summed up by Dick Gregory, exponent of Black Power, 'My answer to genocide is eight black kids and another on the way.'

The Southern suspicion of unconscious Northern racism is not wholly unwarranted. It was encouraged by President Johnson's clumsy remark that five dollars invested in population control was worth a hundred invested in other kinds of overseas aid. The suspicion is however exaggerated and reinforces the dangerous belief that the problem of population is only one of poverty rather than something demanding comprehensive attack.

Failure in Bucharest

This confusion was pitifully evident at the Bucharest population conference in 1974, a UN gathering of ministers and leading family planning agencies which was intended to provide, as one consultant put it, 'the population input for a world-wide strategy for socio-economic development'. The conference proved a miserable failure. Sloganising, myopia and inertia triumphed. The pursuit of short-term national advantage was transparent; the temptation to score political points, irresistible. Almost nothing of substance was agreed; no plan, no action, not even the 'new consensus' many hoped for. Indeed those advocating organised birth control suffered a public defeat.

This was the first ever inter-governmental conference on the subject. Success was thought vital and the preparations lasted nearly two years. The compromise draft plan which emerged from these tortuous consultations was already feeble stuff. It would only have given 'to all who so desire' the information and means to practise family planning by 1985. But even this went too far for the majority of the delegations at Bucharest. Insipid words about 'responsible parenthood' were inserted instead and, for achieving whatever that may mean, no target date was stated.

It soon became apparent that a bizarre international coalition had been formed to wreck the 'plan of action'. Stage-managed by the Argentinians, it included such disparate elements as the Russians, the Vatican, most of the Latin Americans, the French-speaking West Africans, and the Chinese (who found it expedient not to preach abroad what they practise at home). The Vatican took its absolutist view that artificial contraception was wrong in itself. The general refrain was that birth control was an unnecessary and objectionable alternative to economic and social development.

That the poor nations should insist on their need for development is wholly understandable. That they should see birth control as a Western device to stop them becoming similarly rich and strong is sad. That they and their self-interested Communist supporters should use a critical conference about it as little more than a propaganda platform was little short of tragic. Their ritual speech that birth control was 'not enough' was superfluous. No one had claimed it was. Birth control should be *part* of any plan for Southern economic development, perhaps for global survival.

The world community missed an already late opportunity of formally recognising the limited carrying capacity of the earth and agreeing on some of the action this demands. Instead the lines of division were publicly drawn, and the prospects of global action on this front are now slim. In any case we can confidently forecast a doubling over the next few decades. The even more pressing question therefore is whether such gargantuan numbers will be fed.

4   The Second Threat: Food Crisis

Prosperity and famine are never far apart: the rich and poor frequent the same houses.

Somali Proverb

Ours is not just a world of hunger but of unnecessary hunger. There is sufficient food to sustain all four billion of us. The hunger is due to the cruel maldistribution of our harvests. The food crisis is a food scandal. One way and another we of the North consume so much that slimming has become a multi-million-pound business while a third of our fellows are grossly under-fed.

Since 1965 the average American has increased his consumption of grain by about a pound a day. He does not notice it because he eats it mainly in the nutritionally extravagant form of extra beef and chicken. A pound of grain is equivalent to an Indian's total daily diet.

America used more fertiliser on its lawns and golf-courses than India can afford to fill empty stomachs. We of the West have often deliberately reduced our food production for 'sound commercial reasons' while peoples in Asia, Africa and Latin America sit weakly waiting, without reserves of fat in their bodies or grain in their stores, for the next disaster from drought or flood, soil erosion or monetary inflation, pestilence or war.

A victim of a Somali drought said,

The dreadful calamity began in November 1974. During that month the country was utterly dessicated. The shrinking vegetation faded. There was hardly anything for the animals to graze on. Consequently, animals had to drink water on an empty stomach. . . With their bellies curved in and twisted what good is it to water them? I was beginning to despair. In the short space of five weeks, I personally lost 150 sheep. However the sheep were not the first animals to die. It was a horror, a terrifying horror for the cattle. The cattle could not stand the lack of water for a few days as well as the lack of grass. A total of forty head, which was all I had, died. Every week I used to burn them so that they would not rot and spread disease when they decomposed. I continued this tragic process until I had burned the last one. That was the fate of my cows.[1]

By that same month 15,000 people had died in just one region of neighbouring Ethiopia. A witness saw 'children reduced to skeletons, too weak to walk or even talk; old people in advanced stages of tuberculosis — widespread in the area; babies trying to feed from breasts which had long gone dry'.[2] People were breaking off twigs to chew. Many dead lay unburied in the wilderness.

While Africa had too little rain, parts of Asia had too much, too fast. Early and intense rains in June and July 1974 destroyed much of Bangladesh's summer rice crop. About half the country was under water, whole villages were swept away, cholera was reported. Her food deficit of two million metric tons widened to three million and the government of Sheik Mujib (since deposed and killed) was virtually bankrupt. Not much international relief was forthcoming: rampant corruption had dissipated too much of the aid given over the previous three years. A Bangladeshi told me he had seen food relief lorries deliver their loads to black market merchants in Dacca and then used to collect the dead, like litter, from suburban streets.

Meanwhile thousands of Indians were dying over the border in West Bengal. Officials blandly denied reports of starvation, preferring to talk of 'malnourishment'. In Jambusar a reporter saw emaciated children whose lives had been saved at the last minute:

Two-year-old Maheru was a bag of bones, too weak to walk. Over the previous three days, he and his mother had eaten a handful of wheat flour cooked in a mug of water, and a piece of chapatti donated from a neighbour's meagre meal. They sit all day in one mud-walled room. The government-supplied roofing for the rest of the house had been sold for food, as have all their ornaments, vessels and clothes except for a glass, a cooking pot, a ragged blanket, and what they are wearing.[3]

The Marks of Hunger

There has been a serious famine somewhere in almost every year since 1945. In 1971 there were fifteen. Most of mankind has always lived in or close to hunger and has carried the cruel marks of food deficiency. Rickets, due to a lack of vitamin D, deformed the skull, legs, spine and pelvis of many of our own forebears. In parts of South Asia four out of five infants suffer from malnutritional dwarfism. A balanced diet requires a wide variety of nutrients — carbohydrates, proteins, fats, vitamins and mineral salts. Lack of any of them may cause disease. The shortage is often due to ignorance over what to eat or how to cook it, or to superstition, as in regions of Africa where women are forbidden milk and eggs for fear of infertility.

But in many places, foods containing the essential proteins and vitamins are not widely available and where they are, there is often what bureaucrats call 'a lack of effective demand'. That means people are too poor to pay for them. Milk, cheese, butter, meat and fish are generally the most expensive foods. The average intake of animal proteins in the South is about a fifth of that in the North. This would matter little if Southerners had adequate plant proteins. They do not: the *general* level of nutrition is too low.

Protein deficiency can have devastating effects. The disease *kwashiorkor* is found throughout Africa and great stretches of South-East Asia. Its name derives from one of Ghana's languages and means 'the sickness a child gets when the next is born'. It results from the weaning of the older child on to foods which lack the protein of the mother's milk. The stomach distends with 'hunger swelling'. Muscles are wasted, the child becomes apathetic. The skin discolours and some-times peels. There is diarrhoea and anaemia. If the deficiency is prolonged, growth is retarded and resistance to diseases like measles, whooping cough and pneumonia is lowered. In the South these are often fatal. Early treatment with high protein fluids, ideally containing careful measures of skim milk powder, is essential.

Nutritional marasmus is even more serious. It derives from carbohydrate as well as protein deficiency — general starvation. Many of the symptoms are similar though there is no swelling or skin rash, rather an over-all wasting. Fatty layers as well as muscles are thin. The young victim often shows 'Old Man's Face', wizened and shrivelled. Treatment must be swift unless death is to follow from the loss of body fluids.

For children surviving these diseases of poor nutrition there is a strong chance not only of physical but mental stunting. No one is sure how many are at risk. In a passionate address in May 1969 Robert McNamara put it then at about 300 million. He said,

> They live languidly on — stunted in their bodies and crippled in their minds... This is irreversible brain damage. What is particularly tragic in all of this is that when such mentally retarded children reach adulthood, they are likely to repeat the whole depressing sequence in their own families.

There are also specific diseases caused by lack of certain vitamins or minerals. Beri-beri is due to a lack of vitamin B, especially the thiamine component, and results in wasting and paralysis of the limbs and, sometimes, nervous disorders and heart failure. Pellagra, due to lack of niacin, is common among maize-eating peoples. Avitaminosis, from a short-fall in vitamin A, can cause blindness in infants. Lack of iron causes nutritional anaemia and is responsible for over thirty per cent of the deaths of women in childbirth.[4] Lack of iodine causes 200 million to suffer from endemic goitre which enlarges the thyroid gland and retards physical and mental growth. Poor diet also aggravates trachoma, the virus eye disease which afflicts one in eight of our fellows.

Hunger also has profound emotional effects. It distracts the attention of children at school; it demoralises mothers; it reduces the capacity of men and women to work. It condemns to anxiety and lassitude millions who never appear in the formal statistics of major disease or privation.

The Global Distribution of Hunger

A cautiously-worded UN report in late 1974 showed that, of

ninety-seven developing countries studied, sixty-one had a deficit of food energy supplies in 1970 and that in Asia and Africa, twenty-five and thirty per cent of the population suffered significant under-nutrition.[5] It went on to say that, on a highly conservative estimate, malnutrition affected around 460 million people and that within such widely dispersed countries as Brazil, India and Tunisia the poorest twenty per cent ate half as much as the richest ten per cent.

What most contributes to the hunger of the South, however, is the unwitting gluttony of the North. Northerners in general over-eat and suffer the characteristic diseases of so doing. What is worse, they choose a diet which is nutritionally wildly wasteful. The British, far from the North's richest, eat half their protein in the form of meat and dairy products. Throughout the North the demand for these has grown enormously as incomes have risen and its farmers have had to depend even more on feed grains and less on pasture.

It varies of course, but to produce a pound of milk protein a cow consumes up to five pounds of vegetable protein. Some conversion ratios are much higher. A pound of beef or lamb on the butcher's slab may be the equivalent of over twenty pounds of crude protein feed. Much of this, like grain, is quite edible by humans. Moreover the land used for growing animal feed as such could just as well grow human sustenance.

Northerners have been heavily persuaded that a day's hard work demands lots of animal protein. This is just not so. We could get virtually all our needs from beans, peas, oats, nuts and other vegetable and cereal sources. We eat so much protein, especially meat, that we burn it up for energy rather than use it for body growth or repair; so much, indeed, that we invite arteriosclerosis and heart disease. Many communities prosper without flesh foods. Jon Wynne-Tyson says the Hunzas of the Himalayas are renowned for their longevity and freedom from disease, 'Their diet consists of whole grains, fresh fruits, vegetables, goat milk . . . (with) occasional indulgence in goat meat on feast days.'[6]

The hideous waste implicit in the standard Northern diet is made worse by losses of about twenty per cent of output from pests, weeds and inadequate storage and a further six per cent in processing.[7] (Cheese makers throw out most of the whey — about four-fifths of the original milk.) On top of all this, about a quarter of the food which reaches the kitchen is later tossed out with the garbage.

The Northern appetite for animal proteins has startling results. About a third of the world's cereals are fed to Northern livestock. So is a quarter of its fish catch. So is much of our powdered milk, that excellent remedy for marasmus and *kwashiorkor*. Peru's huge annual catch of anchovy could satisfy the protein deficit of all Latin America. It is mostly exported to North America and elsewhere as animal and pet food. The cats and dogs of Los Angeles and Edinburgh have a greater 'effective demand' for anchovies than do Latin American peons. Britain's ten million cats and dogs eat enough protein to satisfy half a million humans. In 1974, as officials were preparing their grim assessments for the UN Food Conference at Rome, a British television commercial was singing out, 'There's never been a better time to be a dog'. Absolutely true, our dogs are fed far better than hundreds of millions of our fellows.

The present world situation is grotesque and dangerous enough. The question is whether we can stop it quickly deteriorating as our numbers explode.

Decades of Success

Until 1972 the prospect looked moderately hopeful. Over the previous two decades population steadily rose by about two per cent a year but food output by around three per cent. This remarkable performance owed most to more intensive cropping of land already under the plough. The area being irrigated doubled and the use of machinery and chemical fertilisers grew swiftly.

Cereals — wheat, coarse grains and rice — are of course crucial: they provide not only a large part of mankind's carbohydrate needs but much protein too. Output per acre over much of the North has tripled since the Second World War — in North America, Western Europe and Japan for example. There were large surpluses especially in the US which has consistently grown such enormous ones as to dominate the world cereal trade and to harbour most of the world's reserves in her granaries.

Most of the countries of the Poor South also kept ahead of their population growth but by the mid 1960s the gap was narrowing. Due to repeated failures of agricultural management, the Soviet Union, and China too, became considerable grain importers. There were two consecutive monsoon failures on the Indian sub-continent, in 1965 and 1966. Six of the seven most populous countries in the world — China, the Soviet Union, India, Indonesia, Pakistan and Japan — had become net importers and Western Europe's massive deficit had stayed about the same — around twenty-five million tons — for thirty years.

The outlook was not wholly dark. Washington placed new emphasis on encouraging developing countries to improve their own agriculture rather than depend on the long term food-aid contracts of the past and the 'Green Revolution' was having some impressive results. New high-yield wheat strains had been created in Mexico to carry much heavier heads on shorter, stronger stalks. They took fuller advantage of fertilisers, matured faster and were more adaptable. Other new cereals were developed in the Philippines, like IR 8, the so-called miracle rice.

The new strains spread rapidly. In five years, from 1965 to 1970, the area devoted to them in Asia grew from 200 acres to forty-four million acres — about a tenth of its cereal-producing land. By the beginning of the 1970s Pakistan became, for a while, a net exporter of wheat. The Philippines ceased to import rice. India was briefly emboldened to declare herself self-sufficient.

The Turning Point: 1972

Since the disastrous weather of 1972 the whole outlook has changed. It affected several subcontinents simultaneously. Total food production fell for the first time in more than twenty years.[5] The harvest of cereals dropped by thirty-three million tons instead of rising by the twenty-five million tons needed. The Russians, hit badly, secretly bought up most of America's grain reserve — nearly a fifth of her total crop — mostly to feed their cattle, pigs and chickens. Cereal prices rose steeply. In 1973, despite record harvests, an economic boom in the North further inflated demand and doubled prices world-wide.

For us these sorry years meant dearer bread and beef, for the South they meant hunger and fear of worse. In Bangladesh a friend saw crows picking over carpets of mouldering bodies. World grain reserves sank to their lowest since 1945 — three weeks supply. Food aid was cut by half. The world's fish catch fell. So did production of protein-rich legumes like soya beans, for many the staple diet.

Then, in 1974, monsoons were late, and, as I said earlier, floods hit some areas, drought others. Famine struck the sub-Sahara, Ethiopia, Bangladesh, India. About four million starved to death — some lying outside stores of grain they could not afford to buy: an image of our time. Prices doubled again and stayed mercilessly high after further failures in Russia and elsewhere in 1975.

Assuming the North goes on consuming more per head, the world's food production must rise by an average of two-and-a-half per cent a year, with the poor countries raising theirs by nearly four per cent a year. (It means we must not celebrate 'record' years but worry whenever we do not have one.) How could this continuous expansion be achieved?

There is plenty of unbroken terrain on the earth but over three quarters of it is inhospitable, waterless or remote. Of the remainder, less than half is cultivated, partly because its soils are leached out or thin but mostly due to financial, geographical and political factors. Some adequate land is wasted but mostly in sparsely populated regions. Landless Indonesians and Bangladeshis could probably extract a fair living, by their lights, off unused American or Australian acres but no invitations have been issued.

Expanded world production therefore largely depends on raising the yield per acre of existing croplands. Here we encounter more difficulties. Much of the richest ground is being lost year by year; in the North to towns, industry and tarmac; in the South to soil exhaustion, erosion, floods and salination. In Java I saw the overcutting of forests lead to the scouring of terraces and the silting up of precious irrigation systems. Some experts believe a quarter of India's tilled land could lose its topsoil in the next twenty-five years and, as her numbers grow, less and less land is left fallow to recover its powers.

Intensified cropping also means using yet more fertilisers. Demand, especially from the North, has been outstripping supply and the major producers have often been suspected of deliberately restricting output. Fertiliser prices have risen over threefold since the oil crisis and some Asian countries have had to reduce their imports and hence their planned harvests. The enormous rise in the price of oil has directly or indirectly affected the cost of almost everything connected with modern agriculture, not only fertilisers but machinery, freight, processing, marketing and pumping for irrigation.

This has made everyone, South and North, suddenly aware of how energy-intensive modern farming has become. It uses at least five units of energy — for cultivation, watering, gathering, drying, transport — for every unit of food energy produced. High protein diets often use more. When oil was a dollar a barrel this could make sense. At fourteen dollars or more it hugely inflates the price of food and pushes Southern millions out of the market.

Apart from these immediate hazards, a terrible suspicion has emerged that 1972 may have heralded damaging changes in the world's climate. Monsoons have been unusually erratic, causing more frequent droughts and floods. The growing season in the Northern hemisphere seems to have shortened; frost boundaries have shifted southwards. Whether we are entering a 'mini ice-age' is fiercely debated among climatologists but a bad weather cycle of only ten years could be catastrophic.

As against all this, various technological hopes have been periodically held out to the anxious. None offer a panacea. The achievements of the Green Revolution have been real but Norman Borlaug, one of its founders, has called them small in relation to total needs. The dangers are real too. There is doubt about how much chemical fertiliser some soils can take without deterioration. There is also a threat of devastating attacks by plant diseases and insect pests when huge areas of the same crop replace the varied patterns of traditional farming. The perils of monoculture were most dramatically seen in Ireland between 1845 and 1847. Potato blight spread swiftly from field to field, rotting the staple diet of the Irish peasantry. When the potatoes went, there was nothing else. A million and a half starved to death and as many again had to emigrate.

Hope has also been placed in new technologies for making palatable foods out of algae, leaves and grass. A factory near

Marseilles is producing protein from petroleum. New foods have been based on oilseeds, peanut meal and soya beans, sometimes spun into textures resembling meat. But none of these are likely to be manufactured at a low enough price or in sufficient bulk to meet the growing food deficit, even if man's gastronomic conservatism could be overcome. Industry cannot succeed where agriculture has failed; the essence of the problem is not supply, but distribution. As Gandhi once said, 'The earth has enough for every man's need but not for every man's greed.'

The Politics of Hunger

The essential point is that greater food production need make little difference to the famished. Millions in the South simply cannot afford what they need. New surpluses would mostly be eaten — as they have since the war — as meats and cheeses on the tables of the Rich North, not least Russia's, and of the prosperous élites of the South.

The food problem is a political problem. It reflects the interests of the comfortable and the cruel absurdities of the systems they naturally seek to preserve. In the market economies of the North, farm output is plainly geared to profit. If it pays to grow more, or less, a farmer will. If it pays to grow feed for cattle rather than food for people, feed will be grown. Moreover our governments are concerned to keep farmers secure in their incomes and solid in their political loyalties. They prefer paying them to keep land in idleness than have what we selfishly term a glut. Between 1968 and 1970 the US, Canada, Australia and Argentina, the four biggest market economy producers, cut their acreages by over a third. In 1973 Washington paid three billion dollars to farmers *not* to grow crops. In 1977 President Carter ordered a twenty per cent reduction in US wheat acreage for 1978. Western Europe piles up 'mountains' of hundreds of thousands of tons of unsold butter, beef and dried skim milk, while the famished of the Sahel strip trees for their leaves.

The South is especially unable to afford the high price of food grown by capital- and energy-intensive methods. The Northern demand for beef is much more 'effective' than the Southern demand for the grains that go into it. In world markets the South is generally an also-ran: it gets what is left over. It is little more than a handy dumping ground for any unexpectedly high surpluses. The tastes and buying power of the rich — not least of the beef-besotted industrial working classes — dominate the scene. In lean years, the world's poor discover that the distress resulting from their own thin harvests is aggravated by the high prices which Northern demand creates on the Chicago and other corn exchanges.

The world food problem is also exacerbated by the huge areas of fertile land devoted to luxury crops like tobacco, coffee and tea and to relatively unnutritious foods like sugar of which most of us anyway eat too much. Some land must be given over to such things and certainly to raw materials such as sisal, flax, cotton and rubber. What is more questionable is whether the developing countries have been wise to place so much emphasis — or allow the North to do so — on the pursuit of these exportable cash-crops at the expense of home-grown nourishment. Throughout drought-ravaged sub-Saharan Africa, what are ponderously termed 'multi-national agribusiness corporations' exploit thousands of the best acres and a large share of the scarce water supplies. This cash-cropping, like the Green Revolution, has done little to help the little man working his small patch. Both tend in practice to encourage large-scale operation and mechanisation. These deprive the peasant of land and the unskilled of work. Because the new high-yield strains require much irrigation and fertiliser, they also require bank credit. This is generally accessible only to the already rich and they get the consequent profits. Large harvests from the big estates then force down local prices, the small men get less and many are forced to sell their labour to the rich or sell their land itself and trek to the cities. This shows how promising technical innovations can cause social tragedy unless the surrounding system is changed.

For reasons like this the critical need is massive agrarian reform. Southern governments cannot much longer depend on the continued availability of Northern grain surpluses or their own capacity to pay high world prices. If they could, their poor could not. The deprived of the South must be given the land and the means to lift themselves out of poverty.

As things are, about three quarters of all land in the South is owned by a fifth of its people. So this problem of the South has to be solved in the South by getting rid of antiquated and oppressive agrarian systems. Large estates would need to be divided up and the law of land tenure reformed to give small farmers greater security. Cooperatives would have to be created for purchasing, marketing, distribution and production. The general provision of easy credit and relevantly 'small' agricultural services is also necessary and schooling in better land use and diet.

That a deliberate reversion from large- to small-scale farming would reduce unemployment is obvious. More surprisingly, it can lead to larger net output of food. The special dedication of a peasant secure on his own ground, as of a gardener to his familiar soil, is potent. Japan's eight-acre farmers, helped by family labour, strong cooperatives, high fertiliser use and small-scale mechanisation, are among the most prolific producers of food — per man and per acre — in the world. China's agricultural achievements have partly derived from similar principles of self-help and communal support, and these same once-suspect ideas are encouraging many Western aid agencies to reformulate their strategies.

However, many Southern governments are prey to vested interests, domestic and foreign, and hostile to serious land reform. Some of their dominant figures are from land-owning classes. The huge estates of President Kenyatta's family have been mentioned. Moreover when Southern leaders have finally sought drastic agrarian change they have often met the fate of Arbenz in Guatemala or Allende in Chile, falling victim to internal opposition or external interference.

What then of the world community's response to the gathering food crisis? A fair test came at the UN Food Conference in Rome in August 1974. The fundamental but sensitive issue of land reform was buried under worthy words, abstract 'targets' and talk of emergency measures. The meeting produced a fine collection of embarrassed diplomatic evasions and few firm commitments to anything. The US, which had previously cut its food aid by two-thirds, declined to increase it. The rich oil-producing states and the Western powers waited for each other to contribute to the Agricultural Development Fund. Some agreement was reached on a 'food watch' to stop the world being surprised, as it was by the crisis of 1972, but most of the participants dispersed in despair.

Without the vast programme of international cooperation on which the Rome Conference so signally failed to agree, the prospects are grave. There will be famines to dwarf those since the war, famines more terrible than those in which up to ten million died in the Soviet Union in the 1930s and up to four million in West Bengal in 1943.

We have been forewarned. We have not reacted. The blindness and inertia of the Seventh Enemy are doing their deadly work. As Dr. Sicco Mansholt, ex-President of the EEC has said, 'Unfortunately we always seem to prepare for a crisis when we are already in its grip. . . It happened with the oil crisis; it will happen with the food crisis — which is certain to come.'[8]

5 The Third Threat: Resource Scarcity

> Man faces the prospect of a series of shocks of varying severity as shortages occur in one material after another, with the first real shortages perhaps only a matter of a few years away.
>
> National Academy of Sciences Report,
> 'Mineral Resources and the Environment',
> Washington, February 1976

Only ten years ago we were worrying about an imminent 'leisure explosion'. And we were wondering what to make of the promised Super-Cities of the Future, those automated, air-conditioned, hydroponically fed megalopolises with their complexes of shining towers and silent monorails sheltered beneath all-encompassing plastic domes. It was a paradise which all would allegedly share, down to the private helicopters and submarines in which to get away at weekends. Ingenuity would triumph over want. Mankind would come into its ultimately satisfying, ultra-hygienic kingdom. As Hegel had said, the earth existed to be appropriated by man.

Within that decade, we have suddenly become aware that man's colonisation of the planet has been consuming its finite resources at a pace which kills such (anyway chilling) visions stone dead. The desirability of rampant economic growth was already being debated, if mainly by the prosperous, in the name of the 'quality of life'. Now its very possibility has become doubtful.

Kenneth Boulding has said anyone who believes exponential growth can go on for ever in a finite world is either a madman or an economist.[1] The earth cannot much longer support what he has called the 'cowboy' economy of the past, the reckless exploitative behaviour of men facing what seemed an open frontier of unlimited riches. Instead we shall need a 'spaceman' economy in which we do not maximise production and consumption as 'income' but respect and conserve the planet's limited resources as 'capital'.

Some argue that our material reserves are not so short for such issues to become pressing until way into the next century, perhaps later. Yet the growing awareness of their approaching scarcity will itself become a fact of momentous political significance. Indeed it has already, since the oil crisis, sent its first pitiless tremors through the world's economic and political structures.

What is essentially in question is how the planet's reserves are to be used and how shared, in whose interests and by what mechanisms. In recent decades the North has been consuming raw materials at a gluttonous rate with no sense of the needs of either the South or posterity. There is a saying among Hereford farmers that they should live as if they will die tomorrow but farm as if they will live forever. We have been ravaging the earth as if there were no tomorrow. This could become a self-fulfilling prophecy. Posterity gets a bad press: some will ask with Groucho Marx, 'What has posterity ever done for me?' The trouble is that no previous generation has had as much power to consume or destroy the inheritance of the unborn.

The Earth's Store
Some resources are 'renewable' in that production can be started again each year. Food, fresh water and forests can be replenished given time and good management. The metallic minerals, the rock phosphates and the fossil fuels — oil, natural gas and coal — are effectively non-renewable. Their deposits in the earth's crust are limited in a nearly absolute sense: the fossil fuels took millions of years to accumulate from the compression and carbonisation of plants.

Judgments about the adequacy of these finite resources are not a matter of geology alone but of geography, technology and economics. We have to assess what deposits, of what richness, are available where and at what sort of cost of extraction. The planet's solid crust averages thirty kilometres in thickness but only the contents of the top one or two are usefully accessible. Most deposits, moreover, are far too poor in concentration to be worth extracting and, in general, the best have already been excavated or are being mined now. More rich finds will certainly be made — in Africa, Australia, South America, Siberia and China, for example — but with demand multiplying, the discoveries would need to be immense and frequent to transform the outlook.

The workings of the market and the wit of man can of course moderate the difficulties. As the price of a fuel or metal rises, it becomes economic to exploit deposits previously reckoned marginal, like the poorer oil-shales or low-grade cupiferous rocks. We can extend our explorations, recycle more of our waste and devise new substitutes. We can learn to conserve the irreplaceable: we are therefore unlikely to run right out of any particular resource. But ending up with a token tonnage is small comfort when millions of tons are required. Cost is vital. You can extract gold and other metals by evaporation from sea water, but the cost in money and in energy is prohibitive. Technical possibility is one thing; economic reality another. We *could* install strawberry-growing greenhouses on Everest.

There are other problems. The cost of exploiting lower-grade deposits of copper and molybdenum is inevitably high but at least their concentrations grade out fairly smoothly, and the tonnages found are compensatingly large. This is not so with most other metals such as lead, zinc, tin, tungsten and nickel. Between the best deposits and the next best lies a gulf. Of some minerals, notably gold, silver and diamonds, there are relatively few sizeable sources, world over.

Nor can the cost of extraction be calculated in purely financial or energy terms. The environmental cost also rises. Pits and quarries have to be dug deeper, greater risks of subsidence have to be run. Resort must be had to even larger open pit workings and strip mines. There are ever greater mountains of waste rock and spoil for disposal, often over fertile land.

The Minerals: How long will they last?
Apart from the odd chunks we heave into space, the minerals never disappear from the planet but, after use, large amounts are dispersed in quantities far too small for practicable

recovery. In the case of iron about half is recovered as scrap and recycled. The rest rusts or is disseminated in waste. As prices rise and methods of recycling become more sophisticated, the rate of loss of some metals will decline. As against this, the rate at which we are consuming them is climbing exponentially and will continue to as long as population and industrial appetite expand.

To make their well-known forecasts the authors of *The Limits to Growth* assumed that five times our present known reserves of minerals would eventually be found.[2] Despite this possibly optimistic assumption, they calculated that at recent rates of growth most of our basic metals would be exhausted within a century — aluminium, lead, manganese, molybdenum, nickel, platinum, tin, tungsten. Several, including copper, gold, silver, zinc and mercury, would be gone within half that time.

There has been much dispute about these and similar estimates but if they are only roughly right, they not only confirm Boulding's diagnosis of a 'crisis of closure' but imply that the South can never expect to industrialise on anything like the scale of the North. Take iron again, one of the metals of which we have most. Mankind is now using four times more than in 1950, all but fifteen per cent of it in the North. *The Limits to Growth* gives iron a life span of just over 170 years. That period would be severely reduced if the Southern three quarters of humanity started consuming it at even half the Northern rate per head and would be further halved when the world population doubles.

Fertilisers, Fresh Water and Forests

The rising price of oil (and natural gas) has already led to shortages of nitrogen fertilisers and the phosphate deposits of Morocco may not last many decades. The capital cost of chemical fertiliser plants is so high that most developing countries have no domestic production and, as prices climb, the South will find it even harder to compete. The North already consumes eighty-five per cent of world output, using up to 300 pounds per acre. India can afford only about fourteen pounds per acre.

There is also a growing scarcity of available fresh water. About ninety-five per cent of the world's water is saline. Of the remainder some three quarters is frozen in glaciers and ice-caps or locked underground. Only about an eighth of the rain falls over land and most of this on inhospitable terrain where it cannot be used or economically collected.

The cost of catching and moving water in the volumes needed is immense. The production of a pound of wheat requires about sixty gallons, a quart of milk about 1,000, a pound of meat about 2,500, often double. Industrial processes are more profligate: about 100,000 gallons are used in making a car.

Water tables in many areas are sinking fast. The shortage is exacerbated by the poisoning of rivers and underground reserves by industrial wastes. Experts believe that careful and extensive water management will soon be essential unless spasmodic local shortages are to become serious and national ones. A UN conference on water held in Argentina in March 1977 took as its motto, 'A generation later may be too late'. It is thought that scarcity will first become severe in South and East Asia, Central Europe and the American South-West.[3] Ultimately there may be no alternative to organising huge movements of either water or people. Artificial rain-making, solar distillation and the desalination of sea water are still far too expensive to make up the shortfall.

Vast areas of the earth's remaining forests are being felled to meet the short-term calls of industry and agriculture for timber, pulp and cleared ground. Deforestation often results in soil erosion, floods and climatic changes. It has reduced rainfall in the Sahara and extended the deserts. Northern China, Southern Europe and much of North America have already lost much of their tree cover. The tropical rain forests are climatically especially important: Brazil's have already been reduced by a quarter or more.

The outlook is dismal. In his plea for the native beech forests of New Zealand, Graham Searle says:

> Many of the most splendid, naturally regenerating forests of the world stand little chance of surviving the century. . . Colossal tracts of tropical forests in the Philippines and in Indonesia have by now been converted into woodchip and pulp. Elsewhere, the forests of India and Sri Lanka, Africa and South America are under the hammer

and axe. In the Pacific region, New Guinea, Malaysia, Australia and New Zealand are next in the queue.[4]

Replanting has been grossly insufficient and done mostly with fast-growing softwoods which damage nutrient balances. The US National Forest Service believes demand for timber and newsprint will double again by the year 2000. Prices of both have been rocketing. New forests, when planted, can take fifty to a hundred years to mature.

The Fossil Fuels and the Energy Crisis

Energy is of course the central issue. Some have dreamed of such bountiful supplies from nuclear power that would be 'too cheap to meter'; a troublesome scarcity of minerals and fresh water for industry and agriculture might then be postponed indefinitely. At worst they could be extracted from the sea. And more materials might be transmuted from others like diamond from graphite or replaced by new man-made substances on a parallel with the plastics.

The dream of cheap energy is at best remote. The world economy overwhelmingly depends on the fossil fuels — about ninety-seven per cent — and the reserves are being run down with lunatic profligacy. *The Limits to Growth* estimated that on present trends, petroleum and natural gas would last about fifty years and coal about 150.[5] To keep up with world demand for oil there would have to be several bonanzas of North Sea proportions *every year*.

The affluent society is energy-intensive. The hallmark of industrial life is the increasing horse-power harnessed by each citizen at work, at home, at play. The average Northerner depends on dozens of energy-consuming machines. The US alone uses well over a third of world energy output. It uses more electricity for air-conditioning than China uses for everything.

Energy consumption has roughly trebled since 1945 and will probably double by 2000. Until the oil crisis we had been gradually moving from an Age of Coal to an Age of Oil. The end of that is now in sight. Should we therefore now embark on an Age of Nuclear Power? We would have to if anything like the Northern energy binge was to continue, let alone be copied by the South. Most of the signs are that the North *is* heading for the nuclear option despite some public protest and some second thoughts by governments. There is growing evidence, however, that this policy will prove impracticable — quite apart from the terrible questions of safety and proliferation to be dealt with in Chapter 7.

Nuclear power stations take about a decade to set up and, although their running costs are relatively low, their capital cost is high.[6] So is the cost of research and development. Between 1965 and 1975 Britain's Advanced Gas-Cooled Reactor Programme cost a billion pounds without producing a single unit of electricity. The energy cost is also high — the amount consumed in building and fuelling a nuclear reactor. The benefits are therefore a long time coming. After decades of research and investment, Britain generates only an eighth of her electricity by nuclear means and in the US nuclear power has probably only just surpassed firewood as a source of energy![7]

There is even doubt over the long-term supply of natural uranium. On current plans, demand might rise three to five fold in the next decade but, according to an expert, Dr. Stanley Bowie, the rate of discovery is clearly inadequate. It is true that some reactors — the so called fast breeders — can produce more fissile material than they consume but with these the dangers of nuclear proliferation would be substantially increased.

Some suggest controlled thermo-nuclear fusion would be a better way of filling the gap being left by oil. Fusion is the process that goes on in the sun — and the hydrogen bomb — releasing energy by fusing two small atomic nuclei together. It should be intrinsically safer than fission and its fuel, deuterium, is abundant in sea water. It may not however be practicable: it requires a temperature of about 100 million degrees centigrade. Nor can the economic and safety aspects be assessed until commercial prototypes are built, possibly by the 1990s.[8] Fusion is therefore unlikely to be seriously relevant before the next century.

Alternative Energy Sources
For all these reasons it looks as if mankind will need increasingly to turn to permanent and inexhaustible sources of energy, not only hydro-electric and geothermal but solar,

tidal, wave and wind generation. These have the huge advantage of using the planet's daily energy income rather than its scarce and buried energy capital. They are also non-polluting. Coal, gas and oil should in any case be husbanded not burned; posterity will need them for their rich chemical content. The alternative sources are, however, beset by technical difficulties and require the urgent research priority previously devoted, perhaps tragically, to the nuclear option.

The greatest immediate benefits could flow from measures to conserve energy. Immense amounts are wasted through out-dated industrial processes, poor insulation and the excessive use of energy-extravagant transport systems. Forthright action could well induce substantial savings. Beyond a point, however, governments are stymied by special interests and public resistance. Two years after President Nixon's energy-conserving 'Project Independence' was launched, America was importing more oil than before — nearly half her consumption. President Carter's energy programme of April 1977 was bolder and more comprehensive but, even without Congress whittling it down, it would not reduce American per-capita consumption to West European levels. And those are anyway greatly excessive.

All in all, neither alternative sources nor conservation are in practice likely to avert an energy crisis. An authoritative international study sponsored by the MIT said the only uncertain factors were whether it appeared by 1981, 1990 or 2004 and whether it measured two or twenty million barrels of oil a day.[9]

The End of the Age of Abundance

Although experts differ about the planet's reserves of raw materials, the age of abundance is almost certainly drawing to a close. Rising costs alone will increasingly afflict the Capitalist economies with inflation, recession and unemployment. Nevertheless, it seems unlikely that either electorates or national ambitions will permit much relaxation of the urge to material growth which is probably also the vital dynamic of the Capitalist system. The Soviet bloc and China are committed to an ideology that likewise denies material limitations and is similarly suffused with mindless optimism.

If this diagnosis is valid, the North will further deprive the South of what it requires to relieve its poverty. If the Club of Rome's estimates of material reserves are even roughly right, there is no prospect of the South even gradually achieving the North's present levels of material consumption. If so, this has momentous political implications. It means that only by deliberate and *permanent* material sacrifice by West and East could even roughly comparable levels be achieved either for the three billion Southerners of the present or the five billion expected by the year 2000.

As the Club's second report makes clear, world stability could only be preserved by a deliberate concerted move from the greedy, unselective and unbalanced growth of the past to an organic kind of growth which would take account of both the material constraints and Southern needs.[10] The vigorous expansion of Southern agriculture would be considered essential while the continued uncontrolled growth of most Northern industry would be cancerous.

The absolute shortage of the planet's basic resources is bound to sharpen the growing North-South conflict over poverty and injustice. It could give the South's Club of 77 (and its OPEC members) a great deal more muscle in its aim of enforcing the redistribution of the world's wealth. To understand this perilous new dimension in global politics we need to look back a little.

The Politics of Resource Scarcity

The geographical spread of minerals and fossil fuels is of course uneven and arbitrary. This was not troublesome while resources seemed limitless; the ordinary mechanisms of trade functioned quite smoothly with little danger of distress and disruption. For the rich, that is, not the poor. Take the sordid story of oil. So long as their economies were based on coal, the Northern nations could largely depend on indigenous supplies. They were not vulnerable to the whim or coordinated design of overseas producers. Even after oil started replacing coal, the US remained especially well placed since she was blessed with large domestic oilfields and the North as a whole had, or seemed to have, such a diversity of sources that it could virtually dictate world prices.

This bargaining power was wielded with especial severity

through the seven biggest multinational oil companies, squeezing the weak and divided Arab and other producers. For a while after 1945 crude oil became cheaper than ever. Western governments firmly backed the multinationals. For instance, after Mossadeq's revolutionary regime in Iran nationalised the British Petroleum concession in 1952, it was toppled with the help of the British Secret Service and the CIA.

1960 saw the beginnings, however, of what the Northern industrial states now increasingly fear — the collective exercise of power by Southern exporters. The chief oil-producing states formed OPEC which gradually forced up the price. By 1968, Sheik Yamani of Saudi Arabia persuaded his OPEC colleagues to bid in effect for a fundamental re-negotiation of the traditional arrangements. So the meteoric rise in oil prices in 1973 was only partly due to Arab fury with the West over its attitude towards the Yom Kippur war. It was the outcome of a long campaign.

By 1974, OPEC had forced the price up from under three dollars to ten dollars a barrel and by early 1977 to fourteen dollars. That hoary old Foreign Office slogan, 'The Arabs cannot drink their oil', which I too had blindly accepted, had got its come-uppance.

The quadrupling of the price of a basic commodity had immediate effects on the Northern economies and was a shattering blow to the illusion of perpetually cheap and bountiful oil, an illusion which had flourished throughout the 1960s despite warnings from Dr. Fritz Schumacher and others. Moreover, the selective but emphatic embargo of supply to the West by most of the Arab members between October 1973 and January 1974 demonstrated not only that the flow of essential resources could be cut off, but be cut off for overtly political reasons. Western governments which for years had treated the Arabs with patronising condescension now found them trying to dictate Western policies and with some success. The fabulous earnings of OPEC members rapidly gave them another formidable source of international pressure on issues they agreed about.

One such is the Group of 77's demand for a New International Economic Order. As I said in Chapter 2, they want a new order, not a new deal; justice, not charity. The

Group of 77 refuse to accept the typically Northern view that the prospects of the poor must depend on the increasing prosperity of the rich. They see the basic problem not as a temporary breakdown of development but as a crisis of the whole system, as 'structural imbalances' too severe for mere patching up.

The Group of 77 wants improved terms of trade, stabilised commodity prices and hence more assured earnings, new codes of conduct for multinational companies and a greater say in decision-making all round. It also wants the mineral resources of the ocean beds to be regarded as the 'common heritage of mankind', not as the rightful pickings of those who can get there the fastest with the mostest — the giant enterprises of the North. (Years of negotiation on this front, about a new law of the sea, have so far made little progress. Unilateral action is being taken or threatened by many powers and the prospects of big trouble brought nearer.)

In a sense however all these are incidental details which could distract us from the South's central aim. As the modern historian Geoffrey Barraclough has pointed out, the Group of 77 demands conditions in which its share of world industrial production, and hence wealth, can be lifted from its present paltry seven per cent to about twenty-five per cent by the end of the century. This would mean the loss of millions of industrial jobs in the North and, in effect, the creation of a new international division of labour. It would involve revolutionary changes in the world economy and ultimately in the North-South balance of power.

Whether to enforce such changes the Southern nations could create OPEC-style monopolies in the supply of other raw materials is yet to be seen. They do not command so high a proportion of the supply of most of them as OPEC does of oil. Financially much weaker, they would also be less able to endure an income-less period in which they refused to export on the old terms. There are also divisions amongst themselves which are already being fostered by deliberate Western tactics. The West, it is true, is not itself wholly united but at the crunch its power is huge and the old economic order will probably be defended tenaciously. The chances are that most Western nations will continue to deploy delaying tactics and make as few concessions as they can get away with. For a while at least the old order will remain essentially intact and, with it, the grinding penury and rising fury of much of the South.

Nevertheless, if it came to it, the Group of 77, with OPEC's power over oil in the background, could probably orchestrate some damaging embargoes on supply. Almost all the world's tin is produced by Malaysia, Indonesia, Zaire and Bolivia. Almost half its copper comes from Zambia, Zaire and Chile. More than half its bauxite — the basic source of aluminium — is mined in Jamaica, Guyana, Malaysia and West Africa.

Moreover, the dependence of the West on Southern supplies of raw materials is steadily growing. Until the 1940s the US was a net exporter. Now it has to import all its chromium, almost all its manganese and two-thirds of its tin and nickel. The dependence of Japan and Western Europe on the South is greater. Moreover, the South's embargoes might be highly selective at first, addressed against the especially recalcitrant. Later they might be comprehensive and include a new OPEC embargo on oil supplies. (Much will depend on whether the radical wing of OPEC led by Libya and Algeria can persuade or overcome the conservative wing led by Iran and Saudi Arabia, much richer and far more cautious.)

The Food Card

The West would doubtless cry 'blackmail', the term used by Henry Kissinger in early 1974 about the oil embargo. Then, when OPEC threatened a further increase in oil prices in September, 1975, President Ford said, 'We don't have to take this lying down — and we won't'.

The abuse — as the West would see it — of Southern resource power might well be answered in the same vein. If OPEC or other Southern producers play the oil or the minerals card, or both together, the United States could play the food card.

The staff of life is rapidly becoming a weapon of power politics. A CIA report of August 1974 concluded that world grain shortages 'could give the US a measure of power it never had before, possibly an economic and political dominance greater than that of the immediate post-World War II years...' At the time of the World Food Conference, in

November 1974, Assistant Secretary of State, Thomas O. Enders said, 'The food producers' monopoly exceeds the oil producers' oil monopoly', and that, 'Food will give us influence because decisions in other nations will depend on what we do.' Carried far, this must amount to a willingness to use starvation as an instrument of economic policy; as a tool indeed for seeing to it that the rich stay rich and the poor stay poor.

The politics of resources also conjure up serious possibilities of military violence. Should the West's 'food power' fail to disarm Southern pressures, it might use force. The industrialised countries' reaction to any challenge to their supplies can be unexpectedly ferocious. Britain's abortive Suez venture in 1956 followed what Eden saw as Nasser's threat to sever 'Britain's jugular'. When the oil crisis broke in 1973 there was immediate Western discussion about forcibly occupying Middle East oil fields. Whether the Russians would have sat idly by is questionable. In February 1975 a member of Kissinger's immediate entourage said, 'If Western dependence on imported oil is not ended in five years, the choice will be between political surrender or military force'.

The possibilities of what President Giscard d'Estaing has called an 'enduring crisis' over resources are clearly legion and awesome. Robert Heilbroner sees 'wars of pre-emptive seizure' among the potential strategies.[11] As resources dwindle, the desire to maintain if not increase the level of national output may lead to desperate acts of self-preservation. A competitive struggle between East and West in seizing resource-rich areas of, say, the Middle East must be a serious possibility. Egypt could be tempted by Libya's oil. Even amongst NATO allies we have already seen tension rise high between Greece and Turkey over the resources under the Aegean and between Britain and Iceland in the 'cod war'. Eventual European conflict over the North Sea is not inconceivable. Far more damaging however would be the North-South 'war of redistribution' between the world's poor and rich, to which we shall return.

6 The Fourth Threat: Environmental Degradation

There is as yet no ethic dealing with man's relation to land and to the animals and plants which grow upon it.
Aldo Leopold,
A Sand County Almanac[1]

All life on this planet is conducted within a thin and fragile envelope of air, land and water not even ten kilometres thick. The entire biosphere depends finally on green vegetation converting solar into chemical energy and maintaining the balance of oxygen and carbon dioxide in the atmosphere. On this foundation are built all the intricately intertwined food chains involving thousands of species. The careless destruction of a single species of predator may lead to a plague of its normal prey and hence perhaps to the defoliation of a whole plant crop.

When Schoharie Valley in upstate New York was a garden of hops it was said the local people 'would shoot anybody who shot a skunk'. The skunk was the predator of the hop grubs. No skunks, no beer. The connections are usually less obvious and less respected. In Southern Oregon the pine forests are in trouble. There has been wholesale destruction of the fisher, big cousin to the mink and possessor likewise of a desirable fur. This has led to an explosion of the fisher's normal prey, the porcupine, which delights in girdling the bark of young pines.[2]

So long as it was numerically minor, the human species made relatively little impact on the biosphere. The natural mechanisms of recovery gradually overcame most of the results of our forebears' assaults by hand, fire, axe and spear. Only in the last two centuries or so has man crashed into biological history as the all-conquering species. Already there are few places on earth that do not bear his marks. In its habitable regions there is almost no natural wilderness left. The man-less environments that challenged the pioneer are no longer there to humble the arrogant or refresh the weary.

We have so multiplied in number and voracity that in an instant of evolutionary time we have altered almost everything. Our poisons have penetrated every corner of the biosphere: DDT has been found in polar bears at the North Pole and penguins at the South. On his raft 'Ra', Thor Heyerdahl found he was drifting past oil slicks and other detritus all across the Atlantic. No one can yet measure the chances of a crippling contamination of the biosphere but plainly our means of life are already corrupting the medium of life. Let us look at the main abuses suffered by each sector of our environment in turn.

The Abuse of the Air

The lungs of country people are usually pale pink, those of city dwellers rather grey. But all air now contains potentially harmful pollutants, mostly from the incomplete combustion of fossil fuels in industry, in the home and particularly in motor engines. They include carbon monoxide, nitrogen oxides, sulphur dioxide, hydro-carbons and various obnoxious particles, solid and liquid. In high concentrations, as in city centres, carbon monoxide can cause acute poisoning, sometimes convulsions and death. In Tokyo policemen have to use oxygen masks at busy crossroads. The nitrogen oxides similarly reduce the oxygen-carrying capacity of the blood. The various hydro-carbons are believed to contribute to the rising mortality from cancer as do the particles of asbestos and various metals.

Some cities have spent fortunes merely stopping pollution getting worse. Los Angeles has eliminated over one and a half million domestic and commercial incinerators, a dozen large municipal ones and over fifty open burning dumps. It has also banned the burning of coal and oil with a high sulphur content. Despite these measures, there has been little over-all improvement since 1960, mainly due to increasing numbers, especially of cars. Air pollution is causing damage to orange crops hundreds of miles to the east. Moon-bound astronauts detected Los Angeles' smoke pall from thousands of miles into space. London's air has perceptibly improved since 4,000 were killed in five days of smog in December 1952. In some parts of Britain however a hundred tons of polluting matter is still deposited per square mile each year.

Air pollution is no respecter of frontiers. Some of Britain's sulphur emissions reach Sweden, increasing the acidity of her lakes. The accident at the Windscale nuclear reactor in 1957 released radioactive isotopes of strontium and iodine which were traced to Norway and Germany.

Another potential hazard is the depletion of the ozone in the stratosphere. Ozone acts as a screen against solar radiations which can cause skin cancer. It has long been contended that supersonic aircraft like Concorde and the Tupolev 144 could, in any numbers, destroy this protective layer through their emission of nitrogen oxides at high altitudes.

More recently there has been anxiety that the chloro-fluorocarbons used as a propellant in many domestic aerosols may have the same effect. It seems ridiculous to suggest that hairsprays or deodorants may harbour an enemy to world health, yet there are several million tons of these propellants already floating in the atmosphere and a further million tons or so are released each year. It has been argued that as each molecule decomposes it releases atoms of chlorine which react with a molecule of ozone and start a chain reaction. Some scientists have ventured that, at recent rates of use, half the ozone layer could be destroyed by the middle of the next century and have urged a universal ban. Others, equally reputable, say this talk of a chemical time bomb is a misleading scare. Whatever the final verdict, it took forty-five years after the introduction of fluorocarbons for the question even to be raised.

The Abuse of the Land

Good soil is perhaps man's most valuable asset, a mysterious eco-system in its own right, which takes centuries to form and can take only a few years to dissipate or ruin. Erosion is a natural process which is gravely hastened by over-cultivation, over-grazing and, as I have said, deforestation. Thanks to John Steinbeck, the American Dust Bowl is perhaps the best known case. Over a succession of dry years the removal of ground cover and rapid spread of machinery combined to expose a thinning soil to scouring winds which left behind a desolate landscape and despairing people.

Similar ignorance and impetuosity has subjected tropical soils from Brazil to Southern Sudan to similar erosion, loss of nutrients and degradation into rock-like laterites. Parts of Asia are losing top-soil fast. Even where agriculture is pursued with apparently scientific deliberation, as in the West, there is much evidence suggesting that soil structures are being strained by the heavy use of fertilisers. Meanwhile, factory farming of animals deprives the soil of organic nutrients, while embarrassing quantities of wasted animal sewage accumulate around the sheds. The decline in the soil's organic content has become serious in Britain and may explain declining yields. As an agriculture specialist, Michael Allaby, has said, 'We are living on our capital, mining the soil'.[3]

Chemical Dilemmas
Modern agriculture has resorted to insecticides and other chemicals of extreme potency. They can seem essential. Insects destroy as much as a third of the world's crops and carry many diseases. The trouble lies in the massive quantities of chemicals used, often before the long-term effects are recognised: DDT was the classic case on which Rachel Carson rang the alarm. Mankind is scattering about 100,000 tons a year. Much is harmlessly broken down but some accumulates in the living tissues of birds, animals and human beings. I am told the level in the body fat of Americans renders them technically unfit for human consumption.

DDT poisons many useful soil dwellers and disturbs the reproductive processes of birds. So do other organic chlorides like dieldrin, aldrin and endrin. Some of the organophosphorus compounds like parathion and malathion are reportedly able to kill through the skin. Pesticides based on cyanides and arsenic are also lethal. Food chains can become death chains: Mexican peasants died when they ate pigs which had fed off corn treated with an anti-fungal mercurised seed dressing. Some herbicides carry dangerous impurities, like the 2,4,5-T defoliant used in cruel abundance by US forces in Vietnam.

These chemicals pose terrible dilemmas. It would be foolish to ignore the benefits, especially in the poorest countries. Unfortunately, illiterate farmers tend to believe that doubling use will double effectiveness. Moreover many of the insecticides are grossly unselective, destroying predators as well as prey and, ecologically, change much more than intended. There is no easy answer, but the slow accumulation of insecticides in food cycles means that it can take a decade *after* a decision to restrain their use before levels in the biosphere begin to fall.

The pesticides are only one category of a vast array of new substances disseminated by the rapidly expanding chemical and petroleum industries. Half a million man-made compounds are now in use.[4] Thousands more are introduced into the environment each year.[5] When the Swedes banned mercuric seed dressings in 1966 they found their sea birds were still accumulating mercury from the effluents of paper mills and chlorine factories. Anxiety had of course intensified since the Minamata tragedy in Japan in 1953 when mercuric wastes from the Chiasso chemical firm were absorbed by shell fish on the mud flats and produced mental derangement, physical deformities and deaths amongst local fishermen and their families. Water-soluble methyl mercury eats away the brain. In 1971 3,000 Iraqis died after eating grain seed dressed with a mercuric fungicide.

The noxious substances discharged by industry include heavy metals, acids, persistent oils, carcinogenic dusts and organic compounds like PVC. Mercury and lead are well-known poisons; nickel, titanium, beryllium, cadmium and chromium less so. New stories about such hazards seem to break every week.

In August 1975, yellow water seeping out of the ground in a low-lying part of Tokyo was found to contain a high concentration of hexavalent chromium, believed to induce cancer. It then transpired that over 500,000 tons of chromium-polluted slag had been dumped in or around the city.

In July 1976 an explosion at a chemical works in Seveso, north of Milan, contaminated the neighbouring countryside with a chemical, dioxin, feared to be more dangerous than thalidomide. It took eight days before the owners publicly admitted that dioxin was involved. It may be years before the human cost can be counted.

In 1977 new cases of neurological damage were being discovered in the State of Michigan caused by the accidental addition of PBB (polybrominated biphenyl — a fire retardent) to animal feed four years before. Polluted milk, meat and eggs had been sold throughout the State before the accident was discovered.

Commercial secrecy adds to the difficulties of government investigators who are often short of staff and legal powers. It took many decades to establish that lung and throat cancer could be caused by asbestos dust. Legal penalties for industrial pollution are sometimes ludicrously light. It is far easier to get imprisoned for stealing a fish than poisoning a river.

Toxicity aside, the sheer volume of industrial, mining and municipal wastes consumes huge areas of otherwise fertile land. By 1970 Americans were annually discarding about seven million cars, twenty-eight billion bottles and forty-eight billion metal cans together with mountains of paper, plastic and other domestic rubbish. Land is destroyed outright by strip-mining and quarrying. By 1980 about five million acres will have been defaced by surface mining in the US alone. Immense acreages are also buried under sprawling suburbs, airports, roads and factory developments or left in dereliction amongst them. In England and Wales about a million acres of farmland is being lost every seven years.

The Abuse of the Waters

Many pollutants emitted into the air or absorbed by the soil are eventually leached out into streams, rivers, lakes and seas. Others are directly discharged into them — massive quantities of human and animal sewage, pulp and paper wastes, detergents, sulphite liquors, phenols, ammonia, oil and the salts of heavy metals.

About twenty-four million tons of waste products containing about 6,000 toxic substances are poured into the Rhine each year. No one swims in Rome's Tiber, said to have a hundred times the safe level of pollution. Industrialised stretches of rivers and canal have burst into spontaneous flame. The notorious Lake Erie is still the dumping ground for Detroit, Cleveland and Toledo.

Many coastal waters are heavily burdened, particularly the land-locked seas like the Baltic, the Mediterranean and Russia's Lake Baikal. The Baltic receives the effluent of seven highly industrialised countries and some areas are so contaminated that fishing has had to be closed down.

Another menace is 'eutrophication', the depletion of dissolved oxygen, which is mostly due to over-loading with nutrients like sewage and other organic wastes. It creates a stinking soup of dead water and can be especially vicious in the south where explosions of aquatic weeds throttle rivers and coastal waters. Irrigation is jeopardised; water transport and fishing are made difficult; diseases spread more easily.

Oil is of course a major pollutant world-wide; between one and two million tons find their way into the sea each year, leaving aside the disasters involving tankers and super tankers. The recent acceleration of off-shore drilling for oil adds to the risks of seepage through accident, collision, malicious damage or blow-outs.

There has been false confidence about the strength and immobility of containers used to dump noxious wastes in the deeps. Old canisters of mustard gas from the First World War have since eroded, yet the US Army sank containers of nerve gas off the Bahamas in 1970 as if nothing had been learned. In 1976 there were reports of seepage from drums of radio-active waste off both east and west coasts of America. Between 1962 and 1970 85,000 drums of it, solidified in concrete, were sunk into the two oceans by the Americans alone.

The oceans can no longer be regarded as a limitless sink. There has been extraordinary complacency about their waste-absorbing capacities. All the world's waters have been rapidly polluted over the last two or three decades and weird things have started happening. There has been an unaccountable explosion of the large starfish, the Crown of Thorns, which has destroyed Pacific corals and hence the surrounding fishing grounds. Another puzzle concerns the 'Red Tides' of a microscopic dinoflagellate off the Californian and Peruvian coasts which produces a nerve poison of extreme power.

Pollution has certainly unbalanced the stocks of various fish species — especially in the shallower inshore waters many of them favour. Over-fishing is as great a threat. Stories about the decline of cod, herring and salmon stocks are becoming common in European newspapers. Britain's east-coast herring industry was wiped out by sonar-equipped purse seiners in the late sixties.

The slaughter of the world's whales is one of the great ecological tragedies of the post-war era. Stocks of the biggest whale, the Blue, collapsed in the forties and are down to one per cent of their original size. The Humpback, Right and Bowhead whale have followed them to virtual extinction. The Fins and Seis are in danger. The Sperm and the Minke are being decimated. Bigger and more powerful ships are employed on the hunt. Attempts to secure international agreement on whaling quotas have had only limited success: Russia and Japan have defied UN appeals for an adequate moratorium.

Threats to the Climate

The sensitivity of food output to weather is high: many crop varieties are 'tuned' to a narrow range of local conditions of rainfall and temperature. Some climatologists believe that only a tiny change in the earth/atmosphere energy balance could lead to a climatic instability perilous for agriculture. Such changes could follow an accumulation of industrial dust in the atmosphere, increases in its carbon dioxide content, widespread alteration of the absorbency of the earth's surface (by deforestation, for example) or the continued injection of man-made heat.

Take for example carbon dioxide. The atmospheric level has increased by thirteen per cent since the start of the Industrial Revolution. Carbon dioxide allows sunlight to reach the earth but limits the re-radiation of the resulting heat into space. This so-called 'greenhouse effect' alone could substantially raise the earth's average temperature.

No less significant is the heat directly generated by the burning of fossil fuels and the operation of nuclear power stations. The earth is effectively a closed system and man-made heat adds to that arriving from the sun, the solar flux. We are permanently warming our thin atmosphere by, as it were, burning the earth itself. The danger of this extra heat disturbing the climate and hence food production, except locally, is not immediate; so far it amounts to a tiny fraction of the solar flux. However, were recent rates of industrial growth to continue for a century or so, the threat could become substantial.

In practice we would be forced to halt or reverse the growth of industry before this point, unless, that is, we found practical means to replace fossil and nuclear fuels by harnessing large amounts of the solar energy that reaches the earth anyway. Climatology is an immature (and under-financed) science and controversy over these issues rages. Nevertheless, the British Meteorological Office has said that 'the whole future of man on earth' may depend on how well we can understand past and future changes.

The Politics of Environment
The rapid growth of environmental consciousness in recent years may mislead us. Most of the successes of pressure groups have been scored on the narrow front of local planning as it affects human comfort or the preservation of endangered species of wildlife. Relatively little has been done to moderate the fundamental insults to the web of life. Neither nationally nor internationally have environmental considerations carried much clout, except where they involve measurable harm to private property. Public property, like the air, is less rigorously protected. Being everyone's it is considered no one's. In traditional economics it is an anomaly: it has no price.

Few enterprises, privately or publicly owned, will voluntarily reduce their profitability or competitiveness for the sake of a common environmental good. Nor does the system expect them to. Directors and shareholders demand 'realism', narrowly defined. Business is about profit. The balance of nature does not enter the accounts. Nor does posterity. The logic of the entrepreneur does not even require the sources of his present income to be preserved. Russian and Japanese whalers are quite prepared to drive the whales to extinction because, after exploiting their existing equipment to the full in a few boom years, they can then divert their capital to quite new projects.

Effective protection of the environment therefore depends on deliberate national or international action by governments. These are generally reluctant or slow to act. Many are closely identified with powerful economic interests. All are aware of the political cost of intervention. Marginal companies may be put out of business and thousands lose their jobs. In times of recession governments are under even more pressure to treat new safeguards as dispensable or 'inopportune'. States always fear to harm their competitive position. Many, especially in the South, claim they are unable to incur the extra costs that regulation involves. Antipollution conventions are therefore slow to be negotiated, even slower to be ratified. The 1954 convention on oil pollution in the Mediterranean did not come into effect for thirteen years. Thousands of tons of oil are still being dumped into what for another reason has been called the 'biggest sewer in the world'.

The international community attempted to take an over-all view at the UN Conference on the Human Environment at Stockholm in 1972. It dramatised the issues but there were bitter rows. One, over the East German question, led to the non-participation of all the Soviet bloc except Romania. The Chinese nearly wrecked the final Declaration with their rigid line on nuclear weapons. Many Southern states claimed the industrialised nations were trying to place a ceiling on the economic growth of the South to perpetuate their own dominance. Little concerted action resulted and a good deal of the momentum behind the conference has since petered out.

There must be some danger of environmental issues eventually precipitating armed conflict. We cannot readily imagine the Dutch and Germans coming to blows over the poisoning of the Rhine, the Swedes and British over atmospheric pollution or the Yugoslavs and Italians over the fouling of the Adriatic. It would, however, be a quite different story if a deadly, perhaps radio-active, pollutant from one state gravely affected another's vital interests.

What are the over-all proportions of the environmental threat? Various chilling warnings have been uttered. Rachel Carson's was a stark vision of a world devoid of insects, birds and other wildlife.[5] Professor Snyder forsees a slow extinction through universal contamination.[6] Paul Erlich has written of an 'eco-catastrophe' involving the death of the sea from the slowing down of photosynthesis by chlorinated hydro-carbons.[7]

I suspect such apocalyptic scenarios are exaggerated but they are not intrinsically absurd. All the factors contributing to ecological pressure are still multiplying fast — population, urbanisation, industrial growth, high pressure agriculture, the hunger for resources and the spread of harmful technologies. Moreover, historically speaking, many of the environmental threats have arisen suddenly. Since 1950 the levels of some man-made pollutants and the scale of physical destruction have been doubling every ten or twenty years. Subject to resource and other constraints, it is not unlikely that the total pressure on the biosphere will be four times greater by the end of the century, perhaps six times by 2015.

Beyond certain levels of accumulation we may abruptly find that a threshold of ecological tolerance has been reached and that a whole series of unexpected repercussions is triggered. The destructive processes could become irreversible before they are fully visible.

That is speculation. The dramatic tragedies may continue to be local. What is certain is that both the poisoning and the destruction of the common environment are reducing the chances of accommodating either the voracity of the rich or the needs of the poor.

7   The Fifth Threat: Nuclear Abuse

> We turned the switch, we saw the flashes, we watched them
> for about ten minutes — and then we switched everything
> off and went home. That night I knew that the world was
> headed for sorrow.
>
> > Leo Szilard describing an
> > experiment in uranium fission
> > made on March 3, 1939.

Fifteen seconds before five-thirty a.m. on July 16, 1945 the
desert at Alamogordo, New Mexico resounded with a giant
crash and a ball of fire surrounded by a huge cloud of
transparent purple air rose over 30,000 feet into the sky.
After the blast wave had passed, Kenneth Bainbridge, in
charge of this first test of an atomic bomb, got up from the
ground, congratulated J. Robert Oppenheimer on the success
of his Los Alamos team and said, 'Now we are all sons of
bitches'.

Atomic physicists had unlocked a crude power of blast and
fire that could eradicate all life and a subtle power of
irradiation that could irreversibly corrupt our genetic inheritance. This apocalyptic event not only created new vulnerabilities and demanded new restraints but transformed the
perspective in which all later generations must think about
peace, war and human survival.

Oppenheimer himself recognised on the instant of the
explosion the tragic dimension of the feat. A passage from the
Bhagavadgita, the Hindus' sacred epic, entered his mind, 'I
am become Death, the shatterer of worlds.' Another witness,
General Farrell, spoke of 'the awesome roar which warned of
doomsday'.[1]

Only thirty years later most people seem to have lost the
proper fear of this now perpetual threat. A curious com-

placency has grown; familiarity has bred passive acceptance of what Martians would see as certifiable lunacies. Yet it is already clear that the next ten or twenty years will see a massive expansion of nuclear energy and weaponry. The tragic myth that 'atoms for peace' can be separated from atoms for war still suits many powerful interests.

The Dangers of Nuclear Power

A conventional nuclear fission reactor of 1,000 megawatts creates in a year about as much radioactive material as a set of nuclear explosions equivalent to about twenty-three million tons of TNT. The scale and intricacy of the safety problems this represents are immense.

Placed in the core of the reactor are fuel rods of uranium 235 and uranium 238. A bombardment of neutrons causes the disintegration of nuclei of uranium 235, resulting in a fierce release of energy and a further burst of neutrons. These in turn cause more and more nuclei of uranium 235 to split. Let rip, this chain reaction causes the explosion of an atomic weapon. In a reactor it is regulated by the insertion of control rods of substances like boron-steel which absorb neutrons, slowing the reaction to a safe level. As the rods are carefully withdrawn the activity intensifies, producing immense quantities of heat which are taken up by a coolant to a heat exchange system. This produces steam which drives electricity-generating turbines.

The reaction transforms some of the idle uranium 238 into the new element, plutonium 239, about the most dangerous substance known to man, and generates about 200 other radio-active products, some of them also ferocious. These gradually accumulate in the fuel elements, reducing the efficiency of the reactor, so periodically the old fuel elements have to be extracted. These can be taken to a special reprocessing plant for a long and tricky exercise in which plutonium 239 and unused uranium 235 (both of them fissile) can be recovered. But, either way, there is a remaining 'hot' and 'dirty' cocktail of waste which must be effectively cooled for hundreds of years and scrupulously stored for thousands.

These thermal, or 'burner', reactors are fuelled with uranium and produce less fissile material than they consume.

Fast breeder reactors, on the other hand, are normally fuelled with plutonium 239 and can 'breed' more of it than they start with.

All reactors and reprocessing plants allow *some* radio-activity into the environment during normal operation. The levels are carefully monitored and measured against inter-national safety standards. Yet, strictly speaking, there are no 'safe' levels, only levels of 'acceptable risk'. As has often been said, there is an inescapable Faustian bargain between the desire for the benefits and the risks to be run.

In the reactor itself there can be leakages through the failure or weakness of hundreds of different components. Control rods have stuck in position, rivets have failed, screws have been jolted out of place, welds have cracked, poor materials have been used to save on costs. In the US alone such failures have caused operating difficulties at reactors in at least eight States. There are dangers from explosion. Liquid sodium, used as a coolant in fast reactors, can burn violently and rupture fuel assemblies, shielding or emergency mechanisms.

The greatest danger is a runaway 'meltdown'. A severe loss of coolant can lead to a literal melting of the reactor core due to the intense heat from the radioactive decay. The molten core can then penetrate the reactor's steel walls and the concrete floor and release large quantities of radio-active material into the earth and air. If not restrained, the mass could sink catastrophically into the ground and grow for perhaps two years. Until this happens no one knows how far the mass would sink through the earth, hence its jocular name; the 'China syndrome'.

The meltdown at the Enrico Fermi fast breeder reactor at Lagoona Beach, Michigan in October 1966 came close to a catastrophic 'runaway'. It amply justified the title of the recent book *We Almost Lost Detroit*.[2] Fortunately the reactor was operating at a very low power level at the time. It took over a year for Fermi staff the locate the cause; ironically, part of a safety device had come adrift. Other fast breeder reactors have often hit trouble of lesser kinds — Britain's Dounreay, France's Phénix and Russia's BN-350. So have plants manu-facturing the plutonium fuel they use. In December 1972 one at Pawling, New York, was destroyed by fire and two explosions scattered undetermined amounts of plutonium into the surroundings.

Human Error
Atomic energy commissions always contend the chances of a meltdown or the like are extremely small but the record reminds us of the unpredictability of human error.

At the big Brown's Ferry station in Alabama in March 1975, a seven-hour fire was caused by a workman using an unshielded candle to detect an airflow. Cables under the control room were set alight, knocking out all five emergency core cooling systems. Fortunately other pumps, not intended as safety systems, proved sufficient to maintain a critical water level.

The most sophisticated safety calculations were nearly upset by one man with a candle. Engineers cannot easily anticipate the actions of an impatient, let alone malicious or suicidal, operative. How do you combat boredom or complacency as nuclear power becomes routine and commonplace? One nuclear commentator, Walter Patterson, has described how around April 20, 1973 one of the largest tanks for the storage of nuclear wastes at Hanford, Washington, leaked 435,000 litres of highly radio-active liquid into the earth.[3] The leak was not discovered for six long weeks. Each week the day-shift supervisor had left it to someone else to review the routine test data. It was the eleventh leak at Hanford. Nor was it the last.

Another problem with reactors is what to do with them after their useful life is over. They remain menacingly radio-active for at least fifty years. You demolish or guard: there is no other choice. The cost of demolishing the ruined reactor at Lagoona Beach was judged prohibitive; its hollow shell is being guarded. Within three or four decades there could be hundreds of radio-active monuments to endanger the inquisitive. Dismantling nuclear processing plants is even more difficult. Believe it or not, the need was not always provided for in the original designs.

Immortal Wastes
Reactor safety aside, even the nuclear enthusiasts concede that the disposal of nuclear wastes poses entirely unpre-

cedented conundrums. Their handling and safekeeping demand precautions capable of being sustained without major mistake or accident for thousands of years — very much longer than any civilisation has ever endured.

British committees of enquiry are not given to exaggeration. The Ashby Report of 1972 said, 'In effect, we are consciously and deliberately accumulating a toxic substance on the off-chance that it may be possible to get rid of it at a later date. We are committing future generations to tackle a problem which we do not know how to handle.'

'High level' radio-active wastes could easily start boiling so they are kept agitated and cooled within special double-walled, stainless steel tanks inside thick concrete chambers. It is these tanks or their replacements which will need to be monitored, adjusted and guarded for millenia, despite revolutions, wars and natural disasters.

The most favoured alternative is 'glassification'; firing the liquid into cylinders of glass or ceramic. There has been talk of dumping these in salt beds, deep mine shafts, ice sheets or ocean trenches. This last is a specially worrying notion because monitoring would be difficult and any necessary recovery might be impossible.

Meanwhile Britain, like France, has been developing waste reprocessing as a service industry. Britain has already accepted wastes from many countries and in 1976 there was a burst of public indignation about it becoming a 'nuclear dumping ground' for Japan. Marvellous how a touch of xenophobia excited people about dangers they previously accepted with docility.

The Level of Risk

The probability of a nuclear calamity may be tiny but the scale of its potential ecological and genetic consequences may be so huge as to make that tiny chance entirely unacceptable. Moreover, the chances of accident seem much higher than those committed to the industry recognise or admit. In the Windscale 'incident' of October 10, 1957, most of the No. 1 reactor's containment devices failed after the overheating of nuclear fuel had led to the escape of radio-active isotopes through the chimney. (Afterwards milk produced in an area 400 square miles around had to be seized and destroyed.)

The Detroit meltdown exceeded what experts had solemnly defined as the 'maximum credible accident' for that installation.

Another 'impossible' accident occurred in the autumn of 1974, when Japan's experimental nuclear-powered ship, the *Mutsu*, sprang a radiation leak on its first voyage. The government had told its not insensitive public that nothing could go wrong. When it did, the ship was adrift for six weeks in the North Pacific. Later it was moth-balled. Public mistrust was not diminished when it transpired that engineers had tried to plug the leak with boiled rice in old socks.

The most disastrous nuclear accident so far occurred in early 1958, in the Sverdlovsk region of the Soviet Union. Neither the cause nor the death toll is known because the event has never been officially admitted. But witnesses say radio-active material was scattered over hundreds of square miles, the whole population had to be evacuated and the area was made useless for years.

It is surely quite staggering that we should expose ourselves to these and worse hazards — and pay out hundreds of millions in nuclear research — before we have stopped the appalling energy waste in our societies or spent even a fraction of these sums on exploring alternative sources.

Opposition to hazardous nuclear energy programmes is intensifying almost everywhere (except in Communist countries where dissent is automatically crushed) and has been encouraged by many distinguished scientists and by several nuclear engineers who have resigned on grounds of conscience. Nevertheless there are already about 200 commercial reactors operating in twenty countries and by 1990 there could well be three times as many in forty or more countries. Nuclear technology is spreading like wildfire, North and South.

The Spread of Nuclear Weapons
On September 23, 1974, four months after India conducted her first nuclear test explosion, Henry Kissinger pulled no punches in a speech to the UN General Assembly,

> The world has dealt with nuclear weapons as if restraints were automatic. Their very awesomeness has chained these

weapons for almost three decades; their sophistication and expense have helped to keep constant for a decade the number of states who possess them. Now ... political inhibitions are in danger of crumbling. Nuclear catastrophe looms more plausible — whether through design or miscalculation; accident, theft or blackmail.

Three months later, Israel revealed she too had acquired the ability to make nuclear weapons.

Any nation with an operating nuclear reactor is well on the way, although full-scale processing and enrichment plants, producing weapons-grade materials, clearly speed things up. India obtained the plutonium for her first ('peaceful') explosion using a small Canadian research reactor and American heavy water provided for peaceful purposes.

More than fifty states already have some sort of reactor. An assessment submitted to President Ford in mid 1976 listed forty countries which could have enough plutonium to make nuclear weapons within a decade. The most likely candidates are those which have strenuous ambitions like Iran, Libya and Brazil and those like South Africa, Pakistan, Egypt, Argentina and Taiwan which have hostile neighbours.

In June 1975 Brazil ordered eight nuclear power stations from West Germany in one of the biggest and most controversial deals of history: the package included uranium-enrichment and plutonium-separation plants despite Brazil's constant refusal to sign the Non-Proliferation Treaty (NPT). Officials denied any military motive; then a General let slip that the deal 'reinforced Brazil's sovereignty and made it lose its fear of the nuclear powers'.

Nuclear technology is very big business. France has been notably cynical, negotiating the sale of fuel-reprocessing facilities to both Argentina and Pakistan. A dangerous deal with South Korea was stopped only by American arm-twisting in Seoul. The Soviet Union has helped Libya which has openly stated her nuclear ambitions. South Africa is believed to have been helped by the Israelis, French and West Germans.

One little-discussed danger of proliferation is that the new nuclear powers are likely to have far less reliable systems for gathering intelligence and making strategic decisions than the mature nuclear powers. Their 'fail-safe' procedures and 'hot-lines', if any, may not work as they should, multiplying the chances of war through miscalculation. Even the threat of a 'local' nuclear conflict could drag in the super-powers. (Incidently, we must assume that *all* nuclear weapon sites, of friend as of foe, are automatically targeted by both American and Russian missile forces. Who knows who you may one day need to 'take out'?)

We must especially fear nuclear arms in the hands of wild or unstable leaders. Hitler might well have made Europe his funeral pyre in 1945. And imagine a later President Sukarno or Amin with an erratic finger on the nuclear trigger. Many more equable statesmen have been known to make eccentric decisions when rattled. President Nixon's 'button' was allegedly disconnected in the last days of his rule.

Another danger is the possible seizure, sale or unauth-orised use of nuclear weapons or substances by people of unsound mind, criminals, bankrupts or dissidents. In the long chain from production to deployment, it has been estimated that for the US alone about 120,000 civilians and servicemen have some access to nuclear weapons or weapon-grade materials.

The NPT, the main safeguard against proliferation, is grossly ineffectual. Many countries have not ratified it and many more including France and China have not even signed. Moreover, the non-nuclear majority regard it as a lopsided bargain. Their agreement not to develop nuclear weapons was obtained by the signatory nuclear powers promising to stop their own nuclear arms race. This would have required, for a start, their agreement to stop underground (as well as surface and atmospheric) tests. After long delay, the so-called 'threshold' test-ban treaty was signed by Washington and Moscow in 1974 but this still permits them to test all the sub-150 kiloton weapons they want.

A new safeguards agreement is urgently needed but the obstacles seem almost insurmountable. The nuclear powers will allow meaningful inspection only of their civil instal-lations. They refuse defence guarantees to the non-nuclear powers and if these produce 'peaceful' explosions, there are no effective sanctions.

The proliferation problem is being intensified by the

threatened spread of fast breeder reactors which would hugely enlarge the global inventory of separated plutonium. It needs only ten pounds to make a bomb and thirty pounds to create a device of Nagasaki power. Even less, as a carcinogen, could kill all humanity. Plutonium is virulently anti-life and its radio-active toxicity is, with a half-life approaching 25,000 years, virtually indestructible. The whole biosphere lies at its mercy or, if you like, at that of the perfectability of man's containment devices and procedures.

Seemingly mindful of all this, in April 1977 President Carter took the most striking initiative for years. He declared his intention to renounce the use of plutonium in the American nuclear power programme, defer the construction of fast breeder reactors and commercial reprocessing plants for at least twenty years, and place an embargo on the export of such equipment and technology.

Being well-endowed with uranium, the US could afford these measures much more easily than many European and other nations which are looking to fast breeders for eventual self-sufficiency in fissile material. Perhaps unfairly, some of them suspect American commercial motives and even a threat of Washington eventually taking an OPEC-like grip on the supply and price of what, in the absence of plutonium, would be their main nuclear fuel, even their main energy source — enriched uranium. But on the best view of President Carter's intentions, the main tasks remain; circumventing Congressional opposition and transmuting a national gesture into an enforceable international agreement.

Nuclear Terrorism

Not the least reason for resisting the use of plutonium is the threat of nuclear terrorism in the coming decades. There are over fifty highly organised terrorist gangs ranging from the Japanese Red Army to Al Fatah, Black September, the Tupamaros and the IRA. They are well funded, well equipped, innovative by nature and swift to emulate each other's techniques. Some of them have 'exchange attack agreements' with each other. The skill, range and ruthlessness of terrorist operations has been seen in the hi-jacking of aircraft, the assassination of diplomats and politicians, the bombings of city buildings, the killings at Lod Airport and the

Munich Olympics and the kidnapping of eleven OPEC ministers at their headquarters in Vienna. The perpetrators often have the suicidal fanaticism of *kamikaze* pilots and Israel's brilliant strike into Entebbe, Uganda, in 1976 was only a small sample of the international complications guerrilla politics might bring. All attempts at the UN to establish an effective international convention to deny sanctuary to terrorists have miserably failed.

If the price of terrorism were no more than a few thousand deaths a year, the strewing of limbs over airport baggage and the occasional diplomatic embarrassment, it would have no place in a study of the global outlook. With nuclear arms it could become a major determinant. The packed cities and technological complexity of our societies make them peculiarly vulnerable to ruthless, selective attack. Nor could a nuclear terrorist challenge be met by 'taking out' its place of origin — no one could know what it was. Nor could the security services always guarantee that any particular threat was a fake.

A gang might steal a ready-made nuclear weapon from a military store. A US Commander in Europe told a meeting in Frankfurt in September 1974 that 'It would be difficult to protect any target which was the objective of a well-trained and properly armed and maniacal group'. It would probably be easier however to seize weapons-grade uranium 235 or plutonium 239 from a nuclear reactor or reprocessing plant or in transit between them.

The technical literature abounds with evidence of poor security. An official of a South Carolina nuclear plant admitted its security system would probably not prevent a band of about twelve armed terrorists from entering. (The invaders could sabotage the installation — or threaten to — rather than steal material. After safety circuits were disabled, a modest explosive charge could break a pipe feeding coolant to the reactor core and hence cause a disastrous 'meltdown'.)

Terrorists might obtain fissile material through silent theft rather than frontal assault. Large quantities are known to have been 'lost' in the US. In 1965 the nuclear fuel fabrication plant at Apollo, Pennsylvania, found it was short of 362 pounds of highly enriched uranium. The AEC spent millions of dollars investigating but finally decided it had been lost through spillage, bad weighing techniques and human accounting errors. In December 1974 a senior official said one plant alone was unable to account for 900 pounds of the same material. In May 1977 the General Accounting Office told Congress that several thousand pounds had been mislaid in US commercial plants over the years.

We should not be surprised, any time now, to hear the first reports of an international black market in fissile material. In 1973 an officially commissioned report said US safeguards against theft or blackmail were 'entirely inadequate to meet the threat'. The Atomic Energy Commission (now the US Nuclear Regulatory Commission) sought to prevent publication. In 1974 a further authoritative study found they were still unsystematic and inadequate.[4] At least American failings are exposed. In Europe it was nine years before it was revealed that 200 tons of refined uranium ore had disappeared on the high seas between Antwerp and Genoa in 1968.

Granted the fissile material, how difficult would it be for terrorists to make a nuclear weapon? A former bomb designer himself, Theodore B. Taylor says it would be comparatively easy. The information required is readily available from public documents; one of the most concise explanations is in the 1973 edition of *Encyclopedia Americana*. In a book he wrote with a Virginia Law Professor, Taylor says: '. . . under conceivable circumstances a few persons, possibly even one person working alone, who possessed about ten kilograms of plutonium oxide and a substantial amount of chemical high explosive could, within several weeks, design and build a crude fission bomb'.[5]

The AEC itself is reported to have secretly commissioned two young and inexperienced physicists to see whether they could design an atomic bomb solely from published literature. They succeeded in six months. They at least had doctorates; an American television film in March 1975 ('The Plutonium Connection') showed how a chemistry undergraduate of twenty designed one in five weeks. He was quoted as saying, 'I kept thinking there's got to be more to it than this, but actually there is not. It's simple.'

There was a cautionary episode at Orlando, Florida, in 1970. A typed and unsigned letter arrived at the city hall on October 27, 1970, threatening to blow up the town with a hydrogen bomb unless the writer were paid one million dollars in cash and granted safe escort out of the country. A diagram of the device was enclosed. An armament officer at the nearby McCoy Air Force Base concluded it could work. The AEC could not confirm that no nuclear material was missing, so the ransom money was put together. It was not paid. The would-be bomber was apprehended first: a fourteen-year-old high school student.[6]

Home-made weapons would be technically 'inefficient' but so what? A small crude device detonated in day-time Manhattan or London could kill 50,000 and blast seventy acres. The threat alone could bring conurbations to a standstill, cause public panic and force governments to accept outrageous demands.

Another terrorist option is a high explosive bomb spreading radio-active dust. Inhaling ten millionths of a gramme of plutonium 239 can cause lung cancer: a few dozen grammes could contaminate several square miles. (For a specific objective, the US Senate for instance, it would be quite enough to introduce the dust into the air-conditioning system.)

The danger of plutonium theft, blackmail or sabotage is so hideous that any society with fast breeder reactors and frequent plutonium shipments would eventually have to impose such total public surveillance and such Draconian security controls — if only on a 'precautionary' basis — that civil rights, democracy itself, would be systematically eroded. Anglo-Saxons, including President Carter, speak of the 'plutonium society'. French dissenters already speak of 'electro-fascism'.

Nuclear War Between the Super-Powers
Fears about proliferation and terrorism must not distract us from the perpetual possibility of nuclear war between the US and USSR. In an all-out conflict between them most of their urban populations would be killed directly and a large part of their rural populations by fall-out. Most industry would be destroyed, government disrupted and the life expectancy of survivors would be reduced. Former Secretary of Defence, James Schlesinger, told a Senate arms control sub-committee in 1975 that a general attack, on military as well as civilian

targets, by 1,200 Russian missiles would kill between ninety-five and a hundred million Americans.

If slaughter alone were the aim, this toll could of course be achieved with far fewer missiles. It would take about half an hour. The race to oblivion is swift and the survival of both nations — and their allies — hinges on the good sense of a few people under incessant pressure.

Nuclear defence doctrines change over the years and the bewildering and sometimes zany logic of first and second strike, measured escalation, collateral damage and the rest has dazed the public mind. So much so that anxiety about the balance of terror is much less apparent than concern about the sexual behaviour of politicians. Essentially however each super-power uses the civilian population of the other as hostage. It is the doctrine called Mutual Assured Destruction, yes, MAD. The calculation is that neither protagonist will throw a first strike if he knows the other will still be able to inflict 'unacceptable damage' with a second strike (from missiles in 'hardened' underground silos and in submarines). According to the sickening arithmetic of our age what is reckoned 'unacceptable' is the incineration of a quarter of the enemy's urban population and half his industry.

The MAD doctrine aims at achieving relative stability in that both sides would retain a lethal second strike capacity even after their cities were reduced to radio-active dust. It is therefore thought of as a war-preventing rather than a war-fighting strategy and explains why 'America equal' is a more sensible policy than 'America first'. Nevertheless there has been a recurrent tendency in Washington to move towards the 'counter-force' doctrine, urged by James Schlesinger in 1974, which seeks to exploit America's rapidly improving accuracy of delivery by threatening Russia's hardened silos. Many believe this could destabilise a precarious balance. Herbert York, a former adviser to Presidents Eisenhower and Kennedy, has described 'counter-force' as 'among the most dangerous proposals I know'.[7]

Similar criticisms have been levelled at Soviet policy. Moscow is allegedly attempting to increase her capacity to detect, blind or attack America's strike forces. Also, by systematically moving her essential industry away from her cities and pursuing an immense civil defence programme, she may destabilise the situation by reducing America's chances of inflicting 'unacceptable' damage with a counter-attack. Nowadays civil defence can be construed as aggressive.

Aside however from the often bizarre contortions of strategic thinking, it is clear that the size of forces poised in the balance of terror is utterly disproportionate to the need. In 1975 the American armed services held a nuclear stockpile containing 10,000 strategic warheads alone with a combined explosive force equivalent to over 615,000 Hiroshimas — over a hundred times greater than that needed to incinerate every Russian city. The Russians' strategic megatonnage is greater still.

By agreement, even without it, both sides could slash their strategic armoury down to MAD levels without loss of mutual deterrence. Subject to anything President Carter may achieve, disarmament has not however been seriously in train. The strategic arms limitation (SALT) talks have so far done little more than legitimise and sophisticate the arms race. In November 1974, for example, much play was given to the Ford-Brezhnev agreement to work for an arrangement limiting strategic nuclear delivery vehicles to 2,400 on each side, of which only 1,320 could be equipped with 'multiple independently targetable re-entry vehicles' (MIRVs). This reassured the anxious while merely preparing to replace obsolete weapons with modern ones. As Congress noted, the proposed figure for MIRVs was higher than either side had yet deployed. Arms limitation was acting more as an induce-ment than a restraint!

Incidentally, the immense array of intermediate missiles, with which Moscow could incinerate Western Europe over-night, are not covered by SALT. Washington does not count as 'strategic' any weapon which cannot reach the US. And we Europeans quietly go along with this. Our witless parliaments and stupefied electorates do not even raise the question.

Meanwhile the arms race continues; some weapons have been deliberately designed as bargaining chips for SALT. New weapon systems may upset hard-won arms-control arrangements and even the balance of power. A frightening example is America's Cruise missile, a thermo-nuclear descendent of the German buzz-bomb, which can be launched from a submarine, surface ship, large aircraft or land vehicle. The Cruise can fly under radar screens and is astonishingly accurate; its 'terrain-comparison' guidance system is said to be able to drop it within thirty yards of the target. If so it could certainly attack Russian missiles in their silos. Washington claims a parallel concern about the 'counter-force' capabilities of the Russians' mobile missile, the SS-20, and their Backfire bomber. (Both sides ought to dread the day when weapons as accurate and *cheap* as the Cruise become generally available, as surely they will.)

Military policy reflects domestic pressures as much as objective needs. The public is easily scared and the military always want the biggest, best and latest. It is natural (if now obsolete) for brass-hats to think in terms of superiority rather than balance. They tend to over-rate the enemy and to be hawkish. They are touchy about the status and therefore the hardware of their own arm of service — land, sea or air. If one gets a new toy, the others must — and will sometimes invent new doctrines to justify it. And no administration willingly exposes itself to charges of neglecting national safety.

The defence industries have a huge stake in high expenditures and constant innovation. It was President Eisenhower, no long-haired radical, who first warned us of the influence of the 'military-industrial complex'. In 1978 the US defence budget was 116,000 million dollars. About one in ten Americans work in or for the defence sector, including half a million scientists and technologists — a quarter of the national total. The Pentagon has intimate relations with the corporations concerned. Hundreds of senior officers have been employed by them on leaving the service. The Pentagon itself employs legions of PR people including 300 lobbyists on Capitol Hill. Wheeling and dealing have their part in all this but more worrying than the corrupt are the short-cropped technocrats possessed by simplistic ideas and downright moralities as they order and deploy their nuclear armouries.

Tactical Nuclear Weapons

The US is believed to have about 22,000 shorter range 'tactical' nuclear weapons spread around the world. At least 2,500 are carried by US ships in the form of bombs, depth charges, torpedoes and missiles. About a third are in the European theatre facing about half that number on the Soviet side, which is far stronger in conventional arms. There is sharp disagreement about the merits and uses of tactical nuclear weaponry but it would certainly destroy large parts of the areas being 'defended'. A NATO war game named Carte Blanche involved the (simulated) explosions of 335 tactical nuclear weapons in two days and an estimated death toll of one and a half million. The toll would be far greater if the Russians deliberately chose city-hugging lines of advance.

The contrivance of 'cleaner' and more accurate mini-nukes is smudging a critical line between nuclear and conventional war. The US Army's 155 millimetre shell could easily be carried in a jeep, yet is capable of destroying everything within a half-mile radius of its detonation. Mort Sahl caught the irony of Western Europe's situation: 'The army has invented an atomic hand grenade. The only trouble is, a soldier can throw it twenty-five yards, but it makes a fifty-yard crater.'

That critical line will be further smudged if the US (or Russia) decides to equip her forces with the neutron bomb, designed to kill thousands by radiation with minimal fire or blast to damage property, whether military or civilian. The neutron bomb would not only maximise death but probably also, as it happens, long-term genetic damage to the survivors and to their children in turn. As Lord Chalfont, a former Foreign Office Minister, has rightly if optimistically said, 'This is a refinement of nuclear madness which we do not need and will not have.'

'Broken Arrows'

With all these hideous weapons there is also the constant chance of accident. Up to mid-1975 the US Department of Defence had admitted at least eleven 'Broken Arrows', major nuclear accidents. (Some observers put the true figure much higher.) In 1958, for instance, a B-47 accidentally dropped a nuclear weapon over Mars Bluff, South Carolina. One of the closest shaves was in 1961 when a B-52 had to jettison a bomb over Goldsboro, North Carolina. Five of the six interlocking safety devices were set off by the fall. Had the sixth catch failed, public opinion might have insisted on the rewriting of Western defence policy: at twenty-four megatons the bomb was 1,800 times more powerful than Hiroshima's.[8] But there is a larger point: in a time of tension any nuclear explosion, accidental or terroristic, could precipitate a full-scale war unless the victim state knew at once its true origin. So could a mistaken reading of the bleeps from an early-warning system. The major nuclear powers, their allies and their neighbours constantly stand at four minutes notice of holocaust.

Neither intellectually nor emotionally have we digested this compulsory backdrop to our lives. Yet how close we have already been to the brink. During the thirteen days of the Cuban missile crisis, President Kennedy placed the chance of disaster at 'somewhere between one out of three and even'.[9]

8 The Sixth Threat: Science and Technology Unleashed

A scientist . . . will always say: 'Publish and be damned'.

Jacob Bronowski

Leonardo da Vinci wrote in his Notebooks that he had suppressed his invention of the submarine 'on account of the evil nature of men'. They would employ it, he saw, to 'practise assassinations at the bottom of the seas'. Leonardo had no doubt that scientific research and its technological application should be subordinated to moral and spiritual values.

In early 1945, while working towards the first atomic test at Los Alamos, the physicist Enrico Fermi frequently told questioners, 'Don't bother me with your conscientious scruples. After all, the thing's superb physics!'[1]

In the intervening centuries the second attitude had become general, if rarely stated with such baldness. Science has become sacrosanct and, despite the shocks of our time, Leonardo's outlook is widely regarded as a sort of blasphemy. Yet, for all the rigour, dedication and courage involved in research, there is a tragic naïvety in the notion that it can be pursued or applied in a kind of moral vacuum. The laboratory and workshop grant no magic exemption from the tortures of responsibility. Not even 'the pursuit of truth' can be wholly innocent. For knowledge brings power and men abuse power; it cannot fail to create new potentials for good and ill.

The eruption of the nuclear dimension into history is only the most dramatic expression of a more general threat to the human prospect. Science and technology have gathered an immense momentum, carrying them far beyond humane direction let alone democratic control. They have done much to reduce the squalor and indignity of previous centuries, yet their very successes have added to their prestige and to our difficulty in directing and restraining them. They have become the most potent agents of a staggering economic and social transformation, the pace of which is still accelerating. And innovation cannot help multiplying the effects of over-ambition and impatience, error and accident, greed and sheer unawareness.

The momentum is not primarily due to the scientist's insatiable curiosity, the technologist's devotion to making things work or even to their shared philosophy of 'publish and be damned'. Science has become something like an auton-omous force, with a driving logic of its own. Science feeds on itself. Once secured and published, knowledge cannot easily be destroyed. And as it grows, new connections are made, more and more frontiers for exploration are opened up. No one can know what lies beyond these frontiers; by definition, discovery is unpredictable. What is certain is that it will constantly provide men with new opportunities to manipulate the environment. These opportunities are avidly seized. Northern society, Capitalist and Communist alike, is mesmerised by the scientific and technological imperative, an unquestioning belief that what can be done should be done. There is a hunger for power and its fruits which is stimulated by a materialist growth-minded ethos and sanctioned by a naïve faith that somehow we shall keep our machines under control.

The number of scientists and their publications continue to explode. Private and state industries pour money into com-petitive and obsessive research and development. Yet no one is really in charge. Neither internationally nor nationally is there a coherent policy or plan of research aimed at meeting the unsatisfied needs of the human majority — mostly rather elementary needs. Perhaps no such over-all direction is possible. But we do not even systematically monitor the profound impacts of past innovations. Bodies like the US Office of Technology Assessment are still in their infancy. Meanwhile we are increasingly baffled by the world we are making and our ruling institutions are exercising powers unimaginable to past generations. Let us look at some examples.

Chemical and Biological Warfare

'*Armis bella, non venenis geri*' said the Romans: 'War is to be fought by weapons not poisons'. Such inhibitions have been considerably eroded as a thriving military technology has spawned ever more chemical and biological weapons (CBW). The First World War saw the use of 100,000 tons of toxic agents. Over a million men died or suffered lifelong injury. Chemical weapons were then used by the Italians in Ethiopia, the Japanese in China, the Egyptians in the Yemen and the Americans in Vietnam.

Perhaps fortunately, biological warfare is dangerous to the attacker as well as the attacked. Infectious bacteria and viruses are not readily controlled; epidemics of plague, cholera and typhoid fever can change direction. The Geneva Protocol of 1925 was meant to outlaw the use of CBW but said nothing of production and stockpiling. The Biological Warfare Convention of 1972 covers these points although it allows research to continue for prophylactic, protective and other 'peaceful' purposes and has no provisions for inspection. It is relatively easy to produce bacteria and viruses in a converted brewery or antibiotics factory, so this threat has been reduced rather than removed.

Far greater menace lies in the potential of chemical weapons for which there is still no equivalent convention. A wide range of agents has been developed and stockpiled that can disorientate, incapacitate or kill on a massive scale. Tear gas, chlorine and mustard gas were the first, then phosgene and hydrogen cyanide and then, some years after the Second World War, the vastly more toxic organo-phosphorus agents.

The nerve gases are militarily the most important. They include sarin, soman, tabun, VX and VR-55. There is also a range of psychochemicals, and, more favoured, various tear gases and skin and lung irritants which can 'flush out' troops (and civilians) to expose them to maximum injury from conventional weapons. It is calculated that a casualty puts more strain on defenders than a corpse. There are also the defoliants and herbicides such as the notorious 2,4,5–T of which over 20,000 tons were sprayed over the forests and crops of Vietnam — the first proving ground for systematic ecological warfare.

The scale of chemical armaments is far greater than the public realises. One estimate is that the Soviet Union alone possesses 350,000 tons of chemical warfare agents. Presumably the US has a chemical arsenal of similar magnitude. The agents are known to have been incorporated in a variety of weapons from grenades, mortar bombs and other projectiles to spraying systems and free-fall and cluster bombs.

Five or ten years after manufacture, most of these weapons and materials are considered unsound or obsolete. They have to be dumped, but where? In the American case great loads have been disposed of in the Atlantic on three occasions without prior study of the consequences.

The need for an effective treaty for chemical disarmament is the more pressing because the technologies involved are neither complex nor expensive. Unfortunately the long-standing problem of inspection and verification has been complicated by the development of 'binary' chemical weapons in which the otherwise harmless chemicals are mixed en route for the target or at the moment of impact. Stored separately, the components would appear innocent to an inspection team. Yet a treaty which exempted binaries while banning other chemical weapons might reduce public anxiety without truly reducing global insecurity.

New Weapons
The hunt for new categories of weapons never ceases. These include land-mobile launchers, multiple warheads, Cruise missiles and anti-satellite satellites which put new strains on already 'old' methods of satellite inspection and existing arms control agreements. The CIA, it transpires, conducted an eleven-year research programme into the effects of drugs as mind-controlling agents which, before ending in 1964, involved human guinea pigs in 154 institutions from prisons to hospitals and 200 *non-governmental* researchers who presumably did not complain. As I write, West Germany is perfecting the BDI, a huge aircraft-carried rocket-bomb dispenser which can wipe out over three quarters of a square mile — massed housing or massed tanks — as effectively as a small nuclear bomb.

The Russians seem especially anxious about means of waging war through weather control. American forces probably hold a clear lead in these methods, having used them to interrupt Vietcong supply trails. Possibilities at issue include not simply flooding an enemy's armies or crops with rain but inducing or harnessing fogs, storms, hurricanes and even lightning, earthquakes and *tsunamis*, tidal waves of extreme violence. All this sounds highly impracticable but, since the triggering operations could be covert, their very possibility could generate unsettling suspicions.

Another new focus of military interest in the US and USSR is the destructive potential of high-energy laser beams. One weapons expert says '. . . it is probable that these two powers are locked in a costly super-scientific struggle to be the first with a practical laser weapon capable of destroying a military target . . . in fact the "death ray" so beloved of generations of fiction writers'.[2] The Russians are alleged by some to be developing a laser-powered proton beam generator which would alter the whole balance of power.

Geographical Engineering
When experimenting with great forces, technologists are prone to underestimate the risks, especially, it seems, about geological repercussions. The Nevada nuclear test site is only 240 miles from the famous San Andreas fault which runs deep under San Francisco and produced the earthquake of 1906. Despite seismologists' fears that another was due, two large nuclear tests were conducted there in 1968 and a third caused a three-mile fissure in the earth's crust. Similar large tests were then transferred to Amchitka, one of the Aleutian islands, only twenty miles from the world's most active earthquake area.[3]

While Lake Mead was being filled behind Colorado's Boulder Dam, 600 seismic tremors were observed in ten years. Larger tremors occurred as the Kariba Dam was filled in the early sixties. Yet, as Gordon Rattray Taylor has pointed out, such experiences have not deterred the ambitious from proposing to dam the Amazon to create an immense inland sea or to run the Mediterranean into the Qattara depression in North Africa.[4]

Perhaps the best known 'geographical engineering' proposal was to blast out a wider Panama Canal with nuclear explosions equivalent to 8,000 Hiroshimas. That idea seems to have been abandoned but the Russians are reportedly planning the nuclear excavation of the Pechora-Kama-Volga Canal to divert waters to the Caspian which now flow to the Arctic.

The Russians have already proved cavalier in the use of nuclear explosives to reverse rivers and many of the boldest ideas have come from them. A Moscow meterologist has suggested warming the far north by putting a dam across the Bering Straits between Russia and Alaska and exchanging cold Arctic water for that of the southern latitudes. Related proposals have included the nuclear penetration of under-water ridges which slow the movement of cold waters; the prolific dusting of black powders to melt the Arctic snows; the dispersal of cloud cover over the central Arctic basin by cloud-seeding; the spraying of aerosols into the stratosphere by aircraft and the diversion of Arctic waters into the Kara Sea.

The main aim of such dramatic measures would be to make vast frozen tundras agriculturally productive. However, repercussions could include radical disturbances of climate and the raising of the world's sea-level. (A rise of only twenty feet would put much of London and New York under water.)

The likelihood of such repercussions is a matter for speculation. But that is precisely the point: no one knows how such gargantuan projects would turn out. It is staggering what risks technologists — or their political masters — are prepared to run. Before the first atomic bomb was detonated some of the physicists involved thought there was a real possibility, however small, of it setting off a chain reaction which could consume the whole earth. A few scientists still believe we run some risk of this 'ultimate catastrophe' with every new nuclear test.[5] Others, you will wish to know, flatly deny it.

The Price of Secrecy

Barry Commoner has shown how excessive secrecy can blind us to potential hazards. For example, it delayed under-standing of the biological effects of radio-active fall-out from nuclear tests.[6] He contrasts statements by two American Presidents. Eisenhower said in October 1956,

The continuance of the present rate of H-bomb testing, by the most sober and responsible scientific judgment . . . does not imperil the health of humanity.

Eight years later President Johnson said of the (partial) nuclear test ban treaty that it had

. . . halted the steady, menacing increase of radio-active fall-out. . . . Radio-active poisons were beginning to threaten the safety of people throughout the world. . . . a growing menace to the health of every unborn child.

Commoner demonstrates that over the years there had been a frightening sequence of miscalculations and oversights by the AEC and others in judging the medical consequences of fall-out, especially of strontium 90. The AEC had said, for example, that the only possible hazard to humans would be through ingestion of bone splinters from butchered meat. By 1956 it admitted that the most important source of strontium 90 was milk — a somewhat more common food.

Nevertheless, to think of bodies like the AEC as composed of ruthless men making frivolous mistakes in a blind pursuit of new death-dealing powers would be to over-simplify. Live to the threats of Soviet power, and urged by government to get on with their job, they might have felt bound to press ahead with atmospheric testings even if they had known the biological dangers. Is it blatantly wicked — by recent standards at least — to accept some thousands of deformities as the price of national survival? At least this choice had the makings of an honest if terrible moral dilemma.

The Impatience of Commerce

Company scientists create ever more new products that are apt to come into massive use before possibly damaging side effects are recognised. Since the 1940s, detergents have largely replaced soap but it was many years before the repercussions were fully understood. As billions of pounds of the stuff descended into rivers every year, the mounds of foam affected both wildlife and drinking water. In the mid-sixties new, more bio-degradable versions were devised but these are troublesome in closed septic tanks and their phosphate content has contributed to the eutrophication of rivers and lakes. Again there was no adequate pilot study.

The case of DDT was similar. It was years before it was realised that it accumulated, first in soils and waters, then up the bird and animal food chains. Through unrestrained use, a wartime miracle suddenly seemed a potential curse.

Neither commerce nor human patience is attuned to what may need to be ten or twenty year test programmes. The hazards for workers in chemical plants are especially acute. As yet there are health standards for relatively few of the thousands of new substances introduced since 1945. Also, amongst the half million chemical substances now in use, are between two and three thousand food additives — preservatives, artificial flavourings, sweeteners, colouring agents and so on. Some, like the cyclamates, have been suspected as carcinogens. So have other domestic products including certain hair dyes.

The flood of man-made substances is creating unique problems for medicine. There are now tens of thousands of poisons to cope with. Nor can any doctor now expect to keep up with the stream of new drugs on offer; there are scores of antibiotics alone, each with its own dosage schedule and side effects. The superficial and emotive pharmaceutical advertisements in the medical journals suggest the companies responsible believe that most family doctors are about as lost in the world of modern drugs as young girls amongst the competing cries of lipstick vendors.

Genetic Engineering
Scientific research is creating quite new dangers. In September 1974 Sir John Kendrew, a Nobel prize winner, said about molecular genetics — genetic engineering — that the situation was analogous to that in nuclear physics at the start of the last war, possibly even more dangerous. He was supporting an unprecedented move by many molecular biologists, from West and East, to erect a worldwide moratorium on certain kinds of experiments in this field. This was a notable breach with scientific tradition. Even so it came eight years after the Australian biologist, Sir Macfarlane

Burnet, had first warned that an artificial microbe could escape from the laboratory and sweep through mankind as myxomatosis had done through rabbits.

These totally new microbes can be created using delicate new chemical techniques to transfer individual genes from one bacterium to another. The same has been done with genes from viruses and even from fruit flies and toads. Eventually such work might help us expunge hereditary diseases in humans through the replacement of defective genes, or enable us to incorporate nitrogen-fixing genes into cereal plants and hence improve the food outlook of a world short of nitrogenous fertilisers. The hazards, however, are immense. By accident or design the molecular biologist could confer penicillin resistance on harmful bacteria like streptococci and pneumococci, or create bacteria that produce toxins or cause cancer. The human gut is full of various strains of the bacterium *Escherichia coli*. If one of these was altered to carry a cancer-inducing virus and then escaped, the result could be biological havoc.

The means for preventing laboratory escapes exist and are already in use for research with, say, the smallpox virus. New safeguards are now being introduced but none are infallible; curiosity, accident or malice will finally overcome them somewhere. Incidentally, in another new departure, scientists at Britain's Porton Down are reported to be experimenting with 'germ warfare' against insect pests. The idea is to infect some of the insects with viral diseases and then release them like a 'biological pesticide' around affected crops. But surely the viral diseases might infect other organisms too, with far-reaching consequences? The mind boggles.

Especially daunting are the potential political repercussions of eventual success in fertilising human eggs in the test tube and transplanting them into the wombs of host mothers. Theoretically this technique could be used to reproduce large genetically 'superior' cohorts from whoever our late twentieth-century masters might consider the best qualified stock. The genetically inferior would of course be compulsorily sterilised. Eugenically this might appear sensible; yet a programme to purge society of inheritable disease and deformity could eventually transform it into something as 'rational' and callous as a battery farm. The idea sounds far-fetched until one remembers Hitler's measures to pro-create an Aryan master race and destroy the 'unfit'.

Technology and Politics

That science and technology are running beyond control is demonstrated not only in what they are doing but in what they are not. Wide areas of human need are neglected while enormous resources are devoted to research and development (R and D) for military purposes, prestige products like Concorde and extravagant consumer goods and services.

Over half of all R and D is military. In the US the federal R and D budget for fiscal year 1976 was about twenty-two billion dollars of which about three quarters was consumed by military, space and atomic energy programmes. Space exploration is surely the classic case of technomaniac extravagance. Considering its tremendous cost, the Apollo programme has produced few innovations or benefits. It was of course exciting. It called for imagination and courage. It was also almost pointless. Pointless scientifically because moon landings achieved little that unmanned satellites with scoops could not. Pointless humanly because it brought no relief to a suffering majority of mankind, apart from the transient kicks of hearing platitudes broadcast from an unusual location.

Of the balance of the US research budget, a large share was allocated to research into cancer, a disease much more common in the North than the South. By contrast there has been little response in America or elsewhere to calls for a concerted attack on bilharzia, for example, a debilitating parasitic disease of tropical poverty which blights the lives of about 200 million people. In fact most medical research is deployed at intellectually stimulating frontiers like organ transplantation, advanced pharmacology and computerised diagnosis and neglects the diseases and disabilities common amongst the world's deprived. We transplant organs while the South waits for elementary medicine.

Likewise most agricultural research is devoted to improving the production of animal proteins and exportable cash crops while the needs of peasant farming get low priority. Research towards the creation of appropriately small-scale tools for village agriculture and industry is starved of funds.

Roughly speaking, only two per cent of the world's R and D effort is applied to the special requirements of the South.

Meanwhile the kind of advanced technology that Northern commerce so earnestly propagates throughout the poor world may bring more harm than benefit. It is ideally suited to providing just what the South least needs — a superfluously wide range of the fancy, the complicated and, with its built-in obsolescence, the perishable or unenduring.

What makes many Northern technologies more seriously inappropriate is that they save labour rather than absorb it. The South's situation is the opposite of the North's: it is short of capital and cursed with unemployment. Advanced technology actually destroys jobs. As we saw earlier, a single mass-producing factory can put thousands of traditional craftsmen out of work.

The Technological Nightmare

The adverse impacts of advanced technology are less subtle and indirect in the North with its vast, crowded conurbations, the soul-chilling tower blocks, the noise and smoke, the commuter agonies and the congested systems of mass transport. Many consider the price worth paying. Some treasure the anonymity of city life. Is the familiar litany of urban discomfort therefore substantial enough to be included in an account of the major threats to the human future?

More than discomfort is at issue. A society driven by the technological imperative makes tremendous demands on our adaptability and has profound effects on our relationships, our personal composure and ultimately on the prospects for maintaining social cohesion. For example, mass production requires the breaking down of jobs into simple repetitive tasks: the daily work of millions becomes meaningless. A worker may use more skill driving out of the car park than he has used all day. Insupportable boredom is a major cause of seemingly idiotic strikes. At a management seminar in London I once heard it proposed that for many assembly line jobs the car makers should recruit mental defectives.

Mass production and mass marketing encourage a massive increase in the size of business enterprises. This heightens the sense of personal remoteness in the work force and weakens any residual sense of identification or loyalty. Men become 'hands' — the rest of the person does not much matter. Parallel 'rationalisation' occurs in the other major institutions, notably those of government. The bureaucratic hierarchies proliferate, the decision makers become more and more distant; as worker and citizen the individual gradually feels more insignificant and helpless. Nor may his home and neighbourhood be the consolations they once were. The modern economy requires a high mobility of labour. In California, the trend setter, people are now said to move home on average every three years. Each move strains family connections (the three-generation family is now rare) and breaks or attenuates friendships.

Most of the indices of social stress seem to suggest an intensification of what Durkheim called *anomie*, a loss of hope, meaning and purpose amounting to alienation from the prevailing social system. Despite the improvements in material conditions, there is a terrible toll of alcoholism and drug-abuse, mental disturbance, divorce and suicide, violent crime and, more recently, of violent dissent. The causes are various but behind the cold statistics, we may hear the cries of anguish and anger of people who cannot or will not accommodate to the unfeeling demands and demoralising pressures of mass society.

Technology is only one of the forces creating mass society but it is probably the most remorselessly dynamic. Its pervasiveness throughout almost every aspect of life and its speed of diffusion is still increasing. Herman Kahn and Anthony Weiner have listed a hundred technical innovations likely to be introduced before the end of the century.[8]

Change, by itself, irrespective of its direction, can create stress. Personal adaptations once made from generation to generation now have to be accomplished within years. Hard-won skills can become redundant almost overnight. In all sorts of ways the rate of change is producing widespread disorientation. It is the condition for which Alvin Toffler coined the term 'future shock' and, as he says, '. . . unless man quickly learns to control the rate of change in his personal affairs as well as in society at large, we are doomed to adaptational breakdown.'[9] There is a substantial possibility of urban-industrial society becoming increasingly uncohesive, unstable, perhaps self-destructive.

We must however remind ourselves that the momentum of the technological transformation owes most to our own limitless appetite for the benefits it brings. We have become addicted to its wares and to the excitement of its constant achievements. Not less disturbing, these achievements engender a reckless belief in technological infallibility.

During the night of November 22, 1975, the American missile cruiser *Belknap* was badly damaged in a collision with the aircraft carrier *J. F. Kennedy* off Sicily and several died. There were questions later as to whether the *Belknap* was carrying nuclear arms but the fundamental point was innocently exposed by a bewildered American official when the crippled cruiser was towed into the port of Augusta. The officers were, he said, faced with a 'psychological difficulty' because a collision between two ships with such sophisticated equipment was 'theoretically inconceivable.'

Our technological society has just this 'psychological difficulty' writ large. Despite the 'unsinkable' *Titanic* and the 'impossible' repetition of the 1965 blackout of New York in 1977, our trust in systems is reducing our capacity to see their limitations and to adapt to their failure. We forget that old tag, 'Murphy's Law': 'If anything can go wrong, sooner or later it will. (And if it can't it still will.)' Man is rapidly accumulating such powers that it is becoming extremely difficult to believe they will not ultimately destroy him.

One reaction to this condition was typified by Lewis Mumford who, soon after Hiroshima, wrote, 'If science itself were the main obstacle to mankind's continued existence, reasonable men, fully awakened to the danger, would demolish science as readily as they would demolish a Congo fetish'.[10]

Such calls may sound brave and bold, yet science is not a destructible object but a mode of thought. Nor is technophobia more rational than technomania. Reasonable men can neither hope nor wish to demolish science. It has, I fear, made human existence permanently precarious but now we can only learn to guide it. And this will need more research not less, especially in ecology (including human ecology) and future studies.

The Six Threats: Conclusion

It will also take more research to establish the relative seriousness of each of the six threats we have sketched and their interconnections. Some of the particular items mentioned under each heading, for instance the alleged fluorocarbon attack on the ozone layer, may prove entirely groundless. Other areas of danger, perhaps the climatic, may have been underestimated.

There cannot however be much doubt that any one of six threats, on its own, could bring havoc. Nor is there doubt that the six threats are more menacing because they are converging fast and are so intertwined as to be mutually reinforcing. Population pressure intensifies the demand for food and for the products of industry. The provision of these puts added strains on scarce resources and on the environment — our reserves of fossil fuels are run down, land is consumed by mines and factories, pollution multiplies. Energy shortage hastens governments' resort to the nuclear option. Pollution and the overstraining of soils reacts back on our food-growing capacity.

With possible exceptions like the control of nuclear armaments, it follows that few of the threats could be tackled effectively in isolation. There is a crisis of the whole system and one of our shortest resources is time. Nevertheless, urgency is a treacherous counsellor; impulsive action based on a false analysis could make matters worse.

There is, for example, no 'technological fix' that can magically transform the outlook. One of the most gloriously zany on offer is curing the population problem by rocketing the human surplus to other planets. Even were another habitable one discovered, it would take so long for our fastest spacecraft to reach it that birth control would have to be exercised on the journey itself! And why even consider paying the immense (if one-way) fare into space when it would cost so much less to look after each other on earth?

It is human choice that decides how technologies are applied and political conditions that largely determine their social impact. Those who rise in spasms of hope that processed plankton or high-yielding seeds will resolve the food crisis have forgotten the brutal truth that the poor have no money to pay for them and the crueller truth that innovation often just makes the rich richer, the fat fatter. Now therefore we must examine the human factor in all this, the Seventh Enemy, and first the question of political inertia.

Part Three
The Seventh Enemy

9 The First Face of the Seventh Enemy: Political Inertia

States as great engines move slowly.

Francis Bacon (1561–1626),
The Advancement of Learning

If mankind is fast heading for multiple calamities most of our national politics and international dealings must be seen as tragi-comic irrelevances. With a third of our fellows destitute and all of us living under a nuclear Sword of Damocles, we of the rich nations are obsessed by secondary problems.

Despite the gathering storm we have refused to reappraise our priorities. Even our worst domestic troubles like unemployment, urban squalor and industrial tension are of small significance in the global perspective, despite the stupidity and injustice they represent. Take inflation. Severe in many Western countries, its persistence could eventually lead beyond hardship to unrest and instability. But for millions in the South, inflation questions hope of life. The rise in the poor countries' import bill for oil alone has wiped out their receipts of foreign aid.

It is true that most of the global perils have been the subject of special UN conferences, including environment at Stockholm; population at Bucharest; food at Rome and the crisis of human settlements at 'Habitat', Vancouver. And, for years, trade and aid have been argued over at New York, Nairobi, Paris and elsewhere. These conclaves, however, have inspired much bitterness and disorder, little agreement and less action. The typical verdicts have had an air of valiant cheerfulness: 'not quite a disaster'; 'not wholly a waste of time'. At one point the Canadian chairman of 'Habitat' was moved to cry out, 'For the sake of God and our children I beg you to stay with what this conference is all about, to do what we can and not try to do what we cannot.'

It is not as if there has been any lack of authoritative warnings. Between 1966 and 1967 thirty world leaders signed a (somewhat misleading) statement saying population was a problem 'no less immediate than that of improving the prospects of peace'. Olaf Palme, then the Swedish Prime Minister, told the Stockholm conference in 1972 that 'what is ultimately at stake is the survival of mankind on our limited planet'. In 1974 the French President said, 'The world is unhappy. It is unhappy because it does not know where it is going and because it guesses that if it did know, it would discover that it was heading for catastrophe.'

Also in 1974, Henry Kissinger said the nations of the world were 'delicately poised' on the verge of a new historic era and that the next ten years would either be 'one of the great periods of human creativity or the beginning of extraordinary disarray'.

U Thant had also given us ten years to forge a global partnership. Why, despite the urgent rhetoric, is there so little urgent action? Why is the international community so slow to combine against common dangers? Why is there such extraordinary inertia?

To answer these questions we first need to see why our governments have so much less freedom of action than is often imagined and why the six threats get so low a priority on their agenda. We must then examine the vital rôle of popular consensus in their calculations, the Western obsession with Communism, and how these and other factors contribute to international torpor.

Constraints on Action

Government is, as someone said of history, just one damned thing after another. Contrary to common belief, administrations do not 'come to power' so much as find themselves in the hot seat. They are more like hard-pressed fire brigades (well provided with smoke-filled rooms) than great construction companies calmly pursuing grand designs. They are reactive rather than pro-active. The ordinary citizen is apt to think in terms of what needs doing; the minister in terms of what circumstances may allow him to do. As Abraham Lincoln said, 'I claim not to have controlled events, but confess plainly that events have controlled me.'

Few governments can act as they like (which can be just as well) and democratic ones must work within an imposing array of constitutional, legal and political constraints. Legislatures are often hostile, awkward or simply over-burdened. The 'checks and balances' of the American system allowed Congress constantly to thwart Presidents Kennedy, Nixon and Ford, in domestic matters at least. In recent times only Presidents Eisenhower and Johnson have not been stalemated over wide areas of policy. Abroad as at home, there are always past agreements, commitments and understandings, legal or moral, to complicate present problems. Tame government lawyers can justify almost any breach of agreement but few administrations can afford to trample on several toes at once.

The struggle to the top in politics is everywhere hard and breeds lifelong loyalties and debts to party or faction, an unshakeable belief by the politician in his own value, and an exaggerated idea of the harm rivals would do in office. Politicians do get to believe much of the nonsense they have to talk. Their own great programmes may constantly need to be deferred but the other lot must be kept out somehow. The politician's first and fundamental instinct is not to act but to cling to office however little he can do with it.

The ruling few must also contend with the pressures of mighty vested interests, especially those of the armed services, industry, finance, commerce and farming and, in the shape of trade unions and professional organisations, of vast numbers of workpeople. In some countries these interest groups are prepared to employ deliberate disorder and violence; in many, corruption; in all, secret influence. Some multinational corporations have carried enormous clout in foreign policy, as in ITT's involvement with the CIA over Chile. Money as such is not exactly impotent; Americans were not wholly surprised by the revelations about Nixon's 'laundered' election funds or the tens of millions that some of its industrial giants had been paying out abroad to secure export contracts.

Governments also have to cope with a wide range of

passive resistance, from Gandhian _satyagraha_ to political strikes and management non-cooperation.

Autocratic governments are not exempt from constraints. All modern societies are so complex and pluralistic that smooth functioning hinges as much on persuasion as *diktat*. Decades of failure in Soviet agriculture have exposed the limits of the Kremlin's authority and effectiveness. The ageing fifteen-member Politburo has to exercise its power through a Central Committee élite consisting of some 240 often crotchety figures whose conservative bureaucracy has frequently obstructed or nullified economic and political reforms. There are factions supporting light versus heavy industry and of agriculture versus both. There is a deeper rift between those favouring détente and the improvement of Soviet standards of living and those elements of the armed forces, the KGB and the Communist Party *apparat* which demand a more thrustful policy abroad.

The effectiveness of modern governments (of right and left) has been notably diminished by the massive growth in their functions, responsibilities and size. The number of civil servants in Britain's central government is about 750,000, a more than fifteen-fold increase since 1900. The US executive branch has over 2,000 departments, agencies, permanent commissions, committees and boards. The men at the top tend to become swamped by detail and executive decision-making, leaving them too little time and energy for major reviews of policy. The strain is often almost intolerable. Lord Crowther Hunt — a political scientist and former minister himself — has said the British machine is in danger of seizing up completely.

Immense and intricate institutions tend to become arthritic. However able the senior people, work is necessarily compartmentalised and fragmented and very few can take a synoptic view. Each official works as if in a little box on a sub-section of policy in which a dozen other departments may also have a voice. The information in question is often unreliable; the equations of choice are complex; departmental aims conflict, and means — men, money and skills — are always limited. Decisions are therefore mostly reached by committee, resulting in half-baked compromises which reflect bureaucratic horse-trading as much as objective needs.

Orders given are not always conveyed or obeyed. Action taken may not have the intended results. And meanwhile the situation again changes; new events and demands call for new decisions.

There is therefore a strong tendency to prefer what the Foreign Office calls 'masterly inaction' — or the minimum adaptive change. Bold ideas cost time and tempers. Initiative on any scale is suspect. Officials are respectful of their hierarchies and seek a reputation for soundness, scepticism, caution, of being 'unflappable'. Those in the British Treasury are renowned for discovering ten problems for every solution.

Granted resolute political direction, most bureaucracies can do a good job: the most telling constraints are the sectional pressure groups. In Britain, the perennial headache of poor industrial relations resisted the guile of Harold Wilson and the determination of Edward Heath alike. Even minor reforms can be successfully resisted. Under fire from the National Rifle Association, Washington seems powerless even to negotiate the disarmament of its own citizens. (They hold forty million handguns alone and inflict 25,000 firearm deaths a year.)

This is not to deny that outstanding individuals, like Franklin D. Roosevelt and Winston Churchill, have sometimes shown a brilliant capacity to get things done. Perhaps no one in our century acted more effectively than Mao Tse-tung. Within thirty years he had survived great set-backs, expelled the foreign imperialists and transformed a huge, corrupt, divided and plundered empire into a unified, centralised, well-nourished and nuclear-armed country of great stature. A farmer's son became — and created — a colossus. Through vision, genius and command he transfigured the lives of a fifth of mankind and the political perceptions of all.

Such revolutionary change is theoretically possible on a world scale. In practice however it could only be achieved in the foreseeable future at the cost of a calamitous world war which, in any case, the revolutionaries would be unlikely to win. For this and other reasons, the initiative for radical change would mostly need to come from (or through) existing governments, especially the Western democracies which allow some flexibility of thought. What can we seriously expect of these however?

The Priorities of Governments

Not only partisan conservatives but prominent liberals have been losing confidence in the effectiveness of 'big govern-ment' and 'big spending'. When leading Western admin-istrations should be bracing themselves and others to meet the six threats, many observers are convinced that they are already over-stretched. Yet it would be an illusion to imagine that, were governments more confident or less impotent, they would readily so dedicate themselves. The idea verges on the laughable to anyone who has worked in them. For a start they do not operate on the relevant time-scale of, say, fifteen to thirty years. A former State Department planner, Frank Snowden Hopkins, shares my own experience,

> As one looks toward the twenty-first century, all nations seem primarily concerned with their own needs and problems, and usually on quite a short-term basis. Prac-tically all diplomatic activity in Washington, for example, focuses on immediate crises and extensive tactical man-oeuvering.[1]

Astonishing as it may seem, very few officials or politicians think it necessary, practical or even possible to think far ahead. In 1975 fifteen senior British ministers were ques-tioned on the time-scale of their department's thinking. In ten of them 'long-term' projections (six years plus!) were made only 'from time to time for internal use'.

In a few specific areas like energy and defence, genuinely long-term planning is inescapable. Some governments have sensibly created 'think-tanks' to extend its scope and com-prehensiveness: Edward Heath established one at 10 Down-ing Street. Typically, however, its main rôle has become that of helping to give coherence to immediate decision-making. Its current head, Sir Kenneth Berrill, has said, 'Your staying here depends on ministers finding it helpful. If you're wasting ministers' time — then you had better be gone'.[2]

What ministers will regard as a waste of time reflects what they reckon to be the necessary priorities. People first want their lives, property and liberties secured against internal disorder and external attack. Then they want the chance to work and higher standards of living and social welfare.

Neither internal order nor external defence are easily or cheaply sustained. The over-all management of a modern economy is another mammoth task, even where the state does not itself, as in Britain, control a third of it. Then the ruling few must somehow hold the ring between rival classes, regions, and groups, each greedy for scarce resources and see to it, whether by law, command or persuasion, that disagreement about the share-out does not lead to stalemate, breakdown or violence.

Most administrations do not and cannot expect to hold power long and whatever the rhetoric about their ultimate aims — the 'Great Society' and the rest — they find themselves swept up in the tide of events. They lurch from crisis to crisis, seizing whatever favourable opportunities offer and defending any advances against their opponents. The present seems quite testing enough without looking years ahead or far abroad for new sources of trouble. As Michael Oakeshott has said, with only a little exaggeration,

> In political activity . . . men sail a boundless and bottomless sea; there is neither harbour for shelter nor floor for anchorage, neither starting-place nor appointed destination. The enterprise is to keep afloat on an even keel . . .[3]

For the most part, therefore, governments must work from month to month, even week to week, making their necessary shabby bargains and coping with whatever demands urgent decision. They are constantly at the mercy of the unexpected; an embarrassing case of espionage, revelations of corruption, an ill-judged appointment or a sexual scandal, leave aside a stock market collapse, a Middle East war or an oil boycott. As Kissinger has said, 'Usually decisions are made in a very brief time with enormous pressure and uncertain knowledge'. He frankly likened his experience to a nightmare, 'You could only pray that the train wouldn't hit you before you ran out of time'.[4]

In this perspective, the six 'long-term' threats simply do not register. The official who is brave (or inexperienced) enough to remind his masters of them would be thought hopelessly idealistic if not mildly dotty. Most Northern governments regard the six threats as either hypothetical, distant or, as with population and food, a menace only to the South. The only one seen as becoming critical and urgent, and that still to few, is nuclear proliferation with energy shortage now edging into second place.

Even these matters are mostly seen in terms of potential national advantage. Factions in both Moscow and Peking would see an energy crisis in the South as providing welcome revolutionary opportunities. Many Southern governments favour nuclear proliferation — to themselves that is — just as several Western ones are all too ready to satisfy them with multi-billion-dollar deals.

It is especially tragic that an era crying out for an internationalist spirit should be one in which the most brazen nationalism thrives. For many, North and South, it serves as an ersatz religion. In the South it stands for modernity too. In the West it is rarely as blatant — or lame — as poor dear President Ford's unconscious imitation of Mohammed Ali at a Wisconsin campaign rally in 1976,

> We are number one . . . the greatest science and technology . . . our military capacity second to none . . . morally and spiritually number one . . . so that America, and all its people, its government, will be number one for ever.

His rival, now President Carter, was asked in May 1977 how much sovereignty the US was willing to give up in connection with today's inevitable economic interdependence. His answer was brisk, 'None'.

Far from Western self-interest being curbed for the sake of the developing world, it is insidious enough to obstruct their shared purposes in NATO. Soviet military capacities have been growing fast, and Europe's southern flank is conspicuously weak. Yet a report in 1975 concluded that NATO members were wasting ten billion dollars a year in competing between themselves in the development and procurement of weapons. The situation is as insane militarily as it is financially. NATO armies have thirty-one different sorts of anti-tank weapons in their inventories, twenty-two anti-aircraft weapons and seven battle tanks. Fuels, ammunition and spares are different. The air forces have twenty-three kinds of combat aircraft. The navies have a hundred sorts of ship of destroyer size or larger, equipped with over forty kinds of guns and thirty-six kinds of radar.

The Need for Consensus

Neither the nationalism nor the myopia of governments are necessarily self-chosen; they are largely enforced by the attitudes of those they rule. Adequacy in office depends on the public's acceptance of the broad lines of policy. Even the Communist regimes have to maintain some degree of willing compliance. The Kremlin knows that the 'valiant vanguard of proletarian internationalism' disguises an ethnocentric Mother Russia who cares first for her own. Mother can get stroppy.

In the democracies, even political survival may turn on keen sensitivity to the public mood. The press, polls and television screen must be studied assiduously. Edward Heath used to reach for the morning newspapers like an addict who had missed his shot.

Much of policy making therefore becomes image making and individual 'performances' are judged by colleagues in overtly theatrical terms. The 'right noises' must be made: tone of voice is half the battle. Every option for action is anxiously weighed by both the 'ins' and the 'outs' for its likely impact, emotional as well as practical, on party supporters, floating voters and the various pressure groups. The merits of an issue often take second place. It may in general seem wise to curb the world arms trade but if cancelling a particular deal means losing jobs and hence votes, which it almost always does, that is simply too bad. And when British forces were withdrawn from East of Suez in the late 1960s it was the result of a Cabinet compromise with the left wing, not of a strategic reappraisal.

The electoral majority want jam today and promises of more tomorrow. Imagine a new enlightened administration deciding that resource shortage required it to create a zero-growth, steady-state economy employing non-polluting methods. This would mean a cut-back in heavy industry and, for some time, a steep rise in prices and unemployment. The political commotion would be immediate, especially from the poor. So the changes would need to be accompanied by work creation schemes, drastic income redistribution and measures to compensate for the weakening of incentives and export competitiveness. It would be possible, in fact, only as part of a long, slow and tortured process of negotiated change.

Few ministers of course dare to challenge the universal creed of growth. One who has is David Ennals, a British socialist, who in January 1976, called it a dangerous illusion, 'In the end it will kill us all'. Speaking of the situation over population, food, resources and environment he said, 'We know what needs to be done to avoid catastrophe; above all, we know that the solutions must be global ones. But are we prepared to do it?' Five months later, one of his colleagues, Lord Shackleton, sounded equally downright, 'Blindly chasing economic growth and material consumption makes matters worse for other nations'. Then, when challenged about Britain's inadequate aid efforts, he blandly said, 'If we want more money for overseas aid, we've got to generate it'.

Most ministers, like most citizens, are scarcely aware of that grotesque contradiction. They see constant economic expansion of any kind as a positive ally to world order. They fail to see that it is constantly enlarging the gulf between rich and poor.

Moreover, democratic politicians can say it is not cynicism nor even 'realism' that requires their surrender to selfish interests. Beyond a point, they can claim to be morally obliged to satisfy the clear demands of those who elect them, however ill-judged these may seem. We cannot escape the paradox that democracy calls for the popular action, not the right one. They may overlap but not often. Democracy (like autocracy) is no lover of generous, internationalist policies. A British Minister of Agriculture told the World Food Conference that he felt responsible to British electors not to starving Indians.

Democracy — and the consensus anywhere — can even be at odds with measures that would benefit all. Imagine proposals to replace the world's present nuclear anarchy with a security system which happened to involve the free entry and movement of Soviet military inspection teams. Even though the arrangements would obviously be reciprocal, any demagogue worth his salt could whip up a public outcry against it. Time and again I have heard ministers say they would willingly do this or that if it would not be 'political suicide'.

The Obsession with Communism

The cause of international cooperation also inevitably suffers in a century in which all political feelings — sectarian, racial, national and ideological — have acquired a special virulence. Sir Geoffrey Vickers has said that never since the seventeenth century has the world been so divided into groups which define each other as enemies not only to be fought but destroyed.[5]

The most bitter of these divisions, between East and West, is a massive distraction from the six threats and Southern needs. Since about 1946 both the USSR and the US have perceived the other as implacable, almost faceless, enemies. Both are utterly convinced their own creed could redeem the world. Moscow has said, 'We shall bury you'. Neither side doubts the wickedness of the other's system. Both insist on being 'number one'. Both are ready for obliterative war. Both are prepared to risk destroying the planet to uphold their cause.

There are surely elements of the paranoid in this obsessive relationship. Each side has fearful secrets from itself. I think I love America but she seems to have forgotten her own revolutionary heritage and become an unquestioning defender of things as they are, or as they suit business. Gorging herself on the planet's scarce resources and groaning with superfluous wealth, she seems almost oblivious to demeaning poverty both beyond and within her borders. Proclaiming the cause of freedom, Washington has supported dozens of obsolete and corrupt tyrannies around the world and conspired to destroy governments it disliked. This is the mentality behind Senator Goldwater's remark that extremism in the pursuit of liberty is no crime. Anything, even a Trujillo-type regime, has been thought better than one like, say, Allende's. And while accusing Communism of arrant materialism, America has sought to cover her own with a philosophy of 'enterprise' and success sanctioned by comfortably adapted, air-conditioned churches.

The Soviet Union has far guiltier secrets. In the name of

socialist humanity it massacred tens of millions between 1917 and 1959, mostly its own citizens. It has effectively regimented the rest, depriving them of their moral and spiritual, as well as their political freedoms. Fifteen million have been incarcerated in the Gulag Archipelago at one time. The shadow of Soviet power still falls darkly over Eastern Europe.

Both camps seem to project their own worst side, mostly unconscious, on to the other. Neither side can accept the guilt of its own failings. So far as these are recognised at all, they are excused as either 'inevitable' side-effects of the system or as necessities for survival against the menace of the other.

The evils of the other side help us forget we all have an internal enemy as real as the external. Our guilt about this, and the fear it carries, is projected on to our ideological opponents who become ever more menacing in proportion to our own gathering self-righteousness. Enemies become monsters, justifying monstrous measures against them. Only in this context does it seem possible to comprehend the superpowers' manic accumulation of overkill capacity (or the Arab-Israeli arms race).

This could sound bookishly remote from the 'real' world of practical politics. Yet George Kennan, a former US Ambassador to Moscow and one of the hard-headed authors of the original policy of containing Soviet expansionism, has reached a parallel conclusion. In the light of what he (rightly) sees as the more profound demographic and ecological dangers, he asked in 1976,

> Aren't we ... being unrealistic in the amount of attention we devote to protecting ourselves from the Russians who, God knows, are not ten feet tall, who have all sorts of troubles of their own, who can't run an agricultural system that really works, who can't adequately house their population, who are rapidly losing their prestige and leadership in the World Communist Movement, and have to reckon with China on their long frontier in the East?[6]

And George Ball, who served with Dean Rusk as Under-Secretary, has said that the threat to Western survival comes not from the Soviet Union or China but from being distracted by them from our responsibilities towards a wider and increasingly hostile world from which the US has been becoming politically isolated.[7]

Inertia and the Dis-United Nations

Being global in scope, the six threats require a global response. Any serious hope of concerted long-term action would have to be found in our only universal forum or one like it. Yet the UN not only mirrors the world's divisions and disorders but raises them to new levels of destructive intensity. The prevailing atmosphere is of sour discord and disillusion. Since its birth its membership has tripled and its budget grown ten-fold. Nevertheless, the benefits have been so few and the proceedings so acrimonious, that almost the only comfort is its survival. Far from accumulating authority as the global crisis has gathered, the UN has descended into frenetic disorder and near-impotence.

In all matters not directly threatening peace the UN has to work by persuasion, through its main instrument, the General Assembly of well over 140 states. Most of these are new (following decolonisation) and all are defiant guardians of their national sovereignty. Each has equal voting rights despite populations sometimes smaller than Manhattan's and annual budgets dwarfed by General Motors'. Votes are often traded for favours. Some have simply been bought. Resolutions are not binding. They are anyway mostly long-winded, convoluted, turgid, incoherent as to priorities and therefore usually pigeon-holed.

Nor is the Secretary-General able to do much more than serve the members, despite the initiative Dag Hammarskjold tried to bring to the office. The UN's bureaucratic apparatus is weak; much of the action agreed on has to be passed to national administrations to carry out. Its own agencies tend to be overloaded, overlapping in responsibility, inexpertly staffed, jealous of their autonomy and skilled at avoiding attempts to coordinate their work.

The new Southern majority has employed the double standard with blatancy. South Africa's racialist contempt for human rights is rightly condemned but friends do not embarrass friends. The extermination of perhaps 300,000 real and alleged Indonesian Communists a few months before

I arrived in Java was largely ignored at the UN. So was the Tutsis' massacre of 80,000 Hutu tribesmen in Burundi. So was India's occupation of Sikkim. So is President Amin's continuing slaughter of his countrymen. So is the continuing persecution of the Soviet Union's Jews. Of course the double standard, like Orwellian 'Newspeak', is endemic to politics. When reporters asked 'Kingfish' Huey Long whether there would be fascism, he instantly replied, 'Sure, but we'll call it anti-fascism'.

Since the oil-price boom, the Arab nations, leading an Islamic bloc of forty, have become pre-eminent amongst the Southern majority and the diatribes have reached a new pitch of outrageousness. In 1975, against Western protest, this majority carried a resolution defining Zionism as 'a form of racism'. Ironically, this perversion was recorded on the anniversary of *Kristallnacht*, the night in 1938 when Hitler's storm-troopers rampaged through synagogues and Jewish homes.

The Western powers have been infuriated by the South's conduct. Kissinger condemned the 'inflammatory rhetoric' and 'procedural abuses' as threatening to wreck the organisation. The American public has sometimes been thoroughly alienated and without US cash the UN would probably collapse. As US Ambassador there, Daniel Moynihan was especially outspoken, denouncing the Zionist resolution as 'obscene'; the Russians for beginning the recolonisation of Africa in Angola; and the Assembly for accepting 'lies' about America and becoming 'a theatre of the absurd'.

This sort of protest betrays a good measure of Western hypocrisy; the double standard is shown by all. Third World manipulation has merely supplanted the Western manipulation which preceded it. And the essential hypocrisy runs deeper. As Hammarskjold emphasised when I talked with him once in Sweden, real power lies not in what he called 'illusory voting victories' but in the immense and largely immune wealth and privilege of the West (and the East).

The UN record is not one of unredeemed failure. It has constantly widened its brief to encompass new issues; some of its debates are sober and creative; the weaknesses of the machinery have been acknowledged. Some of the agencies have done good work as have UN peace-keeping forces and observers in necessarily accessory rôles as in Cyprus and the Middle East.

The UN is useful and could become more so. Yet it would need nothing short of transformation to size up the six threats. Hammarskjold hoped it was in a transitional stage 'between institutional systems of international coexistence and *constitutional* systems of international *cooperation*' (my italics). That was over fifteen years ago. In 1968, Lester Pearson, a former President of the Assembly, said, 'Long and practical experience . . . has convinced me that this transition must be made if we are to escape destruction'.[8] In fact the UN is in greater disarray now than ten years ago. There seems little prospect of it rising beyond its intrinsic weaknesses — lack of authority, undependable execution and, most of all, the predominance of myopic self-interest in almost every calculation of its constituent states.

No Scapegoats

Yet, all this said, we cannot make our political leaders (or diplomats) the scapegoats for the world's ills. We as citizens share their short-sightedness and it is we as individuals who collectively define the consensus from which they cannot stray far. Politicians are individuals and not very different from the rest of us, just more powerful. They have secured that power through a special single-mindedness and a talent for the peculiar crafts of a game they find fascinating. They are rarely blessed with vision or even well qualified. Few ministers when first appointed to major responsibilities have anything like the professional knowledge or skills normally expected by a business enterprise. Edward Heath has said of the late Richard Crossman, for example, that 'When he came to office, he had no knowledge of the machinery of government, had no idea of the informal workings of Whitehall, had no capacity for delegation, and had no ability for handling people'.[9]

Nor do most ministers even find time to secure an over-all view of national let alone world problems. After leaving office, Crossman himself, nothing if not a clever man, acknowledged that 'In the Cabinet I had been as far removed from reality as Olga [his wife], sitting painting a picture in Chelsea'.[10]

My conclusion is not that political inertia is total: constructive change can be gradually brought about. Nor is it that the international community is wholly or intrinsically incapable of meeting the six threats. In theory it might; just. But in practice it shows little sign of doing so and, as the years rush by, the outlook seems bleak. The action demanded would need to be rapid, coordinated and of immense scale. Most important of all, it would require different values and a larger awareness both in the political apparatus and in society at large. Governments and peoples alike have been 'removed from reality'. Political inertia stems in large part from the other face of the Seventh Enemy, our individual blindness.

10 The Second Face of the Seventh Enemy: Individual Blindness

The blood-dimmed tide is loosed, and everywhere
The ceremony of innocence is drowned;
The best lack all conviction, while the worst
Are full of passionate intensity.

W. B. Yeats,
Collected Poems

'In one place nearby the Americans found three North Vietnamese wounded. One lay huddled under a tree, a smile on his face. "You won't smile any more," said one of the American soldiers, pumping bullets into his body. The other two met the same fate.' So ran a Reuter's report in November 1965. An account of another operation that month said a peasant was brought in, briefly questioned by a Vietnamese officer, then shot point blank with a carbine. The US adviser was asked why he had given his approval . . . 'These people could have moved to a Government area. In this war they are either on our side or they are not. There is no in-between.'[1]

At six-thirty a.m. on March 16, 1967, US artillery batteries opened up on My Lai No. 4 hamlet at Son My. Then the helicopters went in, strafing the village. Troops completed the slaughter. Among them was Lieutenant Calley. Over 500 civilians were killed. Men, women, the elderly, the children, the animals; everything that moved was shot. It was an atrocity that sent a shudder through America. The mother of one of the soldiers involved said, 'I sent them a good boy, and they made him a murderer.'

The shock did not run deep or last long. Public opinion polls showed under fifteen per cent thought Calley should be prosecuted. *Time* magazine said sixty-five per cent of its sample of 1,608 individuals denied even being upset by the events. After Calley's conviction the White House said the mail was running a hundred to one against the verdict. The typical reaction was summed up as, 'It didn't happen and besides, they deserved it'. Calley was soon released on parole and was paid 100,000 dollars for his story. No senior officer was even charged.

President Nixon wrote it all off as 'an isolated incident'. But the war itself was one immense atrocity if only because it was almost bound to be fruitless. Despite all the warnings and protests of the minority, the carnage went on, year after year: the raids with bomb, cannon and napalm against undefended settlements in 'free bomb zones'; the 'search and destroy' missions; the defoliation; the forcible removal of civilian populations; the torture of prisoners and 'suspects' with bayonets, bamboo slivers, matches, wires to testicles and nipples, the 'frying' with US field generators.

Spasmodic savagery is a feature of all conflicts. Far more ominous is the systematic erasure of the enemy in modern ones and the glib facility of the rationalisations for it. They range from the absurd idea that political objectives — including the 'defence of liberty' — can justify any means, down to the final abysmal appeal to 'superior orders'. All nations trot out these rationalisations. The British did so over their incineration of Dresden and the French over torture in Algeria. No doubt the North Vietnamese did so too, as they set their hideous booby traps and disemboweled and beheaded their prisoners.

Even when we deplore the events we find it difficult to identify with the afflicted. In 1946 Moses Moskowitz reported on a survey of German opinion,

> The most striking over-all impression is the absence in the German of any emotional reaction towards Jews, be it positive or negative. It was shocking at times to listen to people decrying the evils of Nazism, reciting the horrors of concentration camps . . . without one word of sympathy for the victims.[2]

One American interviewed about the Vietnam carnage said, 'I can't take the responsibility of the world on my shoulders too strongly myself . . . it upsets me. I'm having my problems and can't take this stuff too seriously.'[3]

We may well sympathise, but if we cannot respond with full heart to the overt horrors of war it is less surprising that we pay so little heed to the concealed violence of our world. The corrosive destitution daily endured by a third of our contemporaries in three great continents causes even more suffering, fills even more graves and brings yet more grief and desolation. The North's neglect creates more anguish than its weapons. Provision of fresh tapped water would alone relieve much of the South's burden of disease. As Barbara Ward said to the 'Habitat' conference in June 1976,

> It is simply not possible to underline sufficiently the appalling state of our collective imagination when 300 billion dollars for arms seems normal and three billion dollars for water exceptional.

There was a standing ovation from the delegates — but no commitments to contribute.

The Morality Gap

When my wife and I were in Jakarta our servants lived in our small back garden in sheds which made slave row in *Roots* look a houseperson's dream. As this was standard practice I did not notice. The aged washerwoman shared a two-bunk hut the size of a chicken coop with the gardener's boy. Then, when the cook's woman became pregnant, my wife said we ought to move them out of the ramshackle kitchen shed into our brick-built garage. An obvious answer? My immediate thought was, 'How impractical, the tropical sun will ruin the paintwork of the car!' Mutual neglect can be absurdly banal.

The late Arnold Toynbee, the historian, once warned me — over tea at the Ritz, truth be told — of what he saw as a widening 'morality gap' between man's ever-increasing technological prowess and the obstinate inadequacy of his social performance.

The gulf between what is and what could be has probably never yawned so wide. But can we attribute the extraordinary horrors and perils of our time to some singular wickedness in modern man? I doubt it. As individuals we are not obviously more cruel than our forebears. In many ways we are more compassionate. We would not send children down the mines or tolerate the barbarities of earlier legal codes. A British majority may want hanging back but not for sheep stealing. Nor do we share the bleak indifference of earlier times towards the destitute — not our own. There are minorities devoted to any cause we might name: the young seem specially sensitive.

Yet if our face-to-face morality has not deteriorated, our behaviour *en masse* certainly has. Witness the almost total erosion of traditional inhibitions on the methods of war. Before the nineteenth century, it was generally fought by deliberately limited means for limited objectives. Lewis Mumford has plotted our downward course since then, from Sherman's destructive march through Georgia to the unrestricted submarine warfare of the First World War and on to the Nazis' aerial destruction of Warsaw and Rotterdam. This, as he pointed out, did not make the Allies recoil in horror and concentrate their might on the fighting area. We imitated our enemies' methods. 'This general moral disintegration paved the way for the use of the atomic bomb. Nihilism had set up a chain reaction in the human mind . . . our last inhibitions were removed.'[4]

There is an evident contradiction. From Hiroshima to the onslaught on Hanoi — and recently in Northern Ireland, the Lebanon, East Timor, Cambodia and Southern Africa — hosts of frighteningly well-intentioned individuals have continued to aid, abet or commit quite monstrous acts while speaking of freedom, justice and their own sincerity.

This remarkable moral blindness also shows in our acts of omission. We of the rich countries have not *intended* the distress of the South nor, of course, its dangers for world order. Likewise all but one of the six threats is the unexpected outcome of a multitude of separate, often innocent decisions. The devising of nuclear weapons was wholly deliberate but no parent intends a population explosion or means to contribute to a food crisis. No entrepreneur wants to exhaust scarce resources or to corrupt the air and the rivers. No one meant there to be a global emergency. The 'morality gap' is partly due to a 'consciousness gap'. We have simply not realised what we are doing.

This is not to suggest that awareness of the wider repercussions of our actions is enough by itself to stop us doing harm. So-called intelligent self-interest is not as useful an answer as many suggest. As we noted before, the Indian couple may be acting quite rationally in begetting extra children to help on their land and secure their old age, even though they are also aggravating India's over-all population problem (and fractionally therefore their own). Only if there were nation-wide restraint could they expect net benefit rather than loss from their own restraint. Only then, for instance, might the state accumulate the resources to assure their future by other means.

Similarly it can only weaken a company's competitive position if it voluntarily incurs high extra costs in cleaning up its effluents while others continue to foul the environment. Governments argue similarly — and again 'rationally' — against suggestions that they unilaterally disarm or curb their arms or nuclear sales abroad or stop over-fishing. They say of course that if *they* do not pollute the river, sell the tanks or reprocessing plants, *others* will. Restraint in such cases becomes undeniably self-interested only if the rules of the game are changed, when imposed by superior authority backed up by the threat of force. In the absence of such coercion, appeals to the individual — whether nation, company or person — will be futile. Only moral example could then have any chance of swaying the decision.

There are perhaps three pre-conditions for an effective moral response to injustice or to communal danger (as from the six threats). The first is comprehension of the facts; the second is sound judgment, a confident hold on generous values (encompassing humanity at large and posterity); and the third is a power of sympathy and imagination sufficient in intensity to galvanise us into action. Our time seems to present special obstacles to all three.

Obstacles to Comprehension
Plainly the first obstacle to an understanding of the modern world is its sheer complexity. The pace of change has taken science, technology, industry, finance, economics and war

into an intellectual stratosphere where only the specialist moves with assurance. The lay mind — including the politician's — is often baffled by the intricacy, abstractness and novelty of the concepts used. Then there is our innumeracy, our arithmetic blindness. We are fogged by the millions and billions. (I remember Mr. MacMillan saying it cost 'only' ten million pounds to ready our forces before Suez.) And, as computer use, systems analysis, operations research and game theory have spread, the serious language of public affairs itself becomes technical, mathematical, remote.

The flood of assorted information and clashing opinions we receive must add to our perplexities. Our minds become cluttered with the outpourings of 'spot news' from press, radio and television. The media frantically compete for circulation and ratings. 'Will it grab them?' is the typical question of the news editor. 'Human' stories do; trends, however inexorable, do not. A hundred passengers hi-jacked over Greece rivets our attention; a hundred thousand dead through famine remains a dull statistic. And about the underlying threats the experts often disagree. After all, an expert earns his keep by disagreeing with rivals.

We see little connection between our lifestyle and that of two thirds of humanity. As Barbara Ward has put it, the rich nations suffer a type of 'tunnel vision'. 'Like the elephants round a water hole, they not only do not notice the other thirsty animals. It hardly crosses their minds that they may be tramping the place to ruin.'[5] Speaking in Detroit in September 1974, President Ford said, 'No one can foresee the extent of the damage nor the end of the disastrous consequences if nations refuse to share nature's gifts for the benefit of all mankind.' Great stuff, but he was speaking of the Arab's alleged greed over oil, not America's colossal consumption of everything.

Obstacles to Judgment
Most of us, if asked, would claim allegiance to a universal ethic, Christian, Judaic, humanitarian or other. In practice however we live by much narrower loyalties — family, friends, class, creed, ideology, race or nation. Most of us identify with our own in-groups and are rather indifferent to the out-groups — especially to people who are strange or remote.

It is a very human characteristic. There is something too large, unreal and unmanageable about commands that we love humanity in general. Yet if only in our own interests we should see that mankind's interdependence is no longer a slogan. Group loyalty, including patriotism, has its virtues but is often the excuse for selfishness and, worse, a contempt towards outsiders — blacks, Jews, foreigners, political antagonists.

The hypocrisy of the self-righteous and the dogmatism of the puritans have got morality a bad name. And modern philosopy has been little help. Logical positivism went so far as to write off moral judgment (and religious assertions) as intrinsically 'meaningless'. And the scientific outlook in general is inclined to share a 'reductionist' passion for the simplest, even the grimmest, explanations. Our moral judgments are therefore held to be 'nothing but' the reflections of unconscious motivations or of bodily functions ('it's all hormones') or, in the Marxist view, of the economic structure of society. The determinism implicit in these views is widespread and, in casting doubt on the idea of free will, challenges a basic premise of any morality — that we do have real choice, however circumscribed. Anthropology, as vulgarly interpreted, has also had a corroding effect. The discovery that societies have varying codes of conduct has seemed (only seemed) to justify the idea that there cannot be universal or absolute values. So there has been a drastic loss of intellectual nerve and the very language of duty and obligation has come to sound stuffy, even naïve.

The resulting cynicism has infected the public at large; we constantly hear that 'politicians are only out for what they can get', that 'everyone is on the make'. This is simply untrue but it is no wonder the idea gets about. The prevalent values of consumer-industrial society applaud self-interest as the key to ambition and the dynamo of prosperity. The ethos of instant gratification is shamelessly propagated. 'If you want it, why wait,' said a recent slogan for credit cards. Politicians make the message sound grander. A leading Conservative has called for a 'rehabilitation of the ethic of creative success'. The left is no less enamoured of wealth, if only to satisfy the burgeoning psychology of 'entitlement' amongst a working class blind to the relative riches it already enjoys.

The practice of restraint, what Irving Babbit called the inner check, is widely disparaged. A long line of romantic thinkers has urged us to act on impulse, yield to desire, deny the ancient idea of 'measure in all things' and popular psychology deplores all 'inhibitions' almost on principle! Then, more subtle, there are the tough-minded 'realists' who neutralise morality by saying it should 'be kept in its place'. It is fine, we are told, at home but should not interfere with serious matters of, say, military necessity or international relations. I remember, in 1968, a British minister being questioned about keeping unhappy boys of fifteen or sixteen in the army against their will. He replied, 'Morally I would not defend this system, but in terms of our defence needs, I can see no alternative to it.' This line of thinking (like 'politics should be kept out of sport') betrays confusion — and causes it. Right and wrong ultimately apply to all human behaviour or to none.

The wish to exclude the pious indignation of a John Foster Dulles from the delicate business of diplomacy is of course sensible. A government has to be willing to talk civilly to the devil, whoever its particular devil is. But this is not conscience-less. It is necessary precisely for moral reasons, as the means to preserve peace. To say ethics should play no part in foreign policy exposes us all to the unbridled exercise of self-interest and force. It makes might right.

Some scholar-experts hanker for a 'value-free technology' to solve our problems and think solely in terms of power. During the Vietnam war, a Yale professor proposed to the House Committee on Foreign Relations that the US buy up surplus Canadian and Australian wheat so as to cause famine in China and 'de-stabilise' its government. Noam Chomsky cited this episode in tracing what he saw as the cynicism of many American intellectuals about that war and castigating their pseudo-scientific posings, their increasing recruitment by government and their failure to analyse and expose the lies of officialdom.[6] But beneath this failure is a deeper one, trenchantly denounced in the 1920s by Julien Benda. He showed how in the name of 'realism' the intellectuals — the 'clerks' as he called them — had betrayed universal values and the spiritual truths which are their source.[7]

I fear there will be increasing coldness in the calculations of the world's chancelleries and of their advisers as multiplying numbers and appetites collide with limited resources. Already in 1975 Congressmen from California and other agri-business states sponsored a Bill to cut off food supplies to countries failing to make 'reasonable and productive efforts' to stabilise their populations. (Be sterilised or starve?)

Several scholars go much further. They say that, to survive, the advanced nations will have to adopt 'the ethics of the lifeboat'. The rich nations will find themselves adrift in a crowded lifeboat in a sea of starving millions begging to be taken on board. But if the rich take them in, it is argued, the boat will be swamped and all will be lost. So let the poor drown.

A similar doctrine, 'triage', has been propounded by Dr. William Paddock, a tropical agronomist. This, from the French verb, *trier*, to sort out, is the principle applied in wartime field hospitals when the number of battle casualties overwhelms the available staff. The injured are sorted into three categories; those too gravely wounded to live — the 'can't be saved'; those who will survive without treatment — the 'walking wounded'; and those who will survive only with prompt treatment. Only this last group is attended to. It is considered a waste to do anything about the dying or the walking wounded. Dr. Paddock and others have suggested that afflicted nations should be classified in the same way and that countries like Haiti, Egypt and India (the 'can't be saved') should not receive American food up to or during the coming times of famine.

The 'triage' and 'lifeboat' arguments are repulsive. In any case both are based on a false premise. As I showed earlier, there is ample food to go round if shared fairly. A Jesuit summed it up nicely, 'Before we start throwing people out of the lifeboat we might at least get rid of the golf clubs.'

Obstacles to Sympathy

Obligation is a matter of the head, not heart. To stir us to action we need the imagination of the others' distress and a driving force of sympathetic feeling. However, life in the advanced societies seems to conspire to reduce these capacities. After a hectic day of noisy travel and tiring labour we may suddenly be moved by a (beautifully taken) photograph of a starving infant, but the telephone rings, the car needs fixing, that extra work for the office has piled up, the children are playing hell, the neighbours expect you to call in, the newspaper is still unread and later there's that game on the box. The stream of demands on time and attention is incessant. Information, opinions, entertainments are heaped upon us. We tend to develop the 'grasshopper mind', addicted to immediate sensation. Whenever we seize a few hours' stillness some business somewhere reckons it has failed. Over-stimulation reaches such a pitch that many cannot tolerate the solitude in which depth of feeling matures.

Our immersion in the kaleidoscopic present may even distract us from settled concern with great national ills. In the 1976 Presidential campaign there was a remarkable silence about most of the revelations about America's recent past: shameful and illegal wars in South Asia, proof of long-standing abuse of power by national law enforcement and intelligence agencies at home and abroad and the most profound constitutional crisis since the Civil War.

We become both hooked on change and disorientated by it. The excitement is real; I was once a fan of the urban jungle myself. We want to be where the action is; to know what's new; to keep up with fads and fashions. Our self-exciting industrial system hinges on maximum turn-over, constant innovation, built-in obsolescence, a 'throw-away' mentality. As Toffler says, 'The roaring current of change (is) . . . so powerful today that it overturns institutions, shifts our values and shrivels our roots'.[8]

We are surely also estranged by the abstractness of modern life. The small organic communities of the past with their person-to-person intimacy have been replaced by giant and remote social, political and economic structures in which we have to serve our mostly anonymous functional rôles. We increasingly relate to each other not as whole persons but as instruments for specific purposes. The courtesies decline, neighbourliness withers; in industry we become 'hands'; in politics, 'votes'. In Capitalist and Communist societies alike, man himself becomes a commodity, a dry thing, a cypher in the calculations of corporations or ministries. The dehuman-isation is reinforced by mechanistic thinking. We make a cult of efficiency, unwittingly take machinery as our model and conceal horrors with abstractions like 'body-counts', 'mega-deaths' and 're-education'.

All this deepens a sense of individual helplessness, of powerlessness in the face of great impersonal forces. Some react by turning to the inner world through drugs or dropping out, or searching for revived meaning through Eastern religions or the occult. Others react in anger, seeking miracles from authoritarian leadership or the revolutionary destruction of the existing order. Most just retreat into domestic quiescence, feeling the individual can do little more than look after himself and his own. He feels he must adapt himself as best he may to things as they are, an outlook not discouraged by the prescribers of tranquillisers and psychiatric 'adjustment'.

'The wise man,' said George Bernard Shaw, 'seeks to adapt himself to the world, the fool tries to adapt the world to himself; thus all progress depends on fools'.

Our world systematically eradicates or sedates its fools.

Our Inner Defence Mechanisms

I have described some of the special obstacles to comprehension, judgment and sympathy, yet mankind's situation is so grave that we must look for deeper, less conscious factors to help explain our blindness to it.

We have a profound psychic investment in not taking the reality of the crisis on board. Any psychotherapist will tell you, that his (or her) clients will unconsciously resist the very knowledge they need to resolve their problems. It is as if the client hides from himself that his existing responses and patterns of behaviour are no longer appropriate. And when these are challenged, he often clings on to them more firmly than ever. Recognition of the realities would demand change: change is painful, the unknown is frightening. The existing order — however precarious — is rigidly preserved. The releasing recognition only comes when the client gains confidence that he can use his new awareness constructively.

So it is in society. When people encounter disasters or threats of disaster they find ways of insulating themselves from their reality unless they feel they can do something about them. Hence the contemporary sense of powerlessness is critical: the threats are so vast in comparison with any individual's capacities to cope with them. As Freud said in his later years, 'Life as we find it is too hard for us; it entails too much pain, too many disappointments, impossible tasks'.

One of the defence mechanisms is dazed apathy; another is straight denial. Doctors say the bereaved commonly deny the death has even occurred, and patients assert that their disease 'couldn't happen to me'. Similarly Americans denied the massacre of My Lai. They had too high a psychic investment in the health of the US; such outrages do not consort with the American dream.

If we cannot wholly deny that the threat exists we are apt to avoid it, either by seizing on any excuse to question its scale or proximity or by side-stepping situations, images (or books) that remind us of it. In conditions of actual horror like combat, the avoidance may take the shape of pathological regression; shocked soldiers will fold themselves into the foetal position, a desperate attempt to return to an earlier safety.

In short, the attention and energies that should be used to meet an awesome reality find other outlets. Some take the problem out on themselves; disaster is seen as God's punishment for irredeemable sins. The reaction to the Skopje earthquake of 1963 was of this kind. Others consume their energy in futile displacement activities. They claw uselessly at the rubble with bare hands rather than demand the bull-dozers. Much of today's bottle and paper collecting may be such a displacement, like trying to bail out the sinking *Titanic* with tea cups.

Mass Psychology
In the global perspective, the defence mechanisms we have so far looked at are not at least positively destructive. When fear and frustration turn into a raging anger against a scapegoat — one of the out-groups — the results are very different. History supplies examples in the medieval pogroms or the burning of thousands of 'witches' during the European plagues between the fifteenth and seventeenth centuries. The Nazis of course used the Jews as the 'explanation' of Germany's pre-war ills, as the first focus for their pent-up aggression and as an instrument for contriving national unity. This was an extreme example of mass psychology at its hideous work. An indi-

vidual's unconscious hostilities are normally inhibited or repressed but when immersed in the mass he identifies with it; his hatreds are unleashed, even blessed, by national, ideological and other cries. Merciless violence is then authorised.

In this situation, ruthless leaders can also exploit our apparent need for obedience to authority — the price we are conditioned from childhood to pay for our security. Obedience is a powerful factor: experiments at Yale were claimed to show that, if instructed by someone thought possessed of legitimate authority, nearly two-thirds of normal American adults will unprotestingly administer others with electric shocks they believe potentially lethal.

In conditions of acute stress no nations and few individuals are immune to the degradation of mass behaviour. Before the holocaust, the German nation was counted one of the most civilised. Interestingly enough, although the Nazis openly proclaimed their hatred of the Jews, they felt bound to conceal the scale of the genocide from their citizens. It may therefore be ominous that within three decades a great liberal democracy could daily televise with equanimity the systematic destruction in Vietnam. (Nor, incidentally, did I myself think to raise the slightest question about it as a 'professional' in discussion with a new American ambassador *en route* for Saigon in 1967.)

It is as if we are becoming steadily immunised against moral perceptions. Our attention becomes absorbed by objectives and techniques. Our sympathy flows out to 'our boys' but scarcely at all to the hapless victims of mechanised terror. We allow our political allegiances to justify enormities and the more readily because we persist in believing ourselves individually harmless. Despite the world's evident atrocities, greed, lies, neglect and cruelties, most of us cannot accept that we are in any fundamental way party to them, that in practice or in spirit we all in some degree participate in the evils.

Yet, most of us, consciously or not, are fascinated by crime, torture, sadism, rape, revenge and the diabolical. Look at the headlines, the bookstalls and cinema billboards. As the psychiatrist Anthony Storr says,

> It is a mistake to believe that the ordinary man is not capable of extreme cruelty . . . It is no use pretending that

any of us are immune to sadistic feelings . . . We have to face the fact that man's proclivity for cruelty is rooted in his biological peculiarities. . .[9]

Fighting within other species is usually ritualised. Two rattlesnakes will wrestle without biting. A losing wolf will bare its throat in submission. Only man 'fights like an animal'. Only man is knowingly cruel.

It is a peculiar irony that liberals seem especially prone to deny their own share in evil. Their denunciations often ring with a similar blind hatred to that which consumes the perpetrators. They too, if unconsciously, seek vengeance and simply cannot see that we are all capable of the evil acts they (rightly) protest about. Our most defiantly pig-headed psychic investment of all lies exactly in resisting this terrible fact.

The evils always dwell in 'the others'. This sinister process of projection helps explain our blindness to the atrocities we may personally commit or tolerate in the name of, say, 'freedom' (anti-Communism) or 'justice' (anti-Capitalism) and our corresponding lack of alertness towards the emotionally less satisfying challenges of the six threats. It is our critical lack of insight which, in this and other respects, most sustains the Seventh Enemy.

Part Four
The Next Twenty-Five Years

---

11   A Possible Future

Some men see things as they are and say 'Why?'. I dream
things that never were and say 'Why not?'.

Robert Kennedy
to the youth of South Africa, 1966

If our century has seen the carnage of trench warfare, the
genocide of the concentration camp, the horrors of obliterative bombing and the manic accumulation of overkill, it has
also witnessed saving enterprises like the post-war Marshall
Plan, the willing dissolution of the British Empire and the
emergence of a new West European community from the
ashes of fratricidal war.

There is a yet more relevant example, coming from more
than enlightened self-interest. Before the winter of 1946–7,
Lord Boyd Orr, the first Director-General of the FAO, told
the victorious Allied powers that only if they were prepared
to ration grain could enough be released to avert the risk of
starvation in Asia, Eastern Europe and in a vanquished
Germany. They agreed. Britain, which had somehow avoided
bread rationing throughout the war, joined in.

The Seventh Enemy is powerful, not invincible. Nations
are not wholly incapable of coordinated acts of generosity and
foresight. I have argued that, on past performance, multiple
calamity is likely, not inevitable. Having answered the
question 'Why?', we must now explore a (realistically modest) dream for the future and ask 'Why not?'

The nations plainly and urgently need to cobble together a
minimum programme for world rescue. Can we plausibly
imagine a series of events before, say, 1984, which could on
balance lead to this? What follows is an attempt to create this
scenario for a possible future, one still open to peoples and
governments to choose. It is *not* meant as a set of specific

predictions but as a sort of speculative exploration of the kind of events which could set the human story in a less suicidal direction.

A Possible Future — up to 1984
To be realistic we should first imagine events reinforcing rather than weakening the hold of complacency amongst the world's rich: at the end of the 1970s we can reasonably expect a substantial recovery from economic recession. Energy prices will be universally high but throughout the North unemployment declines, inflation is checked and the refreshed demand for the South's raw materials temporarily blunts its campaign for a new international economic order. An increase in manufacturing investment by multinationals in what they see as politically 'safe' countries like Kenya, Brazil and the Philippines helps somewhat. A re-direction of somewhat greater official aid to the poorest nations helps more. Then from China there are stories of youngsters in gaily printed cottons cavorting to Western pop music and in Russia a growing consumer movement provides cover for accumulating dissent.

Also notable is the rapid increase in the use of automation, lasers, miniaturised computers and robots. The universities are quiet, short hair in fashion. 'Success' seems back in favour. By 1982 Japan — which now introduces the 250 m.p.h. train — has exceeded the American standard of living. Herman Kahn, once derided for his sanguine outlook, is lauded everywhere he goes and much of the literature of doom is remaindered.

Amidst the new Northern prosperity every sign of hope is avidly seized upon but several less happy developments disrupt the mood. A left-wing coup in Thailand arouses fears of renewed US intervention on the Asian mainland. The assassination of the West German Chancellor (by a young woman) sends a shudder through Western capitals. Other temporary shocks include an ugly territorial struggle between Algeria and Morocco which provokes a short East-West crisis. This is soon followed by two more of greater intensity, one in the Horn of Africa and another in the Middle East. Famine strikes South Asia and North-East Africa in 1981. Only a few hundred thousands die, so this, and an ensuing typhoid epidemic in Bangladesh, get negligible news coverage compared with the outbreak of rabies across South-East England, the incineration of part of Rotterdam when a super-tanker explodes and the detonation of a terrorist splinter bomb in Grand Central Station, New York.

We may suppose, however, that by early 1982 a number of government leaders feel impelled to take more notice of the grave underlying situation. Persisting poverty is bringing ever more anger and instability in the South. Energy prices zoom up again and, in the democracies, some surprising electoral gains are registered by the World Survival Movement, founded in London and Brussels in the late seventies. The perspective of many of these leaders is however less shifted by argument, statistics and the familiar string of coups, wars and famines than by particular personal experiences.

For the Yugoslav President (let us say) the critical moment arrives one evening in 1981 when he observes screaming seagulls wheeling over stinking masses of dead fish, molluscs and shellfish in a sea of thick red seaweed formed in a now almost hopelessly poisoned Adriatic.

It is the sight of the peculiarly horrible injuries inflicted by the 'concussion-bomb', a new weapon America has supplied to Israel, that marks the turning point for the Syrian President. This latest Arab-Israeli conflict of November 1981 is brief and inconclusive but the 'fuel-air explosive' tears apart the victims by bursting their lungs.

The British Prime Minister is energised by a terrorist group's successful theft of plutonium from Windscale; on 'expert' advice she had so often flatly denied the possibility. Her Canadian opposite number accidently witnesses a savage food riot during an official visit to Dacca: a youth is slashed down within yards of his trapped car. Sweden's leader retches when he sees the victims of an industrial accident involving dioxin near Stockholm. All over their faces, necks and hands are the ugly symptoms of chloracne — huge blackheads giving off a rancid odour.

In contrast, the critical experience for the Mexican President is one that gives him unexpected hope rather than crystallising his fears. During a tour of the dry backlands of Kenya he sees poor villagers making large cheap cement water jars for catching and storing the precious rain from their hut-roofs. This example of self-help 'appropriate technology' seems capable of transforming life in drought-afflicted regions.

Each of these leaders feels forced to conclude that for the first time the international community must together assess the global outlook as a whole. The initiating heads of government also include those of West Germany, Portugal, Australia and the Netherlands. Crucially, those of Poland, Rumania, Nigeria and India soon join them and then, on the same day, after tedious manoeuvering, the Americans and Russians. In the summer of 1982 a so-called Planetary Commission is jointly established, an international version of a National Advisory Commission. It is not formed under UN auspices since under a half of UN members agree to take part. Some of the national representatives are well-known elder statesmen like Edward Heath, Indira Gandhi, Olaf Palme and Willi Brandt. Each is supported by an able, cautiously sceptical staff and the Commission's secretariat recruits teams of front-rank specialists.

As the work proceeds, directed from the Commission's headquarters uncomfortably installed in, say, Lagos, postures are struck and fiercely opposing interpretations argued. There are press leaks and public rows. Nevertheless, even the most sceptical of the representatives are eventually convinced that the six threats are truly grave, ominously interlocked and therefore the more urgent.

We may reasonably imagine that by the end of 1982 most governments — from West, East and South — are represented in the Planetary Commission; that it now comes under the UN; and that it is instructed to move from diagnosis to treatment, in effect to recommend a World Survival Plan.

One working party concentrates on the question of political structure. An early Norwegian proposal for instituting world government is soon dismissed as Utopian. The problems are too pressing and international divisions far too severe for it. An American witness quotes effectively from a book by two compatriots, 'The nation-state may all too seldom speak the voice of reason. But it remains the only serious alternative to chaos'.[1]

The resulting consensus is that, although the world's bitter divides, not least between East and West, cannot suddenly be bridged, all nations need to take out a sort of limited collective insurance policy for common survival.

A further problem then arises. The insurance policy — the World Survival Plan — will demand substantial material and other sacrifices from the rich nations and hence possibly uneven reductions in defence budgets. This could easily disturb critical strategic balances between East and West and between both and China. Similarly, any disproportionate advantages secured by, say, India or Pakistan would unsettle a local balance of power. Agreement on the Plan therefore hinges on any significant changes in military expenditures being harmonised through a new agency (working through persuasion not, of course, supreme power) charged with sustaining a reasonable equilibrium.

Meanwhile, the other working parties have been earnestly, sometimes bitterly, debating rival proposals for combating Southern poverty and the six threats. By the early summer of 1983 a majority of representatives, including those of the two super-powers, agree on a minimum package to be submitted to governments. This degree of assent has been secured only through much frantic corridor-work, some bribery and several secret agreements.

Then there is a new shock. The Chinese allege in August 1983 that the Russians and Americans intend to use the Planetary Commission's findings to dominate the world in a new and sinister partnership of the rich. The Chinese Commissioner cries out as he quits the conference room, 'The oppressed must unite against the plundering super-powers of imperialism'.

Even after the Chinese have left — taking several smaller Southern states with them — the plenary sessions of the Commission twice reach deadlock and near-breakdown. There are acutely embarrassing press stories. Some of the Commissioners are deeply anxious about the high cost and likely domestic political repercussions of the majority's proposals. At first their apprehensions seem all too justified. Some of their governments refuse point-blank to take the Plan seriously. Many say that, in military terms, it means reinforcing a *status quo* they already find insupportable. The French, and some other governments, which had declined to take part from the outset, claim the whole project is absurd.

Nevertheless most of the major powers finally agree on a further diluted version of the original proposals and find means to bring some of the smaller dissenting states to heel. By October 1983 nearly a hundred governments, now including France, and representing over three-fifths of mankind, agree in principle to meet in New York on New Year's Day, 1984, to sign a Declaration instituting the World Survival Plan.

The Plan involves no new magic ingredients, no elixirs — unless the belated application of some far-sightedness and generosity to world affairs merits this description. Instead, the Plan assembles a vast army of humbly specific and severely practical measures. The nature of some of these has been implicit in our analysis of the six threats. (To lament, say, the paucity of world food reserves is to advocate their radical enlargement.) The full Plan however stretches through several volumes, the collated work of innumerable specialists in each field.

But the over-all conception is significant. The Plan gives priority to ending nuclear proliferation, reducing the already high risks of war and removing the fundamental obstacles, such as ill health, bad housing and destitution, to the long-term development of the South. A ten-year 'basic needs' poverty programme is modelled on one first proposed (and not pursued) by the World Bank in 1976. Its annual cost, as then, is equivalent to about five per cent of world defence expenditure.

At least as much again is allocated to appropriate technical assistance and to job-producing investment — especially in agriculture and small businesses — which is to be concentrated on the poorest nations, regions and classes. Many of the Group of 77's proposals for a new international economic order are also included (the North reconciling itself to much extra transitional unemployment). In addition, the Plan envisages a new, permanently staffed and powerfully equipped International Disaster Relief Organization to make and carry out contingency plans for tackling natural — and man-made — disasters and emergencies of every kind. (This is thought a potent device if only as a symbol of the new global thinking and concern.)

The total annual cost of the Plan is about fifty billion dollars at 1977 prices (equivalent to about a sixth of the world's arms bill). This is enough to make an appreciable difference to the common outlook. Nevertheless the Plan involves no great strides towards disarmament, resource-rationing or the equalisation of incomes between North and South. The nations will not be doing much more than grudgingly adapting themselves to a shared predicament. They agree that only were this first global programme to build exceptional international confidence could really decisive action be taken.

For the Plan to be agreed, however, there is one critical pre-condition, especially for Moscow and Washington: China must drop its opposition and join in too. Otherwise the whole deal is off.

Though still far inferior in its nuclear armaments, Peking is catching up surprisingly fast. By 1983 she has developed an inter-continental ballistic missile of 8,000 miles range and forged ahead with her nuclear testing programme. She has abundant reserves of uranium and lithium ore concentrates. Her gaseous diffusion complex at Lanchow is producing uranium 235 and plutonium 239 on a disturbing scale. Moreover, her vastly expanded civil defence tunnel-networks under Peking, Shanghai, Canton and other cities give credibility to Mao's old assertion that the Chinese 'troglodytes' would emerge triumphant after the nuclear clouds had cleared. Therefore neither the Russians nor the Americans think they can safely restrain their own arms expenditure if China remains free to press ahead with hers.

The fate of the Plan, perhaps the future course of history, now hangs on a single decision to be made in Peking. Can China reconcile herself to *not* becoming the world's third super-power? Will the proposed World Survival Plan miscarry at the last moment or be brought safely to birth with its promise of new beginnings? Is 1984 to open with a triumph for common sense or a monumental set-back?

The Most Plausible Outcome
As the last hours of 1983 expire and statesmen argue urgently in the Chinese capital, our scenario can be completed in either of two ways. We may conclude that with economic pressures and civil disturbances at home and the threat of virtual isolation on the world scene, China finally decides to swallow

her pride and help to build the new scaffolding of world-wide cooperation.

Alternatively, we may reckon that the Chinese leaders will see that acceptance of the Plan would mean tacitly abandoning their proclaimed objectives of China's becoming a super-power and leading a world revolution; that this would expose them to the growing threat from their own left, re-emerging in Shanghai, and that they therefore refuse to grasp the nettle.

The Plan, or something like it, does represent a future we could still choose. My own reluctant judgment, however, is that the negative outcome is much more likely. Indeed my own experience suggests that it would be surprising if the nations got nearly as far forward as this scenario for a possible future has suggested. Quite the contrary; there is a substantial risk of gradual, even sudden, deterioration in international relations in the coming years. Our possible future is one thing, our probable future quite another.

12 Our Probable Future

There is a question in the air . . . whether . . . we do not
foresee in the human prospect a deterioration of things,
even an impending catastrophe of fearful dimensions.
                              Robert Heilbroner,
                An Inquiry into the Human Prospect[1]

It is said of one economics professor that he has a notice on his
study wall saying 'The future is not what it was'. The story
strikes a typically contemporary note. I believe however it
was considered experience rather than fashionable prejudice
which drove me to portray our constructive scenario as
probably foundering when the crunch came.

In this chapter I imagine how the human story might go on
from there. While I still do not mean to predict specific events
(much less simulate one of those disaster novels!), I do
believe what follows describes a likely over-all shape for our
probable future — the downward drift to anarchic calamity.
In 1974 Professor Bernard Feld, as Secretary-General of the
widely respected Pugwash Conferences on Science and
World Affairs, warned that the world was entering perhaps
the most dangerous period in its entire history and, in his
judgment, the chances were greater than evens for nuclear
war to occur within the remainder of this century.[2]

I would put the chances rather higher; but this is not to
imply that the passage to such a disaster cannot be slowed —
or hastened — by our response. It is precisely through
stretching our minds to envisage what is *now* our probable
future that rescuing energies might be galvanised.

Beyond 1984: Drift and Disruption

So let us assume that, when the negotiations for the World
Survival Plan collapse at Peking in the first hours of 1984, not

only is a grand design destroyed but most of the detailed agreements which fleshed its bones go back in the melting pot. The public's bitter disillusion is reinforced by the anger of those who had all along opposed the Plan as naïvely unrealistic (or stupidly unselfish).

By the summer of 1984 several of the progressive world leaders survive this backlash only by swiftly returning to beggaring their neighbours and arming their friends. Nevertheless, there are some reasons for satisfaction. Nuclear war has still been avoided, the East-West détente has held and the economic recovery of the early eighties has been sustained. There is even talk of a new 'belle époque' in the North because, although the wealth gap had gone on widening, the South seems powerless against the staggering might of the West and the basic indifference of the East.

This reviving confidence soon receives a number of seismic shocks. The year 1985 opens inauspiciously when the San Onofre nuclear station in Southern California is sabotaged with high explosive charges. 3,400 die at once and 50,000 are exposed to the radio-active cloud. 'Why weren't we warned?' cry the headlines. (The Bulletin of the Atomic Scientists, which had carried a specific warning in October 1974, instantly trebles its subscription list.[3])

The fatality roll is relatively short but includes a notable visitor, the new American Vice-President, in office only a few days. A plot of some complexity is soon unearthed. During yet another famine the previous year, the West had refused food aid to the admittedly corrupt regime in Bangladesh and to other states, including Ethiopia, which are considered 'unfriendly'. Various terrorist groups, including young physicists and engineers from the Japanese Red Army, had then formed what they called the 'Southern Justice Army' (SJA) to wage a campaign of extortion and retribution on the richest nations of the West.

The SJA was yet to contrive its own primitive nuclear devices but had recently threatened Washington, Bonn, Paris and London with unspecified acts of conventional sabotage unless large shipments of bullion were promptly made over to them. These four capitals strengthened their guard on many vital installations but the threat was not taken very seriously. The idea of a frontal terrorist assault on a nuclear power station hardly seemed credible and it later transpired that there were no effective road blocks at San Onofre. The single guardhouse and the detachment accompanying the Vice-President had been quickly overcome and the charges set and detonated before the National Guard could arrive on the scene. The only comfort was that the wind, though northerly, had not been strong enough to carry the radio-active cloud the sixty-six miles to Los Angeles.

The Collapse of the 'Laager'

A much greater shock to confidence is the collapse in August 1985 of white South Africa. By relinquishing South-West Africa (now Namibia) and remaining aloof during the black take-over of Rhodesia/Zimbabwe, she had greatly shortened her borders and her success some years before in detonating a nuclear device (the Arabs said with Israeli help) had seemed to secure her military position for some time ahead. Since then, however, Pretoria's ferocious police reactions to a series of paralysing strikes in the African townships have so inflamed feeling in black and Arab Africa that by early 1985 a United African Army, drawn mainly from Nigeria, Egypt, Somalia and Tanzania, is established around the borders of the white-ruled 'laager' from Namibia to Mozambique.

Guerrilla attacks have been successfully repulsed for several months but the first African air raid on the white area of Johannesburg transforms the situation. South Africa realises that in a slogging conventional war the whites will slowly be pushed back to a Capetown redoubt and eventually overcome. Nor can she conclusively attack all the well-dispersed African bases and airfields. In July 1985 therefore she threatens Luanda, Lusaka, Beira and Salisbury (now black-ruled) with nuclear reprisals for any further air attack. This reaction seems hysterical to the outside world but, militarily, Pretoria sees the writing is otherwise on the wall.

The African reaction is instantaneous. The United Army has been assembled partly to circumvent further Russian (and Cuban) interference in Southern Africa. Now the African governments think they have no choice but to ask for Soviet help. (The West, after all, seems committed to preserving its heavy financial interests in South Africa.) Moscow at once agrees to make her nuclear-armed Indian Ocean fleet available to deter the South Africans. In consequence, the American President is now put under immense internal pressure to issue a countering ultimatum to the Kremlin.

This right-wing American backlash is precisely what Pretoria has been banking on. Washington has no wish to bail out apartheid but will US public opinion allow a beleaguered white minority to be put down with Communist might? At this point, contrary to orders from the United African High Command, a Tanzanian squadron raids Pretoria itself, incidentally destroying a white hospital and killing a sick member of the now furious Cabinet.

For several days the international atmosphere is as ominous as during the Cuban missile crisis. Soviet and American forces are put on Red Alert. The wires hum and headlines thunder. There are mass demonstrations — for and against intervention — in many cities. America's allies now catch fright. They urge on Washington that South Africa is not Cuba; that there is no threat to America's mainland, and that the defeat of the defiant 'laager' can anyway only be a matter of time. Washington is in a jam and the Russians do not flinch even when a US fleet approaches their own.

Events now move rapidly. The US Secretary of State secretly meets the South African Prime Minister at Bermuda and staggers him by saying there can be no compromise: when it comes to the crunch, the West not the East must have the credit of liberating the blacks of South Africa. If necessary the United States itself will 'take out' South Africa's airfields. However, if Pretoria immediately and publicly agrees to hand over at once to a temporary UN force and to black majority rule within six months, the West will try to persuade the front-line African states to hold off. The West will also guarantee free emigration to Europe, America and Australia for those wanting to leave and financial compensation for personal losses.

As he leaves for home, the South African Premier echoes a remark made by Ian Smith of Rhodesia to Henry Kissinger in November 1976, 'You want me to sign my suicide note'. Many believe Pretoria will rather fight to the finish than accept this deal but, at last seeing their position as hopeless, the South African Cabinet signal their submission three anxious nights later.

A Tale of Four Cities

Psychologically, this sudden surrender of a defiantly entrenched white regime to black pressure has a greater impact on the North than the humiliation of American power at the hands of the Vietnamese a decade before. The shock is deepened by the next major exploit of the terrorist SJA. During the run-up to the US Congressional elections of November 1986, its Indian and Japanese 'chapters' announce they have placed nuclear devices in the harbours of Baltimore, Southampton, Hamburg and Marseilles which will be detonated after twenty-four hours unless a string of extraordinary demands is met. These include the immediate doubling of emergency food aid to India, Bangladesh and Ethiopia and the delivery of named ministerial hostages and political prisoners to Libya together with fifty tons of gold bullion. Attempts to search for the devices will be met, they say, by immediate detonation.

The four powers are stymied. After the San Onofre episode they know nothing will deter the SJA from suicidal acts and British Intelligence confirms that the Japanese chapter has weapons-grade material, partly indeed from the Windscale theft a few years before.

The American President, up against it, impulsively decides to run the risk of a detonation. Without waiting for a thorough evacuation of the Baltimore area, squads of specialist Green Berets sweep in to search every ship in the harbour. One squad, tipped off by a drunken Finnish seaman, rush a terrorist group hiding in the hold of a decrepit Greek steamer. Their device is triggered during the mêlée but does not go off. The President, filmed in his telegenically designed Operations Room, claims he had guessed this and basks in short-lived public glory at his nerve. Privately he confirms to London, Bonn and Paris that only a technical fluke prevented detonation.

Evacuation of their threatened port areas continues but in each there is panic. People with cars overload them with baggage. Others, on foot, throw it off to grab a lift. Roads become congested; horns blare mercilessly; many abandon their vehicles and start running. Army trucks have to bulldoze their way through. Fighting breaks out and pointless looting. In Hamburg, troops kill over 300 when their vehicles are rushed by hysterical workers.

With a few hours to go, the three governments are desperate. Almost everyone urges them to give in. All three have up to 100,000 people still trapped in or around the target cities — the old, the helpless, the lost children and the thousands of adults floundering about looking for them. In outlying towns thirty or more miles from the docks, tens of thousands more sit tight, obstinately refusing to believe they could be affected, whatever the winds might do.

Despite the public clamour, the three Cabinets secretly agree together not to accept the ultimatum. The decision is agonising. The terrorist demands could of course be met, but their service chiefs say surrender will only encourage later and larger threats.

The British decide to say and do nothing in the last hours in case, at the last, the terrorists' appetite for life conquers their political dedication. The French and Germans decide to rush their docks with volunteer troops, believing they have little to lose. The French succeed, just. Marseilles is saved but nineteen minutes before the deadline a brilliant flash across the sky over Hamburg is followed by a deafening crash and a mushroom cloud. Thirty-five thousand die, including many in the German Democratic Republic only thirty miles to the East (a complication the SJA had not foreseen).

Over an hour after the deadline, the British gamble seems to be coming off. Then, in a huge eruption, much of Southampton is razed and the rest ignited. As the cloud spreads east in a gusting wind, radio-active fall-out descends in an arc from Portsmouth to Winchester and as far as the army camps of Aldershot and the tidy avenues of Guildford. From blast, fire and radiation, the final death toll is nearly 70,000. The scenes around Southampton and Hamburg are colour-televised across the North. Millions weep at the livid burns, twisted limbs, molten eyes and blackened corpses. The actions of a few dozen terrorists have transformed the expectations of vast numbers, North and South. And new shocks are under way.

The Great Famine

We may imagine world grain reserves are already stretched by sporadic harvest failures in Russia and South Asia when production in 1987 falls disastrously low. It is a smaller world total than 1972's and now there are over a billion more bellies to fill. Monsoons fail over the Indian sub-continent and floods destroy much of a diminished crop. Drought afflicts Western Europe and Central Africa. Most damaging of all, a combination of uncertain weather and ecological disturbance, due to excessive fertiliser use, shave a fifth off North America's expected harvest. Most of her remaining surplus — sixteen million tons — is snapped up by the Chinese ahead of the Russians and world prices nearly treble over twelve months.

The Soviet Union now has to slaughter half her livestock; so does Britain along with most of Western Europe. Feedstuffs are just too expensive. After a temporary glut of meat, it has to be strictly rationed. The price of fish, soya beans and other vegetable proteins also therefore rocket and many developing countries go bankrupt before they can secure a minimum diet for their people. Famine spreads fast in Central and North-East Africa, the Caribbean and in the Indian sub-continent. It is especially acute in the Philippines where a previously unknown rice fungus rots two-thirds of her second crop.

The death toll in India is staggering. In six months over five million die in Bengal alone. The scenes are as harrowing as those of 1943–4. In December, 1987, after widespread riots and looting, young army officers lead their men in seizing 'Free Calcutta' and five grain ships moored off-shore. The revolt spreads like fire to Bombay and Madras. Within a month the old government, now thoroughly corrupt, collapses and the Indian Army takes over.

The new regime is determined to secure its position by mounting a sea-borne invasion of Burma which has been rich in rice in the four years since she opened herself up to outside assistance and investment. The Chinese, however, then underwrite Burma's defence and immediately the superpowers become involved.

The Arrival of 'Triage'

Despite a recent war-scare between them when a Euro-Communist government finally takes over in Italy, Washington and Moscow jointly resolve to avert what could swiftly degenerate into a nuclear exchange between China and India. This is only done by providing prodigious emergency aid to

New Delhi, against fierce protest from the American and Russian peoples who by now would welcome the mutual decimation of India and China to reduce the still rising human overload.

In an attempt to secure India against further crop failures in the years ahead, the World Bank then mounts the most expensive single development programme in history. After only a few months, it is forced to abandon it. India's sectarian disputes, regional rivalries and lack of managerial personnel create such indiscipline that most of the aid is clearly wasted. Nor does the military regime prove less venal than its predecessor.

Colourful press accounts of all this sicken Western opinion. The aid lobbies, never strong, are not surprised when in September 1988 most Western governments adopt the 'triage' policy. Aid is now to be sent only to countries satisfying harsh criteria. They have to be plainly capable of achieving self-sustaining economic viability within ten years, to have effective population policies and unquestionable executive competence. Other nations, the 'can't be saved', will be left to rot.

Many poor nations cannot possibly fulfil the new criteria. Almost all of them now have brutally authoritarian governments but not even the most callously coercive abortion and sterilisation programmes can be carried through in the anarchic conditions prevailing. Some Western voices urge that 'triage' would be utterly unnecessary if the rich would pull in their belts by another notch or two. They are accused of mindless idealism and the Indian experiment is constantly thrown in their faces. First in Vienna, then in Rome, San Francisco, Oslo, Bonn, Yokohama and The Hague, protesters, young and old, burn themselves alive on the steps of cathedrals, city halls, ministries and other public places. Television laps it up. There are a few learned articles about infectious hysteria and no change in policy.

The Group of 77 hold an urgent meeting in Mexico City later that autumn. Outraged by the new Western strategy and frustrated by years of largely fruitless talks about a new economic order, the South mounts an embargo on supplies of oil and several other commodities to all rich nations opting for 'triage'. They also threaten to seize Western assets in the

South, nationalise the multinationals and expel Western expatriates unless their demands about commodity pricing and debt repayment are met.

For nearly five months the South tightens the screw. The price of oil again trebles but, at the cost of rationing, unemployment and dislocation, the embargoed powers hold out. They find they can live off their fat. (Incidentally, at the new oil price, Norway, England and the newly independent Scotland make a short-lived killing out of the North Sea.)

In the end, the stress on the poorer members of the Group of 77 proves insupportable. The conservative OPEC nations, led by Iran and Saudi Arabia, refuse to go on financing their losses of revenue and, when OPEC finally splits in March 1989, the South's campaign falls to pieces.

The Western powers now make some face-saving gestures over aid and trade, partly to offset a renewed Soviet effort to curry favour in the South and partly to appease sections of their own domestic opinion. Towards the end of the crisis there have been extraordinary scenes, for example, at Denver, Colorado. A mass of young whites, blacks and Chicanos carrying 'Save the South' banners swamp the security guards and seize Stapleton International Airport and the Rocky Mountain Arsenal alongside, with its store of chemical and biological warfare agents. The troops brought in are inhibited from firing with such dangerous stuff lying around and only after three days' parleying do the protesters leave. The long drama is televised live and promises are made which the White House decides to keep.

The Fall of Israel

OPEC has split but its Arab members have remained united in their basic antagonism towards Israel. Egypt's interim 'Sinai Agreement' with her in 1975 and the Sadat/Begin talks of 1977–78 had been dictated by necessity, not sentiment. Quiet on that border had nevertheless lasted longer than most expected. Indeed, apart from a couple of flare-ups, the Jewish state, nuclear-armed since 1974, has seemed reasonably secure. Suddenly, in early November 1989, it is extinguished. Whether hostile or friendly, the nations rub their eyes in disbelief.

In hindsight, three factors have proved critical. First,

although they once got close to it, the Israelis have never been willing to compromise sufficiently with the Palestine Liberation Organisation over the creation of a truly sovereign Palestine State on the West Bank of the Jordan. Secondly, both Egypt and Saudi Arabia have devised their own nuclear weapons. And thirdly, and no less important, the failure of the Egyptian regime to cope with its teeming population and endemic poverty finally leads to a coup by a new generation of angry majors in July, 1989. The previous leaders are strung up along a Cairo street and 'General' Saib announces 'the last Jihad against the Jewish usurpers of Palestine'.

Few take this talk seriously, least of all the Israelis (though they pretend to): it has been the cry of Arab demagogues since the state was founded; it is to deflect the attention of the Egyptian masses from their misery; and so on. This interpretation seems to be confirmed by the announcement of a combined fly-past of Arab air forces, including a powerful Saudi one, over Cairo on October 29, to commemorate the Egyptians who fell at Mitla Pass in 1956 at the start of the Suez war.

On the day before, Israeli radar is therefore expecting intense air activity as Arab squadrons fly south across Syria and Jordan towards the Nile Delta. Over Amman however they suddenly turn and sweep into Israeli air space where, aided by an air armada from Egypt, they launch a devastating three-hour blitzkrieg. Over a third of Israel's aircraft are smashed on the ground and many of her missile sites and all her nuclear facilities at Dimona are destroyed. Arab armoured columns then power in against strong resistance from Israeli forces and settlements and the last Arab-Israeli war has begun.

Having already lost their usual air supremacy, Israel's rulers are divided. The hawks urge an immediate nuclear attack with missiles on Cairo and Damascus and, with long-range aircraft, on Saudi oil fields. The majority protest that this could only invite nuclear retaliation against Tel Aviv and Haifa. (They reckon Jerusalem with its Omar Mosque to be fairly safe.) Israel's big card has therefore been trumped. Nor in the last resort can America counter the Arab nuclear threat without being trumped herself by the Russians. For three days world peace hangs by a gossamer thread; then

Washington backs down. The four-sided nuclear stalemate holds; the war will be fought by conventional means alone.

Here, too, the Israelis always previously held the advantage in both modern skills and old-fashioned dash. Now they are too heavily outnumbered and outgunned. Automated, press-button warfare is much less dependent on the proficiency of individuals. The US flies in great jets laden with arms from NATO supply dumps in West Germany but Israel's defences are steadily overwhelmed. The country is split into two, then three parts and after eight days the Israeli Cabinet sues for mercy. Some units fight to the last man, like their predecessors at Massada against the Romans, but an orderly transfer of power is all for which the politicians can now hope.

The unbelievable has happened. The invincible has been crushed. The lamentations rise as a forty-year experiment ends in a new exodus. Anything, it seems, is possible in an era of nuclear proliferation. Neither courage, nor intellect, nor super-power protection, is any longer an assurance of survival. History offers no guarantees and has no pity.

The 1990s: Decade of Disintegration

Horror elsewhere has arrived less conspicuously but we may assume that by the close of the 1980s much of the South is in a wretched condition. The population of South and South-East Asia alone has risen by nearly a half in only fifteen years and food production has lagged far behind. It is roughly the same picture in much of tropical Africa and Latin America. In many countries there have been savage disorders, sectarian conflicts, insurrections, repressions. In Pakistan, North-East Brazil, Jamaica, Indonesia and Malaysia wildly messianic movements have thrived in the gathering atmosphere of apocalypse. Almost all Southern nations have fallen under the sway of military regimes.

This is not to say the same pattern of poverty and tumult obtains everywhere. By dint of rich resources or of intelligent policies carried out with iron self-discipline, some of the Southern countries have achieved much progress. The result of this, together with the break-up of OPEC in 1989, has been to split the Group of 77 and the frequency of regional wars *within* the South increases in the early 1990s. These include a bloody struggle between Nigeria and Ghana for Togo and

Dahomey, lying between them; Brazil's occupation of Uruguay; the first nuclear exchange in history — short-lived but immensely damaging — between India and Pakistan over Kashmir; and a non-nuclear war between India and Bangladesh over the division of the River Ganges' waters.

There have been much more perilous conflicts in the North. The disruption of world trade strengthens apprehensions about the growing shortage of some resources, notably oil and fertilisers. In 1992 this leads France and Spain jointly to invade Morocco for its immense phosphate reserves and induces NATO to attempt the seizure of some of the Persian Gulf oil kingdoms.

This plan is foiled at the last moment by the Russians strongly reinforcing their Mediterranean and Indian Ocean fleets to back their vocal threat of missile retaliation. Oddly enough, it is against this background of increasing political confusion and division within the South and the North alike that the battle lines of a prolonged North-South war begin to emerge.

The North-South War: First Round

It is of course by definition the poorest countries like India, Pakistan, Bangladesh and Indonesia which are the greatest sufferers from the new Western policy of 'triage'. Written off as 'beyond saving', they become desperate. The Group of 77's purely economic campaign of winter 1988–9 has failed and the South's unity has broken with it. Some of the more extremist Southern governments therefore begin giving secret support to the Southern Justice Army in renewed and more systematic attempts by nuclear and other terrorist means to extort from the West what it refuses to concede voluntarily.

In July 1992, for the first time, nuclear ultimata are issued by the SJA to Japan, Saudi Arabia and Kuwait as well as to NATO members. Japan and the Arab states quickly pay up but in the West the new wave of terrorism has quite the opposite effect to that intended. The West not only sticks by its 'no surrender' policy but the revulsion of public feeling leads to a further drastic hardening of line towards the South in general.

By 1993, suffering her own acute economic problems and

multiplying internal unrest, the Soviet Union severely reduces her aid to her own remaining Southern clients. She therefore becomes the next new target for the SJA which, denied concessions, erases half Leningrad with two nuclear devices in March 1994. The Kremlin, aware that this (all-woman) terrorist group has received covert support from India's military regime, promptly destroys Jamshedpur and two other Indian cities with nuclear missiles. The West too now begins to take violent reprisals against known sponsors of the SJA including Peru, Uganda and Ethiopia.

It is however the immense severity of the Russian response that shakes Southern belief in the policy of sustaining what are still largely sporadic terrorist attempts to extract concessions from the rich powers. A bolder approach is needed and this has now become possible, for the Russians' destruction of Jamshedpur had reunited the South in a shared hatred for the white industrialised world as a whole. In Southern eyes East and West show the same white exploitative ruthlessness.

By the same token, East and West are swiftly acquiring a sharp sense of common interest in relation to the South. This is heightened by shared experience of nuclear attack. The horrors of 1945 never quite got through to the Europeans. The Japanese did not exactly deserve what happened but they had been thought a different, 'fatalistic' people, with whom it was somehow impossible to identify. Now a terrible feeling of vulnerability spreads throughout the white world.

The North-South War: Second Round
Through the summer of 1994, the South licks its wounds and debates strategy. Washington and Moscow are active too. Alive to the quickening North-South polarisation, they are anxious that their counter-measures should not precipitate accidental war between themselves. They therefore start discussions in September 1994 which lead to talk of constructing what comes to be known as the 'Northern Stockade'. It is suggested that, despite their ideological differences, East and West might build their own heavily defended rich white 'laager' against the poor and coloured hordes of the South.

In October 1994, before these tentative talks have got far, China, which is now virtually a super-power in her own right, firmly declares her identity of interest with the world's coloured majority. (This gives the South a nearly five-to-one numerical advantage — if so it can be called — over the North.) One repercussion of Peking's decision is quick to follow. Desperate for *lebensraum*, the Indonesians mount an effective if ramshackle sea-borne invasion of Western Australia.

Rich in uranium deposits, Australia has long since developed nuclear weapons. But so have the Indonesians who also have a far larger army and air force. Canberra therefore appeals to Washington for help in beating back the invaders. At this point Peking counter-threatens missile attacks on Alaskan oil fields and Washington steers clear. Australia is partitioned but few think the rich south-east of the country can remain a wholly white enclave for long.

Heartened by Chinese support and this quick success for direct action, most of the Southern nations agree in early 1995 on a policy of systematic attrition against the now established Northern Stockade. There will be a three-pronged effort: first economic pressure; second, a bigger and better-orchestrated campaign of covert nuclear-guerrilla warfare; and thirdly, where necessary, the threat of direct nuclear attack against at least the smaller of the recalcitrant Northern nations. This last would plainly be hazardous but, with Chinese power behind them, the South believe the North will try to avoid massive retaliation.

We can expect the effects of this renewed and much more comprehensive campaign against the North to be dramatic. Some of the West European economies quickly come close to collapse. Unemployment rises to over forty per cent; social welfare obligations can no longer be met; food riots break out; law and order break down. Under these pressures the last vestiges of democracy are erased. To minimise panic, severe news censorship is imposed. Meanwhile historic divisions reappear: France and Germany (now reunited) come close to war over the Saar and the new 'Government of National Unity' in London orders the re-occupation of Ireland for its food surplus. There are also commotions in Eastern Europe where the Soviet Union relaxes its grip to deal with an unexpectedly bold movement of proletarian dissent within its own borders.

America too continues to draw in her horns, showing unexpected timidity. In a world with twenty-seven nuclear powers, most of them envious and hostile, she is gradually adopting the policy of 'Fortress America' (or 'Lifeboat America' in the now current parlance). In securing her own continent, however, she shows no hesitations. Emergency legislation bans all attempts to 'discredit' the President. In effect, political activity is abolished. In March 1995, shaken by the formation of a left-wing government in Ottawa, the US 'peacefully' occupies Canada and suppresses reports of bloody scenes in Quebec. Three months later, after a series of guerrilla attacks by SJA groups from Latin America, she occupies Mexico too and drives on to establish a (somewhat outmoded) defence line beyond the Panama Canal.

As the South's campaign rises in ferocity the nuclear toll, North and South, grows grimly high and the East-West accord behind the Northern Stockade policy only just survives the crisis of July 1996, when, with American help, Japan pre-empts a North Korean attack by occupying South Korea. As in 1895 against China and 1904 against Russia, Japan shows herself ready to go to any lengths to stop a hostile power commanding the southern port of Pusan, so close to her own shores.

Instead of leading to a clash between Moscow and Washington, Japan's action triggers off another in a long line of border conflicts between Russia and China. This lasts into 1997 and nearly becomes nuclear when Soviet troops are swamped by Chinese numbers. The Russians reckon however that, if victorious, they would be confronted with the impossible task of governing an alien and rebellious population now well over a billion strong. A total war with China was one Russia could lose but never, perhaps, conclusively win.

The same dilemma confronts the North in general as the second round of the North-South struggle grows in virulence with the approach of the new century. The North can never extinguish the Southern masses — not without so vast a pall of world-wide radio-activity that it would itself be destroyed. Nor can the North hope to sustain the peace after any victory less than obliterative; a white-ruled world empire would be intrinsically unstable, whether or not directed by a dyarchy of Washington and Moscow.

On the other hand, the South's campaign is gradually disrupting the vulnerable fabric of the North's elaborately technological economies. The warnings had been there, decades before. When all electrical power was accidentally cut off in 1977, New York had quickly reached the brink of chaos. Now it begins to look as if the whole of the North could be brought to that point. Its various national power grids and intricate systems of communication, transport, water supply, sewerage and the rest are peculiarly open to selective assault and sabotage. Its multiplying nuclear power stations — vital to maintaining industry now that oil is finally running out — prove to be dangerous hostages (and lethal neighbours) in an era of violence. And the South's cause has enough friends in the North — certainly in the former democracies of the West — to hide and assist its agents against the blundering efforts of the now immense security services.

The South in contrast is far less exposed to the guerrilla mode of attack. Its economies and cities are not blessed — or cursed — with elaborate interconnecting systems. It has few plugs to pull out. Only a fraction of its peoples are at all dependent on industry. And, unlike those of the North, they can endure harsh conditions. They have never known much else. The Northern nations have grown soft, addicted to comfort, unused to adversity, guilty about privilege. The Southern nations are hard, durable, adaptable, angry about long denial. Having little, they can lose little. And their climates are warmer, their necessities few.

In short the Northern Stockade is presented with few substantial military or industrial targets and its potentially overwhelming firepower has to be used with immense caution. The South, much weaker on paper, has the strength of its primitive simplicities and by canny infiltration and skilful application can sever one by one the nerves and arteries of its mammoth opponents.

By the end of the twentieth century, hundreds of millions have perished from famine, pestilence and conventional warfare. Tens of millions have died in the various nuclear strikes and exchanges between North and South. The last remaining democracies have resorted to authoritarian rule and the survival of high-technology industrial society is becoming dubious, not only through its vulnerability to sabotage but also through energy shortage. After two decades of escalating turmoil, all six of the underlying threats have gathered rather than lost momentum. (Family planning campaigns were the first victims to disturbance.)

Admittedly, full-scale nuclear war amongst the, now three, super-powers has somehow been avoided. Yet it seems ever more likely. Mutual suspicion between Moscow and Washington remains substantially intact despite the Stockade agreement. A renewed crisis between them over the last reserves of Middle East oil in November, 2000, causes mounting alarm.

If the world survives this threat of holocaust there is another looming ahead. China's nuclear umbrella over the persisting assaults from the South could well finally force the Kremlin or the White House, perhaps both, to order an assault on China's missile bases.

Even that however, as they know, might not provide a lasting solution, quite apart from the incalculable reciprocal injuries it would inflict. White imperial rule of the South would not be feasible for long. The choices open to Moscow and Washington are essentially two. They can jointly surrender to the essential demands of the South, and by co-ordinated sacrifice begin building a more equal world. Or they can persist in the struggle to preserve Northern privileges in the hope that the South will become exhausted before the North. The first alternative seems impossible to contemplate amidst the mutual hatred the previous decade has brought. The hope underlying the second seems increasingly implausible as chaos spreads in the North. The outlook for the new century is blacker than ever. Far from meeting the challenges of a decisive era, the human factor, the Seventh Enemy, has multiplied their menace.

Part Five
The Assault on the Seventh Enemy

13 Countering Political Inertia

Great truths do not take hold of the hearts of the masses.
And now, as all the world is in error, how shall I, though I
know the true path, how shall I guide? If I know that I
cannot succeed and yet try to force success, this would be
another source of error. Better then to desist and strive no
more. But if I do not strive, who will?

Chuang-tse, Fourth Century BC[1]

In the age of the think-tank, brains trust and quick fix, it is
peculiarly difficult for us to recognise that it is probably
already too late to do more than reduce and postpone the
approaching calamities.

Those who still expect the nations to be able wholly to avert
them, seem to place this high hope in one or other of four
potential developments: i) violent world-wide revolution; ii)
rapid peaceful reform; iii) spiritual change; and iv) some
great psychic shock to mankind in general. All four could *help*
us. Even armed uprising could have its place, in South Africa
for example. But could any of the four, singly or together,
save us?

I see no chance of violent revolution proving a sovereign
remedy, whatever its guiding ideology. The counter-
revolutionary forces would be far too strong. None of the
three great power-centres of our time could achieve global
hegemony without global war. And that would be a calamity in itself. Nor would world government, if achieved,
promise any sort of stability. National and regional rivalries and inequities would long persist. The world would
remain restless and fissiparous. War would just become
civil war.

What of rapid reform through international negotiation?
The World Survival Plan, if swiftly agreed and wholeheart-

edly followed through, could greatly improve the outlook but, as we have seen, this seems an unreal hope. The forces of political inertia have persistently trapped the nations in a bottomless swamp of parochial irrelevancies. Their short-sighted selfishness might remind us of a fable by Rousseau. He told how five hungry hunters hid to ambush a stag whose meat would suffice all. Suddenly a hare appeared. One hunter broke cover to seize it. The stag fled.

It is true that outside orthodox politics there have been many encouraging signs of breakthrough as well as break-down. Nevertheless, the forces of breakdown have far the strongest battalions. Innovative work in solar heat collection counts little against the insatiable energy appetites of indus-trial moguls (or the consuming masses) and the immense influence of the nuclear power lobbies. Intermediate technologies offer no fortunes to the bustling entrepreneurs of gimcrack luxuries. Organic husbandry holds no enchant-ment for the agri-business corporations. New ideas about participation, self-help and decentralisation barely give pause to governments anxious to keep their defences strong and interest groups appeased. The intelligence, beauty or moral relevance of an idea is no guarantee of it being taken up. The new thinking and the brave experiments may richly con-tribute to post-catastrophic society, but on a cool calculation they have little effective support now.

The third frequently suggested hope for mankind's rescue is placed in some sort of spiritual change. The need for this may be obvious but nothing less than swift transformation of the public's attitudes could work the political miracle needed. Change of heart is by its nature a slow process, working like yeast within individuals. It would surely be naïve to expect it to sway mass societies within years rather than decades or centuries. And perhaps the notion of a universal spiritual awakening is anyway an idealistic illusion. Has any messiah in history ever achieved it?

The fourth possibility is a profound psychic shock, some cataclysmic event which might transfigure our outlook, jolting us to our senses. However, if psychic shocks were able to do the trick, have we not already missed our chances? Many thought the horrors of the First World War's trenches would produce the needed metamorphosis. Then came the

Second with Belsen and Hiroshima. If these did not transform mankind's consciousness I cannot see famines or nuclear terrorism doing so. In 1945 Lewis Mumford said, 'The moral recoil against the atomic bomb has already begun to take place.'[2] Three decades later, the recoil has considerably diminished, not grown.

A Continuing Crisis

If this assessment of the four potential 'cures' is reasonable, it carries a grave implicit warning that we shall need to act decisively without expectations of doing more than moderating the horrors ahead. We would need to combine what Antonio Gramsci, the Italian Communist leader, called 'pessimism of the intelligence and optimism of the will'.

Some say it is impossible to undertake any serious action when such a dichotomy prevails in the mind; that this tension between a limited hope and a necessary fear cannot be sustained. I think in fact such tensions are inescapable for the rational mind and Chuang-tse's words remind us across twenty-three centuries that they are a perennial feature of the human condition.

Moreover, the warning needs to be grimmer than I have so far said, perhaps grimmer than any previous civilisation has had to face. For the convergence of the six threats seems to herald prolonged convulsions, perhaps without end, rather than a brief period of disaster beyond which might beckon some new age of peace and enlightenment. I agree with the eminent scientist, Lord Ashby, who was the first chairman of the Royal Commission on Environmental Pollution,

> My own hypothesis — it is a gut opinion, I cannot support it with irrefutable arguments — is that we are not just in a crisis; we are approaching a climacteric. Not only up to 1995, or to the year 2000, shall we be anxious about supplies of food and raw materials, and about the equitable distribution of energy and the disposal of wastes, and about the unbridgeable gap between standards of living in affluent nations and what we now call the Fourth World. Nuclear war may bring these anxieties to an end in the Northern Hemisphere; but short of that, these spectres will brood over mankind for the rest of his time on earth.[3]

Professor Harrison Brown, the President of the International Council for Scientific Unions, takes a similar view when, as 'a cosmic gambler looking at the world from afar', he sees a scenario envisaging the rich nations rationally agreeing to eliminate nuclear war and poverty as one which 'verges on the miraculous'.[4]

If we are entering an age of continuing crisis, the warning may be too terrible for most to bear. Psychologists have unravelled the conditions necessary for a warning to be effective. It must be plainly stated, unambiguous and authoritative. It must portray both the best and the worst of what may happen. It must be combined with practical recommendations for action. And the dangers must appear manageable: unless there is a clear prospect of reward the warning will be disregarded, ostrich-fashion.

If this analysis is valid, our generation faces a singular challenge; not just to act boldly and unselfishly but to persevere without illusions that the sufferings will be short-lived, the sacrifices temporary or their results dramatic. It also means acting alone or in small groups, without surprise or grievance that most stick defiantly to old ways and obsolete expectations.

The Individual's Response

It is of course one thing to debate geo-political strategies and quite another to discuss the right response for individuals, each so different in nature, bent and personal situation. Dogmatic prescription would be treacherous; imprudent if not impudent. Anyway, there are no elixirs and I would hesitate to offer even a personal survival kit. (The London financier Jim Slater is said to have listed canned food, a bicycle, a heap of gold South African Krugerrands and a machine gun!)

As individuals we have some influence but little power. We have limited talent and scope, countless rival obligations and have to act within the heavy impersonal constraints of modern society. Nevertheless, in the liberal democracies, we do have freedom of speech, the means to learn and the right to organise. Of over 150 nations barely twenty-five offer these conditions. So our privileges impose a special responsibility upon us.

For which policies should we work? In the context of the World Survival Plan, I have suggested some general directions. This is not however to deny there are genuine dilemmas.

For example, in the light of energy shortage and the nuclear dangers, we might favour deliberate economic de-growth of the materials-crunching and polluting sort. Yet, apart from the obvious political obstacles to de-growth, and the possibility of its causing a self-exciting industrial system to collapse, it is arguable that reduced industrial production in the North would not only strangle the South's raw materials' exports but severely diminish the North's capacity to provide it with financial and other help.

Similarly, those who would contemptuously discard high technology ignore the profundity of the North's dependence on it as well as its tangible benefits. Nor could there be any early hope of weaning a generation of technological junkies into the alternative lifestyle of a simpler (presumably agrarian) economy. Intellectuals sharing a taste for the simple life readily disparage the urban-industrial nexus (having turned down the volume on their mass-produced hi-fi) but the millions are candid in their demand for the incomes and pleasures it generates.

It would be arrogant to evade such perplexities. We have to be pragmatic, weighing the options in each situation as it arises. Nevertheless, one does not need to be a chicken to know a bad egg. We do not know all the answers but we can throw our weight behind those who seem best to have discerned the ills of our time and are striving to devise ecologically and humanly sane alternatives. We can harry our elected representatives. Whether by protest, lobbying, debate, face-to-face persuasion or sheer guile, we can resist the negative and assist the positive wherever we find them.

'Doves of the World Unite'

In the international arena we cannot directly affect events but we *can* help to create a climate of opinion which will eventually bring at least some of the components of the World Survival Plan to birth. This means resisting all forms of national self-preoccupation and ideological obsession. It is ludicrous to be hypnotised by either while the world heads for anarchy. The still widening wealth gap between rich and poor is ultimately more threatening than any missile gap. The trade and aid campaigners are anxious to harness our capacities, from envelope addressing to policy research and public speaking. And perhaps the central message is that we must all wake up to the obvious and radically reappraise our priorities. The new family planning centre at Denpasar, the capital of Bali, the most magical if over-burdened island I ever saw, costs only 30,000 dollars a year to run. Dozens of such clinics could be created for the price of each superfluous nuclear warhead.

The nuclear menace is now so severe that we must insist on an end to anarchic proliferation, the stopping of all nuclear tests, the placing of the processing and circulation of plutonium under international control and the serious negotiation of balanced disarmament. I suspect we must soon go further. The case for considerable unilateral nuclear disarmament is becoming very strong, certainly for the UK and increasingly for the US too. The argument that valuable bargaining cards should not be thrown away for no guaranteed benefit is powerful but we are approaching the point when the poker-play of nations becomes absurd. As Professor Feld has said,

> Under today's conditions it is hard to care less whether the overkill is by a factor of 100 or 1,000. . . The survival of mankind demands a new approach which, with all due respect, might adopt as its slogan: Doves of the world unite. You have nothing to lose but your planet.[5]

We should also resist the now prodigious trade in vastly 'improved' conventional weapons. In the export of arms the US ranks first in the world, the UK third. The South is spending more on arms than on education and health care; a quite terrifying fact. This traffic is stoking the fires of the future. Its restraints would cost the supplying governments some influence abroad, but at home neither jobs nor export earnings need be lost for long. By transferring skills and plant to the manufacture of agricultural and earth-moving machines and medical equipment, the same resources could be deployed to constructive ends. Radar and micro-circuitry also have their peaceful uses.

Incidentally, trade unionists, socialists and all who speak of universal brotherhood have a duty to act accordingly. As it is, the British Trades Union Congress, for example, has a record less than impeccable on questions of racial and sexual equality even at home, and it tinkers and dithers about supporting efforts to establish black trade unions in South Africa rather than decisively withdrawing labour from firms with South African subsidiaries which operate apartheid and pay starvation wages. (It replied with little more than a polite nod when Amnesty International produced a dossier on trade unionists imprisoned for their beliefs by tyrannies of left and right.) The working classes of the Rich North often show just those superior attitudes towards the peoples of the South that they themselves suffered from in the past. At best they are casually indifferent; at the worst they see the world's poor as idle, deceitful, inferior and bloody-minded. In the global perspective organised labour has come close to joining the ruling classes.

Anti-Giantism
In national politics the most urgent need must be to restrain the development of nuclear power — especially of fast breeder reactors — until, if ever, the problems of accident, storage of waste and nuclear theft are close to solution. In Sweden, France, West Germany, Japan and the US, public protest has already made an impact.

Conservation of resources — whether of energy, materials, wildlife or landscape — is vital. It is worth appearing eccentric in rejecting the electric ham slicers and the excessive packaging which is murdering the forests. Municipal authorities can be persuaded to collect waste paper and metals separately for re-cycling and to burn other wastes in specially adapted power stations rather than spoil valuable land by dumping them. Intelligently applied pressure can hasten legislation to stop the polluter or make him pay, and taxation changes could curb the excesses of advertising firms and those making fortunes out of built-in obsolescence.

In these battles what we are up against are not just the peripheral excesses of the economic system but the out-dated and grimly defended idea of 'economic man' in classical economic theory. This is the economics that takes account *only* of market values, of what is bought and sold, and *not* of the costs in noise and filth, in wear and tear to society at large. As E. F. Schumacher once acidly wrote,

> Call a thing immoral or ugly, soul-destroying or a degradation of man, a peril to the peace of the world or to the well-being of future generations; so long as you have not shown it to be 'uneconomic' you have not really questioned its right to exist, grow and prosper.[7]

Schumacher also did more than anyone to focus attention on the related question of size, of the increasing scale and hence remoteness, unresponsiveness and, ultimately, inefficiency of large units whether centralised states, gargantuan cities, mass-production, universities or monolithic commercial corporations. He countered the idolatry of giantism with the famous slogan, 'Small is Beautiful'. As he said,

> . . . People can be themselves only in small comprehensible groups. Therefore we must learn to think in terms of an articulated structure that can cope with a multiplicity of small-scale units. If economic thinking cannot grasp this it is useless. If it cannot get beyond its vast abstractions . . . and make contact with the human realities of poverty, frustration, alienation, despair, breakdown, crime, escapism, stress, congestion, ugliness and spiritual death, then let us scrap economics and start afresh.[8]

More therefore is at issue here than organisational ideas of devolving power from the centre. We have to resist every expression of the icy economic calculus that puts abstract 'efficiency' before personal intimacy. We must boldly put the interests of people before the interests of power or profit.

The Need for Self-Help
In practical terms this also means being wary ourselves (especially on the left) of thrusting too much responsibility — and hence power — upon law, government and other institutions, public or private, and retaining too little our-

selves. Mass society easily de-potentiates the individual, encouraging a trend away from self-help and self-reliance. These crucial values are too often abused to defend the selfish interests of 'the tax-payer' and 'free enterprise'. We should resist the encroachments of the state and big business alike and reassert the individual's capacities and dignity. The movements for worker and consumer participation and for self-help in fields like housing, education and health, embody the conviction that we all have the capacity to make more of our own decisions. A group of women who create their own children's play group, in Bombay, Beirut or the Bronx, are taking a first step towards liberation — achieved by themselves, not for them by others.

These considerations may sound remote from the massive challenge of Southern poverty and the six threats. Yet the inertia of governments derives in large measure from the self-imposed helplessness of individuals. The people who stand up and say no, who reject the lie, who join with others to voice their own needs and do their own thing, are already beginning to break the chains which otherwise shackle us to programmed self-extinction.

All the now influential voluntary organisations had small beginnings: the great development charities like OXFAM, Christian Aid and War On Want; the environmental groups like the Conservation Society, the Friends of the Earth and the Sierra Club; the various movements for population control and for causes stretching from good soil husbandry to international studies.

Amnesty International, universally respected for its impartial professional campaigning on behalf of political prisoners, sprang from a small gathering stirred to action by an article in *The Observer*.

Within a few months in 1976, amidst the bloody turmoil of Northern Ireland, two women created a Women's Peace Movement which became a world story and had enough effect to attract vicious reprisals from extremists on both sides.

Our extraordinary situation is calling on practical creativity as well as the willingness to campaign. Alongside the Vancouver 'Habitat' conference in 1976, there were dozens of techniques on show of how local materials like coconut palm and clay could put elementary shelter within the means of the dirt-poor. At Silsoe in Bedfordshire a hand-operated metal-bending machine has been designed at a hundredth of the cost of the cheapest commercial machine. All over the West, there are experiments with new forms of communal living. One community, in an American city, occupies a warehouse where seventy-five live and about 200 work in a balance of independence and mutual aid. Rejecting the ethos of cold war and space race, yet avoiding the hippy trippy nonsenses of Haight-Ashbury days, they are serious in their various jobs but also free. As one put it,

> We have been taken out of our little mental compartments of 'architect' or 'psychiatrist'. We've come together. And we've realised that we're either going to transform America or we're going to die with America. . . We have seen our enemies and we're looking for our allies. We are no longer 'alienated' from our work because our work is the transformation of America.[9]

Another crucial area for innovation is the university. Concerned citizens cannot get adequate guidance about the global situation from governments (which have an interest in spreading false reassurance) or from the media (which rarely pursue issues in much depth). Only the universities, and a few independent institutes, could provide the synoptic over-views and systematic analyses our situation demands. However primitive they are as yet, both future studies and conflict research warrant much more support than they receive. The appeal for 'relevance' always carries some danger to academic standards but proud (or timid) devotion to the narrowing confines of 'pure' (and safe) research could lead academia to betray a vital need of our time — intelligent if approximate forecasting.

Breakthrough can lead in unexpected directions. At Bemborough Farm, amidst the rolling Cotswolds, hardy but near-extinct breeds of farm stock are being preserved; creatures like the small brown Soay sheep and the Wild White Park cattle brought in by the Romans. It is a living bank of genes on which we may need to draw when protein feed can no longer be imported. And halfway across the world, in the rain forests of the Amazon, anthropologists are seeking to learn from the unexpected skills of 'primitive' people who live in organic harmony with their surroundings.

Our daily practices will be more persuasive than our opinions. We can all live more frugally, more carefully. We can consume less, waste less, make do and mend and acquire new do-it-yourself skills, from elementary mechanics to first aid. (One day they will be essential survival skills.) We can choose a smaller car, or take to a bicycle. We may be able to get an allotment and grow much of our own food; we can all change our diet and eat less meat (passing the savings to charities). All this helps, partly in reducing our demands, partly as self-reliance and example. And we need not be solemn about it. After radical chic, why not survival chic?

But we do need to keep a balance. We must not get so hooked on self-sufficiency, whether personal (impossible) or national (a chimera), that we forget the wider reasons for moving in that direction. Nor should we allow any particular conservationist or ecological cause to become a displacement activity which, by so wholly consuming our energies, dulls our sense of the size of the problems. Collecting 'non-returnable' bottles will not change the course of history.

And nothing less than that extraordinary aim must now be the ambition of the small minority who have seen the terrible direction of events. It is a minority that must employ all its ingenuity and courage. Perhaps its motto could be the order which Admiral Sir Andrew Cunningham addressed to his small Mediterranean fleet in November 1940. Sighting a much larger and more powerful Italian fleet off Taranto he signalled this, 'We are so outnumbered there's only one thing to do. We must attack.'

14 Countering Individual Blindness

> Insight that dawns slowly seems to me to have more lasting effect than a fitful idealism, which is unlikely to hold out for long.
>
> C. G. Jung, *The Undiscovered Self*[1]

We saw earlier that much political inertia results from the blindness of individuals whether as rulers or ruled. I attributed this blindness to three prime causes; failure in comprehending the facts, failure to make appropriate moral judgments and failure to sustain sympathy, the energising power behind all saving action.

The remedy to the first of these failures is obvious. We can repair the gaps in our comprehension of the global crisis only by the hard graft of study.

Our weakened confidence in making moral judgments is a more complex matter, partly owing to the philosophical confusions spread by positivists and relativists who are hostile to the very notion of absolute standards. It seems to me that an ethic is either absolute (and potentially universal) or it is nothing. By its nature it makes assertions about right and wrong which are either true or false. It is not like a collection of arbitrary preferences to be abandoned when found inconvenient.

It is however also true that we cannot irrefutably prove the validity of any particular ethic. Though many have tried, we cannot deduce what ought to be from what is. To look for a safely undeniable foundation for our morality in biology, history, ethology, evolution or whatever is essentially misguided. But if sceptics cannot be proved wrong in holding morality to be no more than a kind of cultural myth, we are equally entitled to live as if it speaks of realities. Indeed, amidst the coldest winds of contemporary scepticism, I think we must affirm as defiantly as necessary that we shall not live as if the universe were soulless and the good had no meaning.

The next question, then, is by which values to conduct ourselves. Judging by the results around us, we have mostly pursued narrow or destructive ones: a fragile world society crying out for justice and a natural environment speaking of depletion and disruption.

Seeing this, many are tempted to call for quite new values. I believe this course mistaken, even arrogant. We need rather to recover some of the old values. Drawing on Joseph Pieper's work, Schumacher suggested there is teaching both subtle and realistic enough to meet the modern predicament in the doctrine of the Four Cardinal Virtues; prudence, justice, fortitude and temperance.

The need for justice and increasingly for fortitude is becoming obvious and the intemperance or immoderation of the consumer society is no less plain. The undisciplined pursuit of pleasure never satisfies us; it can lead to despair. André Gide was right, 'The trouble is one can never get drunk enough'. But temperance, like fortitude and justice, ranks after prudence, the first of the virtues and the mould and mother of the others.

What is prudence? Schumacher said, 'It is not the small, mean calculating attitude of mind which has all but conquered the modern world, but a clear-eyed, magnanimous recognition of reality'. It 'requires that all selfish interests are silenced' and 'presupposes an orientation of the whole person towards the ultimate goal of life'.[2]

The special enemies of prudence are greed and envy. They blind the individual and create both the injustice of the world and the sickness of the environment. They set man against man, and man against nature, by imprisoning him in the material to the neglect of the spiritual. And moderation, properly understood, is not a yielding meekness (much less a suburban caution) but a respect for the wholeness of things, a recognition that the individual's excess can throw a total system out of balance.

But comprehension and appropriate values cannot take us far without sympathy. Calls to love mankind or posterity carry an air of solemn unreality and the 'family of man' is a strained metaphor. We seem able to have an authentic love only for those we know and can respond to as persons. An American friend of mine says he cannot care a damn about the Asian masses, they are too foreign and remote. Yet he also sees that, in a global village, unless the idea of shared humanity acquires some emotional force, we are probably lost.

I doubt whether there is any remedy for absent or deadened sympathy which could be prescribed in cold prose. Our personal suffering and the example of others may slowly teach us; so may works of the imagination. Careful thought can however help by clearing some of the entangling undergrowth from our minds.

It may for example suggest that it is the insistent distractions, frantic pace and progressive dehumanisation of modern city life that most numb our capacities for fellow feeling. Fragmented and meaningless work leads to fragmented and superficial personal relations. We find refuge — and false security — in the calculating intellect or well-paid skill and lose touch with instinct and emotion. We tend to revere the mind that 'works like clockwork', to over-value cleverness and be cruel to failure. Hooked on stimulation, we look to the next satisfaction without dwelling on the last. We are go-getters who never arrive and who forget where we came from. We believe in 'doing' and in our restless hyper-activity have almost forgotten what 'being' is about. Silence threatens; solitude becomes 'loneliness'. It is as if, poor fools, we felt every moment should have a conscious purpose.

A passage of T. S. Eliot comes to mind,

> Where is the wisdom we have lost in knowledge?
> Where is the knowledge we have lost in information?[3]

We become less wise, less known to ourselves and to each other. The springs of feeling do not dry up but their waters become turbulent and muddied. Too little attended to, they sometimes seethe with unlocated anxieties or surge up in a rage that surprises us with its engulfing intensity. These are signs of a loss of contact with our true selves — of who we really are, of what we really want and why we react as we do to events and to others.

This condition reinforces our temptation to immerse ourselves in doing and to use others' conventional expectations rather than our own inner promptings to decide our course of life. We become competitive, obedient to the prevalent values of 'success' and 'enterprise', and treat each other as rivals.

All this tends to generate an excessive concern with our outer fate and our social status or standing. Perhaps it is a vicious circle; perhaps urban-industrial living dislocates our sense of individuality, so we scurry back into the rat-race which both hides and fosters the sense of meaninglessness. Our way of life certainly breeds a sadly shallow prestige-seeking egoism.

This may be obvious but it is a point of some consequence. Egoism is perhaps the profoundest obstacle to love as an animating feeling, for it denies to others the absolute value it attaches to self. The value of others becomes relative, conditional on their use to us.

This is not to suggest we should not love ourselves. If all persons are valuable and irreplaceable, so am I. (The Christian precept is to love others *as*, not *more than*, ourselves.) But if love of self is a pre-condition for loving others, the self in question must be the true self, not that paltry self-deceiving ego of which we are mostly aware.

A Question of Consciousness
This consideration amongst others compels us to see the unique, perhaps terminal, challenge of our time as a spiritual as well as a moral and political crisis. Rarely has so much hinged on our power to love. And we must find ways of preparing ourselves as individuals to face and combat the worst without losing inner composure; of accommodating the pain and the tensions; of keeping going through the blackest despair; of refining an appropriate kind of hope and of retaining a sense of meaning despite the gathering chaos.

If resisting the tide of anarchy ultimately hinges on the individual, it depends in turn on the range and quality of his or her consciousness. If our individual sensibility is narrow of inferior, neither collective effort nor fine ideals, neither sane objectives nor right means, will count for much. Indeed, as the Chinese proverb has it, the right means in the wrong hands work the wrong way.

If however we can enrich our awareness of what the Club of Rome calls the *'problématique humaine'*, we shall begin to re-interpret it, expose hidden aspects, widen the range of possible answers and hence change the actions — or the spirit of the actions — that follow.

There seem to be seven important respects in which the typically contemporary view of things needs to be corrected or supplemented. (In another culture or period the list would be different.) All seven of them run counter to majority thinking and together they would help us achieve that 'clear-eyed, magnanimous recognition of reality' which, as prudence, lays claim to be our touchstone.

As light is the most familiar image for consciousness, it may be apposite, if a rather Victorian metaphor can be excused, to think of them as seven lamps. They are:

1. Rational fear — in opposition to the prevalent unthinking hope.
2. Self-awareness — a recognition of unconscious duplicity in place of a blithe confidence in our ordinary worthiness.
3. A visionary awareness—which transcends what William Blake called the 'single vision' of the science which now dominates our outlook.
4. A revaluation of the feminine — to redress the gross over-masculinity of our culture.
5. A willing acceptance of tensions — in opposition to the modern heresy that they are undesirable and avoidable.
6. An 'ethic of consciousness' — in contrast to an over-idealistic 'ethic of goodness'.
7. A re-awakening to the religious dimension of life — exposing the secular gods we unwittingly worship.

The significance of some of the seven lamps will not be at once apparent but each illuminates a neglected or maligned aspect of experience or reality — fear, the feminine, tension and so on. They are attempts to recover what is too often excluded, attempts to create what we might call an inclusive sensibility.

Part Six
An Inclusive Sensibility:
The Seven Lamps

15 *The First and Second Lamps: Rational Fear and Self-Awareness*

> Fear is the foundation of safety.
> Tertullian

It was reported from Dallas that Jackie Kennedy refused to change out of her bloodstained pink suit, 'Let them all see what was done to him.' First of all we need to be thoroughly frightened by our situation. Fear can be constructive.

This is an idea our time finds puzzling, even abhorrent. We are inclined to think all fears undesirable — abnormal, irrational or neurotic. I pick up a dictionary of psychology to see fear defined as 'One of the primitive, violent and usually crippling emotions. . .'[1] It is no more complimentary about anxiety.

Intelligent fear is the root of true courage. In the British armed services the highest decoration for valour, the Victoria Cross, does not go to the vainglorious who rush into battle, mindless of the realities and their men's safety. It is not for 'men without fear' but for those who have held the fear and used it. We need to have that same rational fear of the six threats and the Seventh Enemy. Fear need not be pathological, hysterical or morbid. It need neither panic nor stultify us.

Unfortunately, in the affluent societies we forget we are finally subject to the same raw human condition as the Hutu of Central Africa, the peoples of the Shan Hills, the aborigines of the Great Victoria Desert or the bushmen of the Kalahari. We forget we have no right to be the world's privileged; that we are not chosen peoples of chosen lands; that it is by chance, not by any special virtue or contract with

God, that we retain our riches and our apparent exemption from the atrocities of life. Our lack of fear is now one of our greatest dangers.

Rational fear is a positive force, a biological function necessary to survival. It heightens vigilance, as in an athlete on the starting block.[2] It makes us alert and watchful. It innoculates us against unreal expectations and embittering disappointments. It reduces the danger of trauma and, I suspect, of resorting to extreme counter-measures during crisis.

The Imagination of Disaster

It is not enough to name the threats. Only the *images* of horror can make the fear real and effective — the swollen bellies and staring eyes, the rioting mobs and ruthless troops, the torture of prisoners and the collapse of cities, the radiation burns and the weeds pushing through the tarmac of silent streets.

Henry James said, 'I have the imagination of disaster and see life indeed as ferocious and sinister'. Most of us do not; and the gap between our technical capacity for perpetrating atrocities and our imaginative ability to confront their full actuality is widening dangerously fast. Robert Jay Lifton, who studied the human effects of the first atomic bomb, thinks we should '. . . attune our imaginations to processes that are apocalyptic in the full dictionary meaning of the word — processes that are "wildly unrestrained" and "ultimately decisive" '. It is, he says, '. . . dangerously naïve to insist that our imaginative relationship to world-destruction can remain unchanged — that we continue to make a simple-minded distinction between psychotic proclivity for, and "normal" avoidance of, that image'.[3]

Apocalyptic Traditions

The sudden emergence of the six threats at the end of the second Christian millenium seems to afford a bewildering relevance to ancient traditions. Since the advent of the Christian era, which coincided with a great conjunction in the zodiacal sign of Pisces, it has been believed that the following 2,000-year cycle would culminate in apocalyptic horrors. The transition from the end of the age of Pisces, the Fishes, to the age of Aquarius, the Water Bearer, and of the brotherhood of man, would be baptised by fire.

St. John, in the Book of Revelation, speaks of the Four Horsemen of the Apocalypse and (though I only noticed this recently) of 'the seven vials full of the seven last plagues' (Revelation 21:9).

For the Hindus, ours is the age of Kali-Yuga, the age of darkness when Shiva poises his purifying fire aloft. Many Indians believe the 1990s will witness an apocalypse. There is a parallel tradition in Central America; the Mayans believe the final destruction of the world is due (and will happen on December 24, 2011!). These myths may enlarge our imagination and move the heart even though they affront the head.

There is some danger of fear paralysing the will to act, indeed of making life seem impossible. We cannot bear very much reality. But complacency, too, effectively immobilises us. We should neither wallow in, nor numb ourselves to, the imaginings of apocalypse. They can spur to action. The nuclear scientist Eugene Rabinowitch described how, walking Chicago's streets in the spring of 1945, he looked up at its great buildings and suddenly imagined a holocaust in which they crumbled. He vowed to redouble his efforts to organise a scientists' petition to head off the dropping of atomic bombs, without warning, on populated areas.

At the last, whatever the risks, we must surely tell the truth as we see it. Not to do so, would be the ultimate insult to our fellow men and perhaps betray an ultimate despair of human nature, a final denial of hope. As Rabinowitch showed, fear can make for new beginnings. The apocalypse also signifies new birth, like the pains of pregnancy. As Spinoza detected centuries ago, 'Fear cannot be without hope, nor hope without fear'.

THE SECOND LAMP: SELF-AWARENESS

After he had been freed from the exceptional horrors of his Japanese prisoner-of-war camp in Java, Laurens van der Post, then a colonel, refused to collaborate with the various Allied war crimes tribunals set up in the Far East. Later he wrote,

There seemed to me something unreal, if not utterly false, about a process that made men like the War Crimes

Investigators from Europe, who had not suffered under the Japanese, more bitter and vengeful about our sufferings than we were ourselves. There seemed in this to be the seeds of the great, classic and fateful evasions in the human spirit which, I believe, both in the collective and in the individual sense, have been responsible for most of the major tragedies of recorded life and time *and are increasingly so in the tragedies that confront us in the world today.* (My italics.)[4]

I have often referred to this high-minded tendency to blame 'the others', to search for scapegoats rather than acknowledge our own share in the world's evils. I believe the self-aware must recognise that every crime finds echoes in us and kindles a secret satisfaction, even if this is often disguised as moral outrage. Unconsciously, the victims, the jury, the judge and the executioner participate in the crime. Psychologically, we are all victims and all murderers. I suspect this unpopular idea is vital to recognising our condition at the depth it calls for. As Jung once wrote, 'Since it is universally believed that man *is* merely what his consciousness knows of itself, he regards himself as harmless and so adds stupidity to iniquity'. (Original italics.)[5]

Modern man likes to think of himself as 'wide awake', 'reasonable', 'realistic'. We resist the idea that many of our actions are the rationalised product of hidden needs or desires. We disdain what hovers so vulnerably between the conscious and unconscious layers of the mind, shaping our perception and filtering reality without our realising it. We constantly tell each other to 'get down to brass tacks' or 'keep our feet on the ground'. We constantly disparage 'mere' feelings, fantasies, myths, dreams and instincts. These rich resources are used for amusement and casual anecdote. As smart know-alls, we repress the primitive child within and become grossly one-sided. Then we may suddenly find that the unattended primitive has gone berserk, has taken us at the throat, from behind, as it did in pre-war Germany.

Contact with the unconscious, not its suppression, heals and makes whole, helps us on the way to maturity, to becoming ourselves, to achieving individuation. It was perhaps not for nothing that we once spoke of 'soul searching', a process more subtle than 'inspecting our conscience'.

The various characters, plots, motifs and places which recur in our dreams are trying to tell us something. The dream is a friend, not to be treated with indifference or disdain, nor, at the other extreme, to be frontally assaulted with naïve dream dictionaries for meanings useful to our shallow ego-ambitions. That, after all, is still to treat the dream life as less than a treasured aperture into the inner creative soul. Better far to 'befriend' the dream, as advocated by James Hillman in *Insearch*[6] and, implicitly, in P. W. Martin's *Experiment in Depth*, another rewarding work for those seeking to renew their inner connections.[7]

Whatever the means, however, fuller self-awareness seems vital to an adequate response to the perils of our time. Without it we stay on the surface of life, blind to the richness of self (and hence to the richness and moral complexity of others) as well as to our own share in the common misfortunes. A clear-eyed recognition of reality demands as much attention to the inner spirit of the knower as to the 'hard facts' of the external world.

We can now see that the 'Jewish problem' of pre-war Germany was largely a Christian or 'Aryan' problem. Nevertheless, most Europeans (and North Americans) persist in seeing the race issue of today as a 'black' problem not, as it essentially is, a 'white' problem. To repress this unwelcome perception we resort to self-justifying evasions and chronic woolly-mindedness. In Britain, for instance, we refuse rights of residence to those we disguise as 'non-patrials' and automatically describe our black and brown fellow citizens as 'immigrants' even though a third of them were born here. Similarly we repress our infantile longing to throw our own responsibilities into the arms of a patriarch by constantly demanding 'leadership' and project on to others our own faults, inadequacies and guilt as in the menacing projections of reciprocal hatred between East and West.

By such unconscious duplicities we preserve a seductive but false self-image. Yet unless we learn to recognise our complicity in the world's evils we shall show no mercy towards our enemies or they towards us. We need a lively sense of human tragedy and this may be a special problem for

Americans, victims as many of them are of the pseudo-innocence of the American dream. As one of their leading historians has put it, 'Two world wars have not induced in them either a sense of sin or that awareness of evil almost instinctive with Old World peoples.'[8]

16 The Third and Fourth Lamps: Visionary Awareness and the Revaluation of the Feminine

> Ours is the first culture so totally secularised that we descend into the nihilistic state without the conviction, without the experienced awareness that any other exists.
> Theodore Roszak, *Where the Wasteland Ends*[1]

Despite stirrings of healthy doubt, modern man still prides himself most on his rationality. He thinks of his affairs as having been rescued from the rule of emotion and tradition to be governed by objective reason in one or other of its many forms — self-assured science, technological deliberation, impersonal law, systematic administration and economic calculation.

But this age of reason is also one of collective insanity. We have enriched ourselves but ravaged the earth. In the quest for truth we have unlocked the secret that can eradicate all life in an instant. In our idiot economic calculus every hideous accident adds to the gross national product as the incomes of rescue squads, repair shops, surgeons and undertakers. These are samples of what we can only call mad rationality.

The Single Vision of Objective Reason
As science gathered its self-congratulatory momentum in the eighteenth century, William Blake cried out:

> —— May God us keep
> From Single Vision and Newton's sleep.

Since his day, objective reason has steadily colonised the

culture of the North and now the South too. We have already seen how science and technology are running out of control. Now we must note how their evident power and abundant rewards have been bought at the price of what the poet Schiller called 'the disenchantment of the world', the driving out of the magic of things. The cold bright light of objective reason has blinded us to larger if more elusive truths conveyed by works of the imagination and religion.

Science operates with spotlight, knife, needle and forceps. Its characteristic focus is sharp; its techniques are division, separation, dissection, simplification, reduction, measurement. Its manner is fearless, intrusive, icily objective. The dedication to the disciplines of empirical evidence and the hunger for discovery are so intense that the purposes served are often overlooked. How else can scientists bring themselves to rot the eyes of rabbits with poison gases; force beagles to chain-smoke; reverse the eyes of kittens or graft additional limbs or heads on to dogs? How else could a (woman) scientist get a prize for a chemical to destroy rice crops? It is all for truth of a kind, just as it is for efficiency of a kind that technologists devise anti-personnel weapons that will implant metal fragments too deep for surgery.

Such scandals may be rare. A few are perhaps inescapable. All are theoretically preventable. Yet they illustrate not only how science cannot in practice be morally neutral but how easily its disinterested objectivity can destroy a more reverent awareness of the observed. As a tool, objective reason is essential. As a disguised metaphysic, often unconscious and always illegitimate, it ignores or denies every level of reality that it cannot itself pin down and manipulate. It sees nothing in the rainbow that is not applied optics and little in Helen of Troy that cannot be dissected on the anatomist's slab.

THE THIRD LAMP: VISIONARY AWARENESS

In contrast there is the subjective mode of knowing, visionary awareness, the mode of the poet, artist, composer and mystic. This is intuitive rather than calculating; synoptic rather than analytic. It transcends rather than reduces. It seeks the mysterious, rich and encompassing symbol rather than the barren precision of the sign. It offers what science can never offer — knowledge *of*, not just *about*, persons. This is something which comes through direct and intimate communication between being and being, through communion not detached observation.

This relation of being to being is the root of art, of human fellowship and of communion between man and nature. It reveals itself in the incandescence of an old boot painted by Van Gogh, in the mutual absorption of lovers and not least in the ways of 'primitive' animists who still know the spirit of the beast, the tree, the stream and the place.

Man and Nature

The Iroquois precede their killing of a bear with a long monologue explaining that they are motivated by need not greed or the wish to dishonour. Such rituals and 'superstitions' help sustain a balance between the human population and the wild. But the Iroquois are not just practising an unconscious ecological wisdom; they implicitly see man as just one dependent creature amongst many.

The single vision of traditional science reinforces quite another view of man's place. Francis Bacon, one of its founders, said the object of science was to restore the prosperity forfeited at the Fall. Nature was there to be dominated, conquered, mastered. But the roots of this attitude, as of science itself, lie much further back in Western history.

If the over-intellectuality largely derives from Greece, the man-centredness seems to have sprung from Judaeo-Christian sources; the belief that Jehovah created man in his own image and nature to serve man's purposes. It is an idea not found in most religions. Roszak puts the blame on Judaism's extreme monotheism which, in rooting out 'idolatry', destroyed mysticism too and made possible so severe a dualism between man and nature as to justify man's dominion.[2] The historian Lynn White Jr. focuses on the destruction of pagan animism by Christianity, in the Western Church especially, and says it was the belief that man had a monopoly of the spirit that seemed to authorise the exploitation of nature. White contends that if science and technology are now out of control and creating a disastrous ecological backlash, then 'Christianity bears a huge burden of guilt'.[3]

Incidentally, this exploitative attitude is obscured, not

ended, if we can only justify our attempts to conserve the blue whale, timber wolf, white cedar or marsh on grounds of ecological balance and therefore ultimate human benefit. We are then succumbing to the same man-centred arrogance, in the subtler form, as those who would consume or destroy them for today's profit. (We are also committing intellectual fraud since it is doubtful whether more than a few per cent of the higher plants and animals are of economic use.) Nature can only be saved through an unconditional love for the land and the wild, for their own sake.

Single Vision and the Technocratic Society

A characteristic result of single vision as it touches human society is the astonishment of housing-experts and other well-educated idiots that the people they have slotted into their frigidly impersonal tower blocks are soon screaming to be let out. Only mad rationality could account for the artificialities and spiritual desolations of the modern metropolis or the tendency of technocrats to talk about justice in terms of 'trade-offs' and freedom in terms of 'parameters'.

It is arguable that advanced industrial society, like its partner the administrative state, is *inherently* technocratic. Politics, production, education, almost every service whether public or private, is controlled by perennial anonymous experts with their passion for efficiency, order and conformity. As Max Weber saw over sixty years ago, it is the dictatorship of the officials, not the proletariat, that is marching on.

The technocrats are paternalists who are absolutely sure of what we need. Any dissent or difficulty must be due not to error but to 'failures of communication'. Democracy becomes the occasional right to choose between the contrived images of Tweedledumb and Tweedledumber. Education becomes a machine to mould the young into the shapes the public and private corporations most like, gratefully submissive workers and infantilised consumers.

As time passes and discoveries multiply, the technocrats hanker for yet more manipulative technologies — new psychotropic drugs, universal electronic surveillance, eugenic controls. Their unspoken ambition is the Ministry of Well-Being, the guarantor of compliance and temple of psychosocial engineering. Russia's political prisoners are already placed in 'therapeutic isolation'. Single vision points us down a road leading to a techno-fascism prettified with a little safely institutionalised 'participation' from token persons.

A rebellious former priest, Ivan Illich, has mounted an especially telling attack on current ideas of objective social progress. His key idea is the convivial society, one in which human relationships are enhanced, not destroyed.[4] He shows how many modern systems, from education to medicine, from housing to transport, not only destroy personal relations but, beyond a point, produce opposite effects to those intended.

Modern transport, for instance, effectively increases the distance between people. But perhaps the owner-driven, otherwise empty, private car stranded in a city traffic jam is almost too obvious an example. Take, therefore, education. In the South especially, such exaggerated value is placed on high qualifications for the élite that the success of the few is built on a pyramid of inevitable deprivation and failure for the many. The training of a Peruvian doctor costs several thousand times more than that of a Peruvian peasant. Such fantastic disproportions turn education into a scarce resource. For the few it is the cement of privilege; for the many (through its absence) it is the rationale for feelings of helpless inadequacy.

But is not the high-grade Peruvian doctor necessary? Quite possibly not. Firstly, says Illich, he will treat the city rich, not the country poor. Secondly, advanced medicine is itself becoming a major threat to health. Illich demonstrates the staggering and increasing prevalence of iatrogenic — doctor-induced — diseases, disabilities and depressions. He also exposes an ethos in which medically protracted suffering is substituted for natural painless death and a heart transplant can be accounted a success even though the patient died.

Illich's arguments are sometimes extreme but he is no Luddite, no arbitrary destroyer of innovations. The telephone, for example, is a convivial instrument; it brings people together, person to person. And he does, I think, conclusively demonstrate that the revolution we need is less political than cultural — the overthrow of the common technocratic assumptions of right and left and the redefinition of social objectives in terms, above all, of personal intimacy and meaningful work (work which is nearer to making than just doing).

The Subtlest Needs

No part of life is safe from the technocrats. They are making us increasingly dependent on their (ever changing) dogmas about how to conduct our sex-life, rear our children, foster our mental health, make friends, enjoy our prefabricated leisure and adapt (oh, always adapt) to the insults and assaults of the system. When people are so often subliminally told to distrust their own instincts and skills, their self-respect and spirit are bound to suffer.

Language itself is dessicated by enslavement to objective consciousness. It suffers from what has been, horribly and fittingly, labelled 'scientisation'. We do not 'want a home' but 'require accommodation'; do not 'make love' but 'have intercourse'. The subtlest needs, experiences and joys become coarsely categorised things; and things for possession. As Emerson warned, 'Things are in the saddle and ride mankind'. Once, when dining with Illich in London, I felt he too was struggling against the infectious blight of academic abstraction. Our language becomes counter-intuitive, sapping the juices of awareness and personal response. If the rich inheritance of common speech is extinguished, so also will the last remnants of our confidence in our private insights. Rilke saw this in the Duino Elegies, '. . . and even the noticing beasts are aware that we don't feel very securely at home in this interpreted world'.

Meanwhile, the visionary awareness of a St. Francis, a Wordsworth or a Dylan Thomas, when not patronised as 'poetic licence', shivers against the icy winds of intellectual scepticism and common neglect. Likewise, the priceless heritage of the animist is rejected by the high priests of science. Jacob Bronowski's verdict upon the primitives was that, 'they have failed in culture . . . because they did not create a mature view of nature, and of man too'.[5]

We, the culturally 'mature', have been carrying out a systematic death sentence on these 'failures'. The European occupiers of North America slaughtered the indigenous Americans and their buffalo brothers with equal indifference. By 1920 there were only 200,000 Indians left across the emptying prairies and even these were forbidden by law to teach their arts and rituals or to invest the rocks with the perceptions preserved from their timeless story. Today, in the Amazon, Africa, South Asia, Iran and elsewhere, the destruction (or 'modernisation') of primitive cultures continues. Few if any seem likely to survive another couple of generations to *show* us the wisdom of man-within-nature.

No scientific vocabulary could preserve the vision of these peoples or convey the power of their all-embracing rituals which whisper the unknowable through the richly ambiguous symbols of poetry, dance, song and art. No textbook could capture the meaning of the squaw's hymn to the earth as she takes its clay and fashions and fires the pot she calls 'good', not 'beautiful'.

No Way Back
We have eaten the fruit of the tree of knowledge: I see no way in which we can fully recover the animist's vision of wholeness. We certainly cannot do so by *rejecting* science or any other of the forms of objective reason. They are vital to intellectual discipline and to sustaining a now complex social order. We must however contest all claims (and concealed assumptions) that science holds a *monopoly* of the truth, that its reality is the only reality.

Roszak suggests science itself could be transformed into a sacramental vision of nature, into a science of the 'rhapsodic intellect'. He shares Seyyed Hosein Nasr's view that science could learn to contemplate nature as a mirror reflecting a higher reality, a vast panorama of meaningful symbols.[6] I see the beauty but doubt the validity of this idea. (I suspect it is a cop-out.) Scientists do need to be less narrow, more synoptic and holistic in approach, but I cannot see how laboratory discipline and visionary awareness can be welded together. Our sensibility has to be inclusive enough to embrace *both*, as separate avenues to different aspects of the truth.

THE FOURTH LAMP: A REVALUATION OF THE FEMININE
From Bangkok to San Francisco, from Greenland to Borneo, I have heard women protest about male prejudice and sexual inequality. Remedy for this injustice is essential if only because population restraint largely depends on women's

decisions and hence on their status, self-esteem and expectations.

So much is slowly being accepted. Yet if women have been grievously disparaged and under-valued so also has a distinctively feminine cast of feeling and thought which is to be found in varying degree in both women and men. We must counter the grossly over-masculine character of modern consciousness and hence of modern society.

If women need to be liberated, so does the feminine. Paradoxically, however, most of the fiercest liberationists see the idea of the feminine as at best an empty myth and at worst an insidious rationale for male chauvinism. The idea of the feminine can certainly be misused but those who reject it are implicitly selling out to the patriarchal systems, values and attitudes which are driving our world towards moral bankruptcy and self-destruction. An over-masculine world needs changing much more than sharing.

The Patriarchal Society

Merdeka (Freedom) Square in Jakarta is dominated by a giant stone column called the *lingam*, the sign of male conquest. It is an apt totem for a typically nationalist society and one in which the President is always called 'Pak' or father. There is a close connection between nationalism and male domination. The link was declared proudly by Goebbels in the 1930s: National Socialism was a 'masculine movement'; the great sphere of politics 'without qualification must be claimed by man'.

Capitalism, including state capitalism, has likewise been made by men, in the image of man: a world of smoke-stacks and pylons, pumps and pistons, cannons and missiles; a world ruled by urgency, aggression, appropriation and conspicuous display. Its most recent associates, militarism, bureaucracy and technology, are likewise governed by rigidly impersonal hierarchies and cold cerebration. Together with nationalism and capitalism, they create an increasingly institutionalised form of mass society in which not only women but the majority of men perform to the orders of a minority of dominant males (some of them in skirts), who supervise work or dispatch to war.

It is therefore saddening to find so many women demanding their just but tainted share of the commanding heights of an otherwise unchanged pyramid of feelingless authority. If it remains tied to the masculine drives of competition, materialism and Faustian conquest, the Women's Movement will not only inherit but consolidate the existing structures of national and international exploitation.

The Maternal Orientation

The liberationists are of course right to ascribe the long subjection of women mainly to the impact of the surrounding culture. The typical male-centredness of Western society can be traced back not just to the Reformation's re-emphasis on typically masculine values, such as the work ethic, but to the patriarchal ethos of Christianity (as of Islam) which originally derived from Judaism. All three of these religions not only worship a deity imagined as male but see women as naturally subordinate, and are indeed unwilling even now to receive them into the ranks of their priestly leadership.

Patriarchy is not fore-ordained. There were many goddess religions in the ancient world and a few matriarchal, or at least matrilineal, cultures have survived into modern times. The Menangkebau women of Sumatra are still admired throughout a vast archipelago for their independence and dignity.

Nevertheless there are characteristic differences between the sexes which I believe are genuinely innate, deriving from women's special functions of bearing and rearing children. Their nature is to nurture. The rôle demands a close protectiveness and patience and a sensitive awareness of emotions and unspoken needs. It requires family-centredness, secure and continuous personal relations, and the investment of sex with love. The maternal orientation gives women (typically, *not* invariably) a particular feeling for nature and the organic — perhaps also for place. For almost all human history women were tied and immobilised by their children's dependency, while the men went off on the chase. Women probably therefore invented agriculture where the cyclical, seasonal patterns of seed-sowing, growth and harvest mirrored their own rhythms of fertility and reproduction.

None of this suggests a subordinate rôle or innate inferiority in women, much less an inequality of rights. If anything it means that the prime needs of mother and family dictated the rôle and outlook of man as hunter-gatherer. Her immobility caused his adventurousness; her sense of the particular provoked his sense of the general; her instinct required his logic. Feminine receptivity is served by masculine assertiveness. The sexes and their characteristic strengths were inter-dependent and remain so. There is no sense in falling backwards into the opposite sexist heresy by elevating woman or the feminine principle into a contrived superiority.

It should be recognised too that men themselves have paid a high price in personal intimacy and emotional satisfaction in conforming to the cool and over-cerebral style required by the patriarchy. The hyper-masculine ethos makes men hide their anxieties and vulnerabilities — especially from other men. And undemonstrativeness in turn can sap the sources of feeling. Men therefore have a personal as well as a general interest in re-appraising their stiff inheritance.

I agree with my former Whitehall colleague, James Robertson, about the necessity of a new flexibility of rôles and balance of power between the sexes — and a re-thinking of women's liberation.[7] I suspect however that the shape of the human future will depend even more on how far we can, in both sexes, revive typically feminine characteristics of thought and outlook. For example, something of the maternal orientation may be essential if we are to counter the masculine rape of nature and patriarchy's indifference to human intimacy. Unless we now nurture all, there may be no future for any.

The Feminine in Thought

We need to re-integrate the special qualities of the feminine in thought itself; the thought that diagnoses our condition and shapes our policies. It may sound absurd that any deliberate process like thinking, bound by rules of evidence and logic, can have any connection with gender. Yet the idea is ancient. It is expressed in various forms in most religions and by Aristotle, Aquinas and Dante: the masculine and the feminine must be harmoniously combined to fashion an undistorted view of reality.

The spirit of the masculine intellect, probing, piercing and penetrating the secrets of nature, is plainly close to the 'objective' single vision of science. In contrast, feminine knowing comes through receptivity, not assertion; through intuition, not analysis. Like the communion between mother and child, it is non-rational (not irrational). It is a mode of knowing associated with love rather than power and is therefore closely related to visionary awareness.

Some men are of course strongest on the feminine side (and some women on the masculine). But the larger mind, like the wholer personality, incorporates the feminine without being overwhelmed by it. It is the mind of Dante, Shakespeare, John Donne and Goethe and, at their level, of today's synoptic thinkers. It holds the masculine and feminine, the objective and visionary, together, without either achieving dominance.

This is a difficult and highly controversial subject. Readers who wish to follow it up may like to be directed to Karl Stern's engrossing study of the parallels between our culture's flight from the feminine and the abnormal relationships with women of many of the most significant European thinkers since Descartes.[8]

The Rôle of the Carnal
Just as there are intimate connections between mind, heart and body so there are between knowledge, love and carnality. All these connections seem to have been dislocated in the modern era. The unbalanced masculine intellect has not only sundered itself from love as another route to knowledge but increasingly separated love between people from sexuality. In Western society, for instance, both commerce and mass culture tend to present the highest carnal satisfactions as the exclusive reward of those choosing the right vodka, deodorant or manual of sexual technique.

The tearing up of carnality's roots in love and relatedness may however be traced back to a devaluation of the erotic ever since St. Paul saw it as a handicap to the spirit. The seriousness of the psychological split this caused is seen where sex is rejected in puritan fear or disgust at one extreme and 'liberated' in permissiveness and promiscuity at the other. Both sides label sexual desire 'animal' — by the one to tame it, the other to let it run wild. One would repress it; the other pays no respect to sublimation, restraint or the feminine instinct to wait. Neither side sees coitus as, at its highest, a sacramental joining with nature, a coming together of body, heart and mind. Yet this is precisely when it embodies the mystery of the knowing of beings — of I-Thou — and when it exemplifies the creative self-abandonment needed to save our world.

The Recovery of the Feminine

The revaluation of the feminine aspects of our sensibility throws unexpected light on both our outer and inner condition. It can liberate women as women, not as ersatz men who would merely bolster up a disastrous masculine technocracy. It can help men to quieten their compulsive restlessness (concealing the homelessness of a Faust or Don Juan) and to recover their potential for expressiveness and relatedness. It might also help to wean us from the competitive lust for acquisition and from our wilful denial of our own and the planet's limits. It could refresh our awareness of our roots in nature and community and help mature our view of society's best purposes. It may therefore have a larger relevance to our response to the Seventh Enemy than conventional attitudes even begin to comprehend.

But again no neat synthesis is possible; the integration of masculine and feminine is slow, painful and never complete. Nor, indeed, should it be completed. The masculine and feminine need each other and the tensions between them must be accepted not denied.

17 The Fifth and Sixth Lamps: A Welcome to Tensions and the Ethic of Consciousness

> Tension is now given the same bad name as sex once was. It has to be endured, coped with, lived with, as if it were a misfortune.
>
> H. A. Williams, *Tensions*[1]

With their special feeling for the absurdity of death amidst life, Mexicans take savage pleasure in the tale of the peasant who 'cured' his drinking companion's headache from an excess of *tequila* by emptying a revolver into his head.

In much the same way, our own craving for ultimate solutions is creating ultimate problems. Mankind has yet to learn a curious but crucial lesson, that the pursuit of any single idea or value always leads not to a single truth but to a paradox; to the uncovering of two opposite and contradictory forces. The Mexican's unqualified compassion leads to a cure which is also death. Humanity's compulsive quest for certainty is contriving unparalleled uncertainty. And no doubt as our circumstances become more patently desperate, people will be tempted to seek ever more desperately for some single remedy, whether ruthless action to erase perplexity or a mystical quietism in which to ignore it. Each extreme will be equally averse to holding and utilising the tensions which are vital to rational thought and action.

That tension is necessary, indeed valuable, is not a common view. We are constantly told to relax, ease up, stop worrying, to put an end to doubt and inner conflict. This is the message carried by the purveyors of tranquillising muzak, of pills and media pap, of political panaceas, of pacifying dilutions of the religious creeds and of the proliferating paperbacks on coping with stress. Tensions can be harmful but are not usually less so by being evaded, whether by leaping to extremes, by doping them down, or by denying their existence.

We live in a universe of opposites and the tensions between them; a universe of positive and negative charges, matter and anti-matter, male and female. Without such polarities there would be no cosmos, no life, no movement, no change. History itself reflects this. An age of classicism gives way to one of romanticism; puritanism is followed by licence; prophets are succeeded by Popes and revolutionaries by administrators. Each swing of the pendulum is a necessary reassertion of part of the truth and usually an excessive denial of another part. Witness the recent revolt of the young against much of their parents' world.

Paradox and the Counter-Culture

The hard-headed, down-to-earth ethos of the ministry, the military machine and the vast conglomerate is hostile to doubt and mistrustful of ambiguity. Yet this conventional Northern culture of management, precision and 'fixes' has been breeding an unconventional generation whose counter-culture delights in disorder, imprecision and riddles. The uptight have spawned the hang-loose. The ethic of materialist success has been succeeded by the ethic of spiritualised 'failure'. The domination of the word is replaced by the cultivation of touch, cry and gesture. Nominal adherence to the orthodox religions gives way to intense expeditions into Zen, the occult and astrology, the I Ching and divination.

The counter-culture has had many strands, from the flowerchild, hippy and beat to the New Left radical, but they have shared the same anarchic style and still re-interpret with perverse, sometimes glorious, thoroughness the 'individualism' that their parents espouse in words but rarely in life. They reject the hard areas of science and technology for the softer, 'caring' professions. They replace over-controlled sexuality with the love-feast. Calculation, traditions and measure are out. Contemplation, happenings and ecstasy are in.

Of course the counter-culture has its own contradictions and excesses. It exploits what it denounces as an exploitative society. Its songs of protest become golden discs. It spouts cant phrases like Herbert Marcuse's 'repressive tolerance' while taking maximum advantage of hard-won freedoms. It sentimentalises love and condemns the genuine necessities of power. At its revolutionary extremes its hatred of the world's self-righteous systems of concealed violence, slips into the equally self-righteous politics of indiscriminate terrorism, into finding new ways, in Camus's words, 'to make murder legitimate'.

The counter-culture illustrates how every movement of protest or reform can swing too far, often turning into its opposite — bringing about what it most deplores. The mad rationality of the established order is not best met by contempt for *all* categories and boundaries, for *all* restraint, form and reason. Unbridled licence invites repression; suffocating order provokes rebellion.

The Razor Edge

As Thornton Wilder said, every good thing stands at the razor edge of danger and must be fought for at every moment. That might make a good motto for the inclusive sensibility. I am trying to outline. Each of the four special needs of contemporary consciousness I have so far dealt with is poised on this razor edge.

Nowhere is this clearer than with fear and the apocalyptic imagination. With too little fear we lack vigilance and urgency. With too much we equally destroy the will to act. The extreme optimist thinks nothing needs to be done; the extreme pessimist thinks nothing can be done. Both are blind to part of the truth; both lead to inertia. Both therefore are manifestations of the Seventh Enemy. The opposites of fear and hope can only be held together in a rational fear which allows that measure of fear — and hope — which the situation objectively requires, no more, no less.

So it is with the other three lamps. In quest of self-awareness one can slide so far into the unconscious world of dream and fantasy as to lose touch with workaday realities. One can become so intoxicated by the liquors of visionary awareness as to lose all critical control. One can so over-react to masculine hyper-activity as to drown in a sea of inert feminine instinctuality.

THE FIFTH LAMP: A WELCOME TO TENSIONS

Whatever direction it takes, the growth of consciousness brings no final resolutions, no sense of certainty. It exposes hidden contradictions and opens ever more conflicts and perplexities. We *accept* the tensions because we cannot honestly or rationally ignore either side of the multiplying dilemmas. Indeed we positively *welcome* the tensions because they signify close contact with reality, the absence of illusion, and because without constant alertness to them we could not sustain a healthy equilibrium. Here we have found the special rôle of 'magnanimity' in the 'clear-eyed, magnanimous recognition of reality' which is our guiding thought.

Tensions and Politics

In its best sense, politics is an activity almost definable by its concern with articulating and negotiating conflicts, whether between rival interests, factions, priorities or principles. In this respect politics is the civilised alternative to force and, in both logic and practice, no single one of its aims, certainly no political ideal, can be pursued without sacrifice of another. There are no failure-proof prescriptions for resolving the competing claims of freedom and order; liberty and justice; equality and incentive; individualism and solidarity.

It is the naïve hope for the impossible — and undesirable — end of such tensions that constantly threatens the survival of politics. It is what fosters that idiotic talk of gathering the 'best minds' to run 'Great Britain Limited', as if pure intelligence could do what professional parleying and persuasion cannot. It is what encourages nice soft-headed Americans to plead for the 'healing of the divisions' in their society when some of these may need *amplifying* before the profound injustices between its races and classes are registered and remedied.

Politics is a noble craft precisely because it accepts and channels conflict. It needs continuous defence against the perfectionists and sloganisers who try either to repress awareness of differences or to act them out in suppression or rebellion. Compromise, often denounced, is of its essence: the only 'solutions' in politics are the death of politics. Civilised government is of the divided people by the divided people and for the divided people.

If domestic tensions are held, democracy can survive. If

international tensions are held, no one reaches for his gun. The best we can ever hope for is a precarious harmony between different voices. The attempt at unison, national or international, ends in the bloody barricade, the political prison camp, the repressive empire and the mass grave.

Tensions and the Individual

Similar considerations apply within the life of an individual. The rational learn to live with competing truths and ambivalent emotions. They recognise that where there is rebellion there is also bondage; that the capacity to hate is necessary to the power to love; and that, just as no statement can comprise all the truth, almost none is wholly false. They know that when we strongly assert something, it is wise to consider what precisely we mean to deny.

Disorder in the mind, as in society, is often the result of attempts at adaptation which are appropriate in kind but faulty in amount. Every cure can also be a killer. The blind worship of reason and thrustful action has taken mankind to the edge of calamity. A complete reversal to a blind acceptance of instinct and passivity would tip us backwards into the same darkness. Our task is simply to continue treading the tightrope and there is no resting place.

THE SIXTH LAMP: THE ETHIC OF CONSCIOUSNESS

When visiting friends at an Israeli kibbutz in the Negev Desert in 1957 I was stunned to discover that it was refusing membership to any of the impoverished oriental Jews who had recently flooded into the country from Morocco. They were mostly illiterates who had been living in the caves of the Atlas Mountains. Their entitlement to a roof and work seemed undeniable. The kibbutz, however, decided that people ignorant of Zionist and Socialist thought did not qualify to share its communal life. It even refused to employ the Moroccans for the summer harvest. It agreed that, without extra hands, much of a heavy crop might rot in the fields but insisted it was wrong to 'exploit' human labour for cash.

The Moroccan families were desolated and mystified by the response of their new Socialist compatriots. No wonder. The kibbutzniks' decisions were not due to any selfishness, cultural snobbism, hypocrisy or any other ordinary moral failing. They were a product of a defiant hold on high principle. The human call on compassion and compromise was drowned by the stern voice of conscience insisting on the ideal. By conventional reckoning their motives were honourable, their actions impartial, their attitude entirely sincere.

So much the worse for conventional judgment. Viewed as a whole, their behaviour deserved James Thurber's verdict on a Broadway play, 'It only had one fault. It was kind of lousy'.

The sincere are much too readily forgiven, especially by themselves. Too often, they are a menace. The nuclear weapons designer and the military strategist have the best of intentions. The industrialist, pillaging and polluting the earth, is often well meaning. The concentration camp commander really believes his society needs purging and, after closing the gas chamber for the night, writes affectionately sentimental letters to his children. As David Riesman put it, the sincere man is the one who believes his own propaganda. He fools others but, more treacherously, himself.

It is no excuse to mean well. It is no defence 'genuinely' to believe some of the things we allow ourselves to believe. To claim that 'our conscience is clear' is to raise the question of how it could possibly have reached that strange condition.

The Ethic of Goodness
These seem to be sound reasons for questioning a fundamental premise of conventional morality, the priority given to goodness rather than wholeness.

Although there are many voices within the Christian (and hence Western) tradition, the overwhelming weight of its moral doctrine has for two millenia been pressed towards goodness. It is essentially perfectionist. The underlying dogma has been that God is exclusively good and this belief has allowed no place for evil in the divine person or in individual conduct. 'Be ye therefore perfect, even as your Father which is in Heaven is perfect' (Matthew 5:48) has been the central theme.

Thomas à Kempis is likewise perfectionist in his instructions for our 'Imitation of Christ', where Jesus is seen as sinless rather than whole. Much else in the Christian tradition persuades us not to touch evil, scarcely even to mention it. Evil is taboo. We get the impression that evil is not intrinsic to human action and that it is just the absence of good rather than its equally real and inescapable partner.

Essentially the same view is shared by atheist Marxists, who seem to see intrinsic goodness in the oppressed proletariat, and by agnostic humanists, who expect a natural human innocence to emerge when reason has finally overcome the obfuscations of creed. Almost everyone cries with shared naïvity, 'Deliver us from evil.' It is a quite impossible ideal.

First Be Conscious

The ethic of consciousness says our first and over-riding obligation is to know what we do. It claims this is even more important than to act rightly. What is most evil is to act unconsciously.

This interesting idea has a long ancestry. One of its sources is a saying attributed to Jesus but banished from its place at Luke 6:4. It is preserved with other non-canonical material in the Codex Bezae, believed to be a fifth-century Graeco-Latin manuscript of the Gospels published in Paris and presented to Cambridge University in the mid-sixteenth century. It says, 'If thou knowest what thou doest, thou art blessed, but if thou knowest not, thou art cursed, and a transgressor of the law'.[2]

Here the supreme criterion is explicitly that of consciousness — not convention, not commandments and not 'goodness'. It is the foundation of an ethic which accepts, rather than denies, the reality of evil within the whole man. It permits, even encourages, us to recognise and to become what we are, rather than constantly to seek an impossible perfection.

Even more than the other components of our inclusive sensibility this idea lies on the razor-edge of danger. Theoretically it could justify the deliberate evil-doer. In practice, however, it is not the villains' charter it looks. It does not say, 'Do what you like.' It says, 'Do what you will if you really *know* what you do'.

Far more dangerous than this is the condition of self-deceiving indifference, let alone blind virtue. If we block off our entirely natural feelings of hatred and anger we fall victim to neurosis or make a deadened response. If, at the other extreme, we let these feelings loose by acting them out without restraint, we may cause havoc. We have to sustain an awkward, always unsteady, balance between love and hate which is not a copping-out indifference. As one of Graham Greene's characters remarks, 'I would rather have blood on my hands than water — like Pilate'.

The ethic of consciousness usefully complicates our judgments. It exposes our otherwise unconscious complicity in the abuse of moral language. Behind the slogan 'freedom' we find napalm; behind our 'property rights' we discover intolerable inequities and so on. It cautions us against all simplistic clarion calls. It enables us to see, for example, that both East and West are trapped in exploitation, superfluous wealth, unassuaged guilt, self-serving hypocrisy and moral confusion. The West has special virtues but we must identify the many evils in which we ourselves collaborate, even if we cannot extricate ourselves from them.

Above all, the ethic of consciousness can sharpen our sense of the morally ambiguous. Someone politically way out to the right of Genghis Khan may do far less actual harm than some trendy lefty who leaves a string of broken hearts behind him as he pursues his latest heroic campaign for Bangladesh. Nor would any averagely sensible crook even consider incinerating the planet, in the name of democracy or anything else.

Even the act of giving is not safe from pollution. It may be an unconscious power-ploy, an aggressive act demonstrating one's material or moral superiority. Such introspections should not stop the giving (hunger cannot afford much pride; it just wants the bread) but they keep us alert to what we are actually thinking, feeling and doing from day to day. May we not, for instance, turn others into terrorists by our own extreme political passivity? Our inaction may generate another's despair of gradualism and persuasion.

We have to sophisticate our judgments without becoming inert. The paradoxes have to be lived with. In the name of peace we treat with the militarists. In the name of humanity we have to go on aiding Southern semi-tyrannies. In the name of development we have to subsidise the corrupt and bankrupt; in the name of international neighbourliness we continue to help the uncompassionate.

The intrinsic duality of politics — of all action — has to be sustained. It involves both compromise *and* power. We and our rulers, like Machiavelli's Prince, have to be both fox and lion. The prim liberals, naïve pacifists and 'New Age' idealists fail to see that an entirely conflict-free society would be a menagerie of tamed creatures. They are political prudes. They try to suppress the fact that, in a perennially wicked world, violence is not always criminal or psychotic but often constructive and essential.

For instance, in the mid-1960s I soon found I had no serious twinge of conscience over the secret, systematic and illegal incursions by British forces into Indonesian territory in Borneo to pre-empt President Sukarno's efforts to seize Eastern Malaysia by 'confrontation'. I had been flown into Sabah by the RAF for a personal briefing by the general in charge of our side of this undeclared war. After a few days, meeting the people of Sabah and Sarawak whom the Indonesian army were intent on 'liberating', I suddenly realised that both my sincerely unbending pacifism of former years and my priggish rectitude about international law had quite evaporated. Given half a chance, I should have joined our clandestine troops in their ruthless jungle ambushes.

I had belatedly recognised that not only enforced restraint but deliberate aggression (or counter-aggression) is sometimes justified. Others may reach a different verdict; my point is that the ethic of consciousness, which has us question every motive and every easy assertion of our 'sincerity', may be vital to steering us away from disastrously naïve policies as well as helping us to live less restlessly with the permanent imperfections of others and ourselves — the things indeed that make us whole people rather than flawed paragons.

Final Polarities

Both the welcome to tensions and the ethic of consciousness have much to do with working willingly within our human limits, our finitude. They reinforce our awareness that what one once half thought was the untidy, troublesome preparation for life is life itself, and that the present reality must always be one of fear within hope, decay within growth and death within life. Now we confront these final polarities and ask where we may find the strength to live honestly, actively and gracefully within the dying of this civilisation, just as men have always sought a way of living towards their personal death without losing their joy in life.

18   The Seventh Lamp: A Re-Awakening to the Religious

> The world is fragile. Handle it with prayer.
> Graffiti at Camden Town Underground Station,
> London 1977

When, a few years ago, a priest was asked why he went on working in a European slum, he replied, 'So that the rumour of God may not disappear completely'. He saw us, as many do, as living in a godless age. Yet all ages, including this, are ages of belief. Man is a religious animal. What alters is less the prevalence or strength of piety than its objects of devotion. The God who is dead, or dying, is being replaced by troublesome demi-gods called Prosperity, Scientific Progress, History and the Revolution and assorted idols like the Machine, the Manifesto and the Flag.

These secular religions can slake much of man's psychic thirst for meaning, purpose and dedication but only in distorting ways which have gross results. False gods have to be unmasked. For this reason alone, it seems essential that we wake, or re-awake, to the truly religious dimension of life, not necessarily by subscribing to any specific set of beliefs (within which many merely go back to sleep) but by seeing life in its ultimate contexts such as finitude, tragedy, comedy and love.

In many parts of the world the secular faiths, like Communism and nationalism, have continued to gain converts (or conscripts). In the West, however, beneath the confident carapace that an impersonal competitive culture makes obligatory, former beliefs, religious and secular, have been losing their potency. In many people there is deadness and torpor heading for cynicism and blank despair. Life is half-lived; passed through with little sense of direction or spiritual content. In the end — to the common danger — life can seem more expendable than treasurable.

Yet there are also some signs of a healthy reaction, especially in the counter-culture; not least a growing recognition of the absurdity of the modern impatience with the mysterious and the immeasurable and a blunt refusal to accept the impoverished view of man and the world which science, misused as a metaphysic, has so damagingly spread. The renewed quest for the spiritual is pressed along a thousand routes, many of them exotic and bizarre, some of them fraudulent. (The frontier always did gather eccentrics, outlaws and confidence tricksters plying colourful elixirs.)

Having explained almost everything, we realise we understand almost nothing. Once-proud sceptics are confessing to a bewildered emptiness; a sense of impiety, of aching separation, even of sin. Some are trying again to speak of the strange centrality of love and the astonishing possibility of grace and redemption.

Many who feel uncomfortable with the vocabulary of the churches are being persuaded that our most haunting concerns are essentially religious. We may begin with anxiety as to how Planet Earth's fragile envelope of life is to be preserved, only to end up with the conclusion that this will finally depend, not on technology or economics, but on how far we can restore our reverence for life and our joy in creation for its own sake. Likewise, many are discovering that only at the religious level can they hope to be sustained, as finally isolated individuals, when courage fails. Only there can the symbols be found which establish and sanctify a world that is meaningful to us; a world making some sense of suffering and evil and offering, it is said, a new fount of vitality and a new reach of freedom.

The Rediscovery of the Transcendent
Much, perhaps most, of this renewed exploration of the spiritual is happening outside the institutionalised religions. Neither they, nor Marxism and liberal humanism for that matter, have found it easy to join in dialogue with a generation live to the prospect of holocaust and possessed of a sharp nose for the patronising, the inauthentic, the evasive and the lie, however beautiful. Few of our would-be mentors,

including the new voices from the East, seem to respond to our bleak, even tragic, condition with the appropriate initial anguish or the dismay which comes close to despair. A church which is not on the rack has surely lost touch with the contemporary realities. And unless it knows the depths it is hard to find it a plausible guide to the transcendent.

By the transcendent I mean the ultimate spiritual reality which is the source of our being and of all love, beauty and goodness (and in some sense perhaps of all evil too). The transcendent, then, is that final truth which lies behind all religions but which none of them can make captive.

It seems to me that all world-views must be relative and all religious doctrines at best dim pointers to what we cannot possibly know. This is what discredits the missionary imperative and makes of, say, the long Christian effort to convert Asia a kind of scandal. At the other extreme some see the relativity of faiths as an invitation to compose some theosophical amalgam. I am doubtful about this approach too. Our nature seems to ask for a single and coherent set of symbols, a whole story, usually springing from our own culture, rather than a collection of fragments however vivid.

There is however a middle course deriving from a profound mutual respect not only between the great religions but between all who show what the late Paul Tillich used to call 'ultimate concern'. Perhaps that respect, that sense of a shared witness to the transcendent, could yet become the basis of what might be thought of as a new and radical ecumenism.

In Greek, *oikoumene* meant 'the whole inhabited earth' or 'humanity'. In that original sense, ecumenism is mankind's most urgent priority — the reconciliation of the divisions not only of creed and ideology but of race, sex, caste, class and culture; the overcoming through love of all the walls of separation and mutual oppression.

As is dramatised when right-wing Latin American Catholics torture left-wing Catholic priests, this 'horizontal' cause of collective liberation is in conflict with the 'vertical' mission of individual piety. We may all be torn between the claims of action and prayer, between the bugle calling us to the battlefield and the bell summoning us to the sanctuary. This is yet another pair of opposites to tear at us and in a sense what we seek is a vessel or myth to contain the tensions and the pain they bring. 'You have given us the cross,' a woman said after one of my lectures (which had not mentioned religion) 'but where is the encompassing circle?' I had to say I did not know but had begun to see the significance of the question; that, in the life of the spirit, opposites can only be held, be contained, by transcending symbols.

An individual's quest for the transcendent may involve great insecurity and a readiness to be driven to strange, even disturbing ideas. But faith has meaning only over against doubt, so perhaps it could eventually take on greater, not less, significance within the shambles of modern culture, where every prompting of the heart is swiftly met by the acids of the sceptical mind. There are rich traditions going back as far as ancient China to suggest that it may be precisely in the abyss, in the experience of meaninglessness, that the transcendent appears. Perhaps secularism is making a desert from which we may learn to take the 'way of unknowing', entering that 'dark night of the soul' which is too easily written off as depression.

The 'unknowing' is more than a matter of purging all the gross or refined concepts we use in trying to talk of God. It is spoken of as a holding and opening of the whole person. In this journey into solitude and emptiness we live fully wherever we happen to be, moment by moment in the 'here and now' — an emphasis found in Christian mysticism, Zen and psychotherapy. And, paradoxically, the point of knowing God is said to be the point of total ignorance, the point when the darkness so dazzles as to become light; the point when all but the true self has been left behind.

This last is the importance of many of the fundamental religious texts. The aim is the discovery and mastery of self rather than the mastery of the world. This is not, however, to show indifference to the world's course; it is rather to move inwards the better to act outwardly. The American Cistercian monk Thomas Merton showed how shrewd and illuminating people can be about the great political issues without losing touch with the immediacies of life and spirit.

The Call to Openness
The way of unknowing may perhaps be seen as a way of openness to experience; not as a way of grim denial or cool

stoicism but of free questioning and eventually of smiling acceptance. What does this mean in practice?

The way of openness means openness to doubt, to anxiety, to guilt and to despair. But it is not what some of us might masochistically tend to make of it: it is as welcoming to comedy as to tragedy, to birth as to death.

It means an openness to whatever thoughts may come, however capricious. Is God, too, suffering and finite? Blasphemy? Yet as Camus said, every blasphemy may be a participation in holiness.

It means an awareness *as they occur* of all instincts, impulses, feelings and desires, but without necessarily acting them out, something I have been slow to learn.

It means openness to the symbols from art, myth, fancy, fantasy and dream which may make religious experience out of otherwise pathological suffering.

It means openness to the signals of transcendence, of the holy, wherever they are found. And open not least to the numinous spirit of places where generations have worshipped; open to what can be felt from the ancient stone menhirs of Filitosa to the fire-temples at Persepolis; from the red, wind-worn temples of Petra to the maze-like catacombs of Rome; from the great ninth-century Buddhist temple at Borobudur to the smoke-blackened chapels of the Welsh valleys.

The openness extends to sensation in the smallest particulars, to the weight, shape, colour and texture of wood, stone and fruit; to the movement of water; to the catness of the cat; to the subtleties of smell and sound, to the pre-verbal experience of the child in us. (Perhaps we should 'become as little children' in point of wonder rather than impossible innocence.)

It means seeing things in their 'suchness' as Buddhists say. Every manifestation of life is a miracle but so is all inanimate existence.

It means openness to others in a love which is not a soft or sentimental aquiescence in their desires but expects of them too that they become themselves.

I am speaking, perhaps a little idiosyncratically, of deeply personal matters that to many will seem light-years away from the diplomatic emergencies falling on the Resident Clerk's desk. But I have become convinced of their critical relevance to the global prospects. I do not think there are any serious problems which are not ultimately challenges to our capacity to love. Love is the best motivation and finally the only valid one. It is dynamic and strong; the secret of moral force. At its highest it also seems to be indivisible. If we truly loved anything — whether it be music, plants, mountains or primitive peoples — we would love all. And the precondition of all love is the escape from egoism. Preoccupation with the false self has to give way to love of the true self. Without that, our new and unprecedented destructive powers will sooner or later eliminate our species.

It has to be said again: it seems that, most of all, the way forward lies through the open acceptance of oneself, through love of oneself, of the whole self — the dark repressed side as well as the light. This is an idea we find especially difficult, that we often treat ourselves unjustly and unlovingly, that we often repress exactly what is most gentle or giving in us.

Even when the dark side contains much evil, that too must be loved. Our very language suggests why. The words 'whole', 'heal' and 'holy' have one root. The whole is the healed. And becoming wholly oneself, becoming fully individuated, may, we are told, put us in touch with the larger reality, the holy. The quest for true self becomes the finding of the ground of all being. Nicolaus of Cusa made God say to man, 'Be thou thyself, and I shall be thine'. It is a staggering idea and a hopeful one.

Experience confirms how the sense of being stripped bare may free us to open us to others. It can allow compassion, previously bottled up, to flow across the most divisive boundaries. This has been evident of late in Northern Ireland where it has taken an atrocity-laden civil war to expose Protestants and Catholics to their common humanity. This gives new meaning to the ancient paradox that in losing we may gain; that in dying to ourselves we may live more fully. Death may also signify new life, like a snake losing its old skin or the flower dying around the seeds swelling for the new season. Destruction and chaos can herald creation.

A Purpose to Disaster

Could a similar paradox underly the global situation? A close friend, Irene Champernowne, was sure of it. She knew she was dying of cancer when she wrote me the following as I began writing this book,

> I could not face my 'life' now quickly diminishing if I did not know and experience the other side — the opportunity for a greater LIFE within the diminishment. What seems like tragedy and suicide in the world may contain a LIVING truth if we can see it. The intuition of its presence might change the course of history.

And she continued,

> I am more and more convinced that the horror of it all is a terrible necessity to drive us to consciousness of our position — the only chance of salvation is consciousness.

Irene was familiar with the many myths in which the creative spirit, like the Hindus' Shiva, destroys the old to make way for the new, in which death is never an end but another beginning. And as one open to the tragic sense of life, she knew to her depths how death is implicit in life, the skull beneath the skin. However, her perception owed most I believe to her psychotherapeutic work. The image of death in a dream usually prefigures change. The threatened 'I' is the old self obstructing the new. What the neurotic sees as dark and dangerously unknown is often the new life struggling to break through the old. Viewed in this way, even a suicidal impulse may be a drive towards transformation, crying out that something must give way.

Might the six threats and the Seventh Enemy, therefore, be seen as not wholly menacing or 'evil' but as partly 'good' in disguise? Certainly they declare, as nothing else could, how profoundly questionable and self-defeating have been our ruling values and expectations. The threats are insisting that we face their reality. Perhaps then the closer we come to nuclear suicide in the coming years, the greater will be the chances of a profound change in man. Mankind's nightmare may literally foreshadow a rebirth.

A connected thought has been explored by theologians who have returned to the prophetic tradition which sees history as having a direction, as leading to a day of judgment in the *kairos*, the pregnant time, the fulfilled time. Religious socialists in pre-war Germany argued that each period of great historical change sets special tasks (and offers special gifts). It may, they thought, take relatively few individuals to tip the scales at the *kairos* — the right moment — and for humanity to be transformed *with* its new technological powers rather than to destroy itself by their means.

It cannot be doubted that an élite can act as a creative minority, a spiritual yeast or catalyst. Fundamental change only occurs in and through individuals. Collectivities, like classes, nations and alliances, are always inferior in behaviour and potential. Deaf and clumsy, they always try to hold on to yesterday's truth, yesterday's interests. They know nothing of the quest for meaning and learn little from suffering. Only individuals can point a new way by a willing sacrifice — a making sacred. And only they can create unselfish arks of survival.

Yet these are perilous ideas, easily abused. Precisely in proportion to the high potential of the individual and the élite there is the terrible threat of *hubris*, of overweening pride. No one is more vulnerable to it than the spiritual leader. But it may be possible — if again on the perpetual razor-edge of danger — for an élite to act in humility. Perhaps some of those who are thought today's eccentrics or cranks, heretics or outcasts, may yet guide us through the maelstrom and fashion a safer, more durable if always imperfect, post-catastrophic society beyond it. Meanwhile, even the 'Cassandras' have their rôle. Cassandra was not shunned because her prophecies turned out to be wrong but because they proved right.

The Place of Laughter

A re-awakening to the religious must include a special recognition of laughter. As Harry Williams, that sparkling theologian turned monk, has shown, laughter is a great redeemer, a kind of resolution in itself of the rival forces that tear at us.[1] In healthily laughing at ourselves we abandon false dignity, false pride, and simply accept and enjoy whatever we are — anything but the super-person our sometimes melodramatic contrition implies. In true mirth we momentarily overcome the paradox of having to try to defeat the false self while knowing we can never succeed. Laughter is realistic and unaggressive, and enables us to laugh lovingly at ourselves and others, just as we are. It is a sign of grace; not the decoration on the cake of spirituality but a fundamental ingredient, vital to its wholeness. That perhaps is why someone said we should judge a philosopher by the quality of his laughter.

We need to joke, to laugh and to play. Man is *homo ludens* as well as *homo faber* — the playing as well as the making creature. Play makes its own rules and frames of time outside the 'serious' world of daily life and grants temporary exemption from the demands of what Heidegger called 'living towards death'. Play too can therefore be seen as a participation in eternity, an affirmation equivalent to the joke on the scaffold. Play with people, with ideas, with the opposites, is a creative activity, like the dance. And we should be willing to play with what in Yiddish is called *chutzpah*, the cheeky zest of the man who, having murdered his parents, throws himself on the mercy of the court on the grounds of being an orphan!

Beyond Despair

The comic and tragic are opposite facets of the same human finitude and we must be prepared to see disasters as potentially either. Even in Dachau, it seems, jokes would unaccountably break through the horror. The regaining of the religious perspective which acknowledges the levity as well as the gravity of life is what could perhaps most humanise our response to the converging crisis, drawing us back from the humourless ranks of the earnest ideologues, fitful idealists and worthy fanatics who so multiply the harm. And perhaps in the end we shall find, as did Dietrich Bonhoeffer before the Nazis hanged him, that all historical events are in some sense 'penultimate' — finding their final significance, and that of our part in them, in a reality transcending all we see as mortals.

Neither this nor anything else I have said is meant to suggest we may acquiesce in avoidable evils. We must rise against them with our full power and do all we can to shake the drowsing conscience of mankind. Spiritual change has always been slow, so unless there is a miracle that we have no right to expect, many calamities are now probable. But our own choices may yet reduce or postpone them. Much can still be saved.

Terrible truths need not immobilise us. The finest kind of courage is rooted in realism. It refuses defeatism as firmly as it rejects unthinking optimism. For some, it may lie waiting on the other side of despair. Our most vital need is consciousness, light on the reality of our situation, global and individual.

One day in 1780, the proceedings of the Connecticut Assembly were threatened by an outbreak of panic when an unprecedented darkening of the sky suggested the arrival of a much-prophesied Day of Judgment. Then a member made this ruling, 'Either this is the end of the world or it is not. If it is not, our business should proceed. If it is, I prefer to be found doing my duty. Let lights be brought'.

Notes on Sources

Where possible paperback editions of source material have also been given.

INTRODUCTION
1. John Maddox, *The Doomsday Syndrome* (Macmillan, London, 1972)
2. Karen Horney, *Self-Analysis* (Routledge and Kegan Paul, 1970)

PROLOGUE
1. Dylan Thomas, *Collected Poems 1934–1952* (J. M. Dent and Sons, 1952; Aldine Publications, 1971)
2. Hugh Thomas, *The Suez Affair* (Weidenfeld and Nicolson, 1967; Penguin, London, 1970)
3. Op. cit.
4. Anthony Eden, *Full Circle* (Cassell, London, 1960)
5. Op. cit.
6. *The Times*, August 27, 1956

1. THE APPROACH TO CHAOS
1. Robert Heilbroner, *An Inquiry into the Human Prospect* (Calder and Boyars, London, 1975)
2. Robin Clarke, *The Science of War and Peace* (Jonathan Cape, London, 1971)
3. Stockholm International Peace Research Institute, *World Armaments and Disarmaments, SIPRI Yearbook 1976* (M.I.T. Press, Cambridge, Mass., 1976)
4. D. Meadows et al., *The Limits to Growth* (Earth Island Publications, 1972; Pan, London, 1974)
5. M. Mesarovic and E. Pestel, *Mankind at the Turning Point* (Hutchinson, London, 1975)

6. Barbara Ward and Réné Dubos, *Only One Earth* (André Deutsch, London, 1972; Penguin, London, 1972)
7. E. F. Schumacher, *Small is Beautiful* (Blond and Briggs, London, 1973; Sphere Books, London, 1974)
8. Theodore Roszak, *Where the Wasteland Ends* (Faber and Faber, London, 1973; 1974)
9. Rachel Carson, *Silent Spring* (Hamish Hamilton, London, 1963; Penguin, London, 1970)
10. John Maddox, *The Doomsday Syndrome* (Macmillan, London, 1972)
11. Cited in D. Meadows et al., *The Limits to Growth*, op. cit.
12. Michael Allaby, *Inventing Tomorrow* (Hodder and Stoughton, London, 1976)
13. Robert Heilbroner, *An Inquiry into the Human Prospect*, op. cit.
14. Alexander Solzhenitsyn, *The Gulag Archipelago* (Collins/Harvill Press, London, 1974; Fontana, London, 1974)
15. Anthony Storr, *Human Aggression* (Penguin, London, 1971)
16. Angus Martin, *The Last Generation* (Fontana, London, 1975)

2. NORTH AND SOUTH: A COLLISION COURSE

1. Peter Donaldson, *Worlds Apart* (BBC Publications, 1971; Penguin, London, 1973)
2. *World Bank Atlas* (The World Bank, 1976)
3. Robert McNamara, 'Address to the Board of Governors', International Bank for Reconstruction and Development, September 1975
4. Op. cit.
5. Solomon Encel et al., eds., *The Art of Anticipation* (Martin Robertson, London, 1975)

3. THE FIRST THREAT: POPULATION EXPLOSION

1. *Scientific American*, Volume 231, Number 3, September 1974
2. Mahmood Mamdani, *The Myth of Population Control* (Monthly Review Press, 1973)
3. *Survey of World Needs in Family Planning* (Inter-

national Planned Parenthood Federation, London, 1974)
4. *People*, Volume 1, Number 5 (International Planned Parenthood Federation, London, 1974)
5. *Scientific American*, op. cit.

4. THE SECOND THREAT: FOOD CRISIS
1. I. M. Lewis, ed., *Abaar: The Somali Drought* (International African Institute, London, 1975)
2. Op. cit.
3. *The Guardian*, June 6, 1974
4. Lester R. Brown and Gail W. Finsterbusch, *Man and his Environment: Food* (Harper and Row, New York, 1972)
5. 'Assessment of the World Food Situation, Present and Future', UN World Food Conference, 1974
6. Jon Wynne-Tyson, *Food for a Future* (Davis-Poynter, London, 1975)
7. Robin Roy, *Wastage in the UK Food System* (Earth Resources Research, London, 1976)
8. *Newsweek*, November 11, 1974

5. THE THIRD THREAT: RESOURCE SCARCITY
1. Mancur Olson and Hans Landsberg, eds., *The No-Growth Society* (Woburn Press, London, 1975)
2. D. Meadows et al., *The Limits to Growth* (Earth Island Publications, 1972; Pan, London 1974)
3. *Ambio*, Volume III, Number 3–4 (Royal Swedish Academy of Science, Stockholm, 1974)
4. Graham Searle, *Rush to Destruction* (A. H. and A. W. Reed, Wellington, Sydney and London, 1975)
5. D. Meadows et al., *The Limits to Growth*, op. cit.
6. John Maddox, *Beyond the Energy Crisis* (Hutchinson, London, 1975)
7. Amory Lovins, *World Energy Strategies* (Friends of the Earth, London and New York, 1975)
8. Op. cit.
9. *Energy — Global Prospects 1985–2000* (McGraw-Hill, New York, 1977)
10. M. Mesarovic and E. Pestel, *Mankind at the Turning Point* (Hutchinson, London, 1975)

11. Robert Heilbroner, *An Inquiry into the Human Prospect* (Calder and Boyars, London, 1975)

6. THE FOURTH THREAT: ENVIRONMENTAL DEGRADATION
 1. Aldo Leopold, *A Sand County Almanac* (Oxford University Press, Oxford, 1966; Ballantine, London, 1971)
 2. Alan A. Love and Rhoda M. Love, eds., *Ecological Crisis* (Harcourt Brace Jovanovich, New York, 1971)
 3. Michael Allaby, 'British Farming: Revolution or Suicide', in *The Environmental Handbook*, ed. John Barr (Friends of the Earth/Ballantine, London, 1971)
 4. Barbara Ward and Réné Dubos, *Only One Earth* (André Deutsch, London, 1972; Penguin, London, 1972)
 5. Rachel Carson, *Silent Spring* (Hamish Hamilton, London, 1963; Penguin, London, 1970)
 6. Ernest E. Snyder, *Please Stop Killing Me* (Signet, London, 1971)
 7. Alan A. Love and Rhoda M. Love, eds., *Ecological Crisis*, op. cit.

7. THE FIFTH THREAT: NUCLEAR ABUSE
 1. Robert Jungk, *Brighter than a Thousand Suns* (Gollancz and Hart-Davies, London, 1958; Penguin, London, 1962)
 2. John G. Fuller, *We Almost Lost Detroit* (Reader's Digest Press, New York, 1975)
 3. Walter C. Patterson, *Nuclear Power* (Penguin, London, 1976)
 4. Sandra Stencel, 'Nuclear Safeguards', Editorial Research Report No. 19, *Congressional Quarterly*, November 15, 1974
 5. Mason Willrich and Theodore B. Taylor, *Nuclear Theft: Risks and Safeguards* (Ballinger, New York, 1974)
 6. Sandra Stencel, 'Nuclear Safeguards', op. cit.
 7. *Bulletin of the Atomic Scientists*, Volume XXX, Number 3, March 1974
 8. *Bulletin of the Atomic Scientists*, Volume XXXI, Number 5, May 1975
 9. Theodore Sorensen, *Kennedy* (Hodder and Stoughton, London, 1965; Pan, London, 1966)

8. THE SIXTH THREAT: SCIENCE AND TECHNOLOGY UNLEASHED
   1. Robert Jungk, *Brighter than a Thousand Suns* (Gollancz and Hart-Davies, London, 1958; Penguin, London, 1962)
   2. R. T. Petty, ed., *Jane's Weapons Systems 1976* (Jane's Yearbooks, Macdonald and Jane's, London, 1976)
   3. Robin Clarke, *The Science of War and Peace* (Jonathan Cape, London, 1971)
   4. Gordon Rattray Taylor, *The Doomsday Book* (Thames and Hudson, London, 1970; Panther, London, 1972)
   5. *Bulletin of the Atomic Scientists*, Volume XXXI, Number 9, November 1975
   6. Barry Commoner, *Science and Survival* (Gollancz, London, 1966; Ballantine, London, 1971)
   7. *The Sunday Times*, September 8, 1974
   8. Hermann Kahn and Anthony Weiner, *The Year 2000* (Macmillan, London, 1967)
   9. Alvin Toffler, *Future Shock* (Bodley Head, London, 1970; Pan, London, 1973)
   10. Lewis Mumford, *The Human Prospect* (Secker and Warburg, London, 1956)

9. THE FIRST FACE OF THE SEVENTH ENEMY: Political Inertia
   1. Andrew A. Spekke, ed., *The Next Twenty-Five Years; Crisis and Opportunity* (World Future Society, Washington, 1975)
   2. *New Scientist*, January 8, 1976
   3. Michael Oakeshott, *Political Education* (Bowes and Bowes, Cambridge, 1951)
   4. *The Observer*, June 19, 1977
   5. Geoffrey Vickers, *Freedom in a Rocking Boat* (Allen Lane, 1970; Penguin, London, 1972)
   6. *Encounter* magazine, September, 1976
   7. George W. Ball, *Diplomacy for a Crowded World* (Bodley Head, London, 1976)
   8. *The Listener*, December 19, 1968 (BBC, London)
   9. *The Listener*, December 11, 1975 (BBC, London)
   10. Richard Crossman, *The Diaries of a Cabinet Minister* Volume I, (Jonathan Cape with Hamish Hamilton, London, 1975)

10. THE SECOND FACE OF THE SEVENTH ENEMY: Individual Blindness
 1. Cited in Richard A. Falk, Gabriel Kolko and Robert Jay Lifton, Eds., *Crimes of War* (Vintage Books, London, 1973)
 2. Op. cit.
 3. Op. cit.
 4. Lewis Mumford, *The Human Prospect* (Secker and Warburg, London, 1956)
 5. Barbara Ward and Réné Dubos, *Only One Earth* (André Deutsch, London, 1972; Penguin, London, 1972)
 6. Noam Chomsky, *American Power and the New Mandarins* (Chatto and Windus, 1969; Penguin, London, 1969)
 7. Julian Benda, *The Betrayal of the Intellectuals* (Mayflower, London, 1960)
 8. Alvin Toffler, *Future Shock* (Bodley Head, London, 1970; Pan, 1973)
 9. Anthony Storr, *Human Aggression* (Penguin, London, 1971)

11. A POSSIBLE FUTURE
 1. David Calleo and Benjamin Roland, *America and the World Political Economy* (Indiana University Press, 1973)

12. OUR PROBABLE FUTURE
 1. Robert Heilbroner, *An Inquiry into the Human Prospect* (Calder and Boyars, London, 1976)
 2. *Bulletin of the Atomic Scientists*, Volume XXXI, Number 1, January, 1975
 3. *Bulletin of the Atomic Scientists*, Volume XXX, Number 8, October, 1974

13. COUNTERING POLITICAL INERTIA
 1. Cited in P. W. Martin, *Experiment in Depth* (First published 1955; Routledge and Kegan Paul, London, 1976)
 2. Lewis Mumford, *The Human Prospect* (Secker and Warburg, London, 1956)

3. Lord Ashby, *A Second Look at Doom* (Southampton University, 1975)
4. Cited in Robin Clarke, ed., *Notes for a Future* (Thames and Hudson, London, 1975)
5. *Bulletin of the Atomic Scientists*, Volume XXXI, Number 1, January 1975
6. Cited in Geoffrey Vickers, *Freedom in a Rocking Boat* (Allen Lane, 1970; Penguin, London, 1972)
7. E. F. Schumacher, *Small is Beautiful* (Blond and Briggs, London, 1973; Sphere Books, 1974)
8. Cited in Judson Jerome, *Families of Eden* (Thames and Hudson, London, 1975)

14. COUNTERING INDIVIDUAL BLINDNESS
1. C. G. Jung, *The Undiscovered Self* (Routledge and Kegan Paul, London, 1958)
2. *The Ecologist/Resurgence* Joint Issue, November 1974
3. T. S. Eliot, 'Choruses from "The Rock" ', *Collected Poems 1909–1962* (Faber and Faber, 1963)

15. THE FIRST AND SECOND LAMPS: Rational Fear and Self-Awareness
1. James Drever, compiler, *A Dictionary of Psychology* (Penguin, London, Revised edition, 1964)
2. Charles Rycroft, *Anxiety and Neurosis* (Allen Lane, London, 1968; Penguin, London, 1968)
3. Richard A. Falk, Gabriel Kolko and Robert Jay Lifton, eds., *Crimes of War* (Vintage Books, 1973)
4. Laurens van der Post, *The Night of the New Moon* (Hogarth, London, 1970)
5. C. G. Jung, *Civilisation in Transition* (Routledge and Kegan Paul, London 1973)
6. James Hillman, *Insearch* (Hodder and Stoughton, London, 1967)
7. P. W. Martin, *Experiment in Depth* (Routledge and Kegan Paul, London, 1976)
8. Henry Steele Commager, *The American Mind: An Interpretation of American Thought and Character since the 1880s* (Oxford University Press, Oxford, 1960)

16. THE THIRD AND FOURTH LAMPS: Visionary Awareness and the Revaluation of the Feminine

1. Theodore Roszak, *Where the Wasteland Ends* (Faber and Faber, London, 1973; 1974)
2. Op. cit.
3. Cited in Robin Clarke, ed., *Notes for the Future* (Thames and Hudson, London, 1975)
4. Ivan Illich, *Celebration of Awareness* (Calder and Boyars, London, 1971)
5. Theodore Roszak, *Where the Wasteland Ends*, op. cit.
6. Op. cit.
7. James Robertson, *Power, Money and Sex* (Marion Boyars, London, 1976)
8. Karl Stern, *The Flight from Woman* (Allen and Unwin, London, 1966)

17. THE FIFTH AND SIXTH LAMPS: A Welcome to Tensions and the Ethic of Consciousness

1. H. A. Williams, *Tensions* (Mitchell Beazley, London, 1976)
2. Montague Rhodes James, trans., *Codex Bezae: The Apocryphal New Testament* (Oxford, 1924)

18. THE SEVENTH LAMP: A Re-awakening to the Religious

1. H. A. Williams, *Tensions* (Mitchell Beazley, London, 1976)

Index

About the Author

Ronald Higgins was the first child of a celebrated Scotland Yard detective and a brilliant, self-taught dressmaker. He graduated with honors from the London School of Economics, of which he is now a Governor, and subsequently taught sociology at Oxford University. He then entered the British Diplomatic Service. His career took him from Copenhagen, through the Middle East, and then to Southeast Asia as Head of Chancery. He also traveled the world as a member of Prime Minister Edward Heath's personal staff at the Foreign Office.